2012

American Tuna

CALIFORNIA STUDIES IN FOOD AND CULTURE

Darra Goldstein, Editor

American Tuna

THE RISE AND FALL
OF AN IMPROBABLE FOOD

ANDREW F. SMITH

UNIVERSITY OF CALIFORNIA PRESS
Berkeley   Los Angeles   London

University of California Press, one of the most distinguished
university presses in the United States, enriches lives around the
world by advancing scholarship in the humanities, social sciences,
and natural sciences. Its activities are supported by the UC Press
Foundation and by philanthropic contributions from individuals
and institutions. For more information, visit www.ucpress.edu.

University of California Press
Berkeley and Los Angeles, California

University of California Press, Ltd.
London, England

Library of Congress Cataloging-in-Publication Data

Smith, Andrew F.

American tuna : the rise and fall of an improbable food /
Andrew F. Smith.

p. cm. — (California studies in food and culture ; 37)

Includes bibliographical references and index.

ISBN 978-0-520-26184-6 (cloth, alk. paper)

1. Tuna—United States—History. 2. Canned tuna—United States—
History. 3. Fish as food—United States—History. 4. Tuna fisheries—
History. 5. Tuna fisheries—Environmental aspects—History. 6. Tuna
industry—History. 7. Cooking (Tuna) I. Title.

TX385.S65 2012
641.3'92—dc23   2012000822

Manufactured in the United States of America

21 20 19 18 17 16 15 14 13 12
10 9 8 7 6 5 4 3 2 1

Contents

Preface

Tuna histories usually begin in the Mediterranean, and for good reason. Tuna spawn in the eastern Mediterranean, and each year they migrate through the Mediterranean to the Straits of Gibraltar and then head out into the Atlantic Ocean. Since the migration is an annual event, fishermen can predict within a few weeks when the fish will be passing near their shores. As soon as migrating tuna are spotted, fishermen flock to their boats and net as many fish as possible before the school moves on. Once in the open ocean, tuna have widely divergent migratory patterns, making their capture much more problematic.

For several thousand years fishermen in the Mediterranean have caught and consumed tuna. It comes as no surprise that ancient Greek and Roman texts make numerous references to tuna, and images of the fish appear in art and on coinage. References, artifacts, and archaeological digs have documented tuna's history for thousands of years, and the fish's continued popularity in southern Europe and northern Africa is yet other reason to begin tuna's history in the Mediterranean.

American tuna history, however, is not about the Mediterranean; it is mainly about the Pacific, where humans have caught and consumed tuna for more than 40,000 years, according to the latest archaeological evidence. Virtually all of the tuna that Americans have consumed for the past century—and still eat—comes from the Pacific. Unlike the relatively well-documented Mediterranean tuna history, however, American tuna history is scanty until the twentieth century, and the record that survives is filled with paradoxes. These incongruities and the questions generated by them are where I began my research:

Although tuna was plentiful off the east and west coasts of North America, early Europeans who arrived in America rarely ate the fish until the twentieth century. As they ate most other seafood, why not tuna?

In the late nineteenth century, tuna captured the imagination of sport fishermen, who skillfully used rods and reels to land specimens that could weigh up to a thousand pounds. Catching such creatures was such an adventure that newspapers and magazines published articles and amazing stories about tuna-fishing exploits in the late nineteenth and early twentieth centuries. What these sport fishermen did not do with their catch, however, was eat it. And neither did most other Americans at the time. Why was this?

Fish canning began in America early in the nineteenth century, but the first canned tuna didn't roll off the assembly line until 1903. When it did, Americans showed little interest, and most cans were returned to the distributor. Within a decade, however, sales sky-rocketed, and by 1918, tuna was the second most popular seafood consumed in the country. What gave tuna its "jump start," and how did it reach the top of the culinary popularity charts in just a few years after having been ignored for centuries?

Throughout the early twentieth century, tuna fishing was dominated by foreign-born immigrants, particularly Japanese-born fishermen living in the United States. How was it possible for Japanese Americans to dominate tuna fishing? And why did their influence and involvement disappear so abruptly?

During most of the twentieth century, Americans ate canned tuna, which remained steadily popular as a low-cost, high-protein source, a staple child's sandwich filling, and "diet plate" mainstay. Few Americans would ever have considered eating raw fish of any kind. By the 1970s, however, sushi, tuna tartare, lightly braised tuna steaks, and other dishes made from raw tuna were the rage of America's culinary scene. Tuna also made the transition from economical staple, a favorite of dieters and the middle and lower classes, to haute cuisine served in America's finest restaurants. Today, virtually every city in the nation has at least one and often many sushi bars and Japanese restaurants. People of all backgrounds also grab sushi packs for a quick office lunch, or they indulge in an *omekase*, or "chef's choice" high-end sushi-bar dinner. How could Americans change what appeared to be a very common culinary prohibition? And how could a cheap, working-class food reach the nation's top tables in such a short period of time?

By the late 1940s, Americans ate more tuna than any other fish or seafood, and the tuna industry consisted of hundreds of large tuna clippers and dozens of canneries offering many different brands. The industry employed thousands of fishermen, boat owners, cannery workers, ship construction crews, truckers, company executives, salesmen, and promoters. Tens of thousands more Americans owed their jobs indirectly to the tuna business—an incredible feat for a fish that was consumed by mainstream Americans for just a few decades. How tuna rose to the pinnacle of culinary stardom is examined in the introduction and the first five chapters of this book.

The American tuna tale, however, does not end there. Despite its incredible success at midcentury, the American tuna industry quickly faded. Today there are only three major canned tuna brands sold in the United States, all of them foreign owned. While some American tuna boats still operate out of U.S. and foreign ports, and a number of small canneries and "boutique" tuna operations survive, they catch and can only a small fraction of the tuna Americans eat today. The reasons for this decline—and the controversies associated with it—are examined in the final four chapters.

Today, controversies continue to swirl around tuna. These include concerns about potentially toxic levels of methylmercury in tuna; bycatch problems, such as the dolphins and sharks that are caught and die in tuna nets and long lines; and overharvesting of tuna in general and Atlantic bluefin stocks in particular. The controversies will likely continue to provoke conflict well into the future. My approach to them is descriptive and explanatory rather than normative in hopes that a better understanding of these issues will improve decision making in the future. Tuna controversies also lead into broader issues, such as those related to industrialization of the American food system, international law, environmental concerns, racism, and global economics, which are only touched on in this book.

Chapters are organized thematically and overlap chronologically. The narrative of tuna's fortunes, misfortunes, and controversies over the past century is filled with a host of characters—sports enthusiasts and creative cooks, fishermen and clipper captains, graduate students and research scientists, hardworking immigrants and hard-hitting advertisers, industrial-strength canners and high-end epicures, Japanese restaurateurs and American novelists, cold war politics and global economics, chemists and nutritionists, fisheries' experts and worried environmentalists, as well as frugal consumers and sophisticated aficionados. It's a great, action-packed story with surprising twists and turns. I hope you enjoy it.

Acknowledgments

I would like to express special thanks to the professional staff at the Inter-American Tropical Tuna Commission, Scripps Institution of Oceanography, La Jolla, California, for their interviews and comments on early versions of chapters. I would also like to thank August Felando, former manager of the American Tunaboat Association for three decades, for his help with information about the tuna industry, and his reviews of chapters 2–4; Dan Dupill, Principal Librarian, Central Library/Los Angeles Public Library; Dan Strehl for copying tuna booklets in his collection; Mark Zanger for his e-mails on early American tuna consumption; Charles Perry, then of the *Los Angeles Times,* for locating early references to tuna in California; Lisa Penner, Archivist, Clatsop County Historical Society, for information about the tuna industry in Astoria, Oregon; Linda Johnson, Archivist, Reference Coordinator, California State Archives, for her help with incorporation papers for various tuna companies; the Inter-Library Loan staff at New York University for the dozens of sources they acquired for this book; Jan Longone, Curator,

American Culinary History, Clements Library, University of Michigan, for locating and copying an early tuna recipe booklet; Rachel Laudan, author of *The Food of Paradise: Exploring Hawaii's Culinary Heritage*, for her help with tuna in Hawaii; Janet Clarkson, author of *Menus from History: Historic Meals and Recipes for Every Day of the Year*, for her help with early references to tuna in the United States; Kathleen Wall, Colonial Foodways Culinarian, for early tuna references; William Woys Weaver, culinary historian and author of many books, for his help with early tuna references in Philadelphia; Rebecca Federman, Librarian, New York Public Library, for her help with the library's menus; Joseph Carlin, Food Heritage Press, for his several e-mails on tuna; Barry Popik for locating citations on tuna sandwiches, tuna noodle casseroles, Tuna Surprise, California Rolls, and other important tuna references; Lynne Olver, librarian and creator of the Food Timeline, for her constant help with tuna references; and Mike Dantona and his father, Frank Dantona, for their information on tuna sportfishing and their encouragement to write this book.

I have greatly appreciated the comments, suggestions, and reviews of Clark Wolf regarding tuna tartare and related dishes; Colman Andrews, regarding Japanese restaurants in Los Angeles, and chapter 5; William Perrin, Southwest Fisheries Science Center, La Jolla, California, regarding the tuna/porpoise controversy, and chapter 8; William H. Bayliff, Inter-American Tropical Tuna Commission, La Jolla, California, on several chapters; and especially Witold Klawe, Inter-American Tropical Tuna Commission, who has sent tuna-related materials to me for more than a decade. All comments, suggestions, and reviews have been much appreciated, even though not all were incorporated in this book.

Prologue

For thousands of years vast schools of tuna have frequented the Atlantic, Pacific, and Gulf coasts of what is today the United States. Until the twentieth century, however, few Americans had ever tasted the fish. The first evidence for anyone actually eating tuna in North America dates to just a few thousand years ago in the Channel Islands, just off the Southern California coast. Precisely who these people were and what happened to them is unknown, but they did catch and eat tuna, at least on occasion, as tuna bones are found in abundance at some archaeological sites. Later, the Chumash and Gabrieleño (or Tongva) Indians settled on the coastal mainland of Southern California. Both groups built small oceangoing boats in which they sailed 30 miles or more into the ocean, and groups of these Indians frequently visited and sometimes lived on the Channel Islands. They too occasionally caught and ate tuna.[1]

European explorers and colonists who arrived on the Pacific coast of North America noted the abundance of aquatic life. Fray Antonio de la Ascención, a member of the Barefoot Order of Nuestra Señora del Carmen in Cabo San Lucas, reported in 1602 seeing huge schools of tuna off the coast of Baja California.[2] A century later, another Jesuit missionary, Father François Marie Picolo, recorded that indigenous people in Baja "fish for sardines, anchovies, and tunny-fish, which can be taken by the hand on the borders of the sea."[3] Although indigenous peoples in the area left no written record, they did carve petroglyphs into rocks and cave walls, and hundreds of miles inland, archaeologists have found images of tuna, which suggest that those who carved them were familiar with the fish.[4]

In the late eighteenth century, Spanish missionaries and settlers arrived in Alta California, near what are now the cities of Los Angeles and Santa Barbara. They found that the local Chumash and Gabrieleño Indians had a highly developed fishing culture with excellent boat-building skills and sophisticated fishing techniques. The Indians ate many kinds of fish, including, on occasion, tuna.[5] The Spanish Catholic colonists were of two minds about the Indians and fishing. On the one hand, fishing was necessary to provide food for (meatless) Fridays, fast days, and Lent. On the other hand, the colonists from Mexico, whose dietary mainstays were wheat and beef, were much more interested in employing the Indians on their *ranchos*. It is likely that colonial Spanish and Mexicans in Alta California ate tuna, but if so, no such references have been found in their surviving records. Fish just wasn't an important foodstuff in colonial California. As one observer noted in 1826, "Fish are not much sought after in California in consequence of the productions of the land being so abundant."[6]

The second group of American tuna eaters was also of Asian origin, but they arrived on a very different trajectory. About 2,000 years ago, Polynesians, originally from Southeast Asia, arrived in what eventually became American Samoa; hundreds of years later, other Polynesian groups from the Marquesas Islands landed in the Hawaiian Islands. Based on archaeological evidence and the reports of early European explorers, both groups ate tuna and developed a language that distinguished different tuna varieties and tuna-related species.[7]

FISHY VEAL

When European colonists arrived on America's east coast in the seventeenth century, they were amazed at the wealth of fish and seafood in coastal waters. In 1672, John Josselyn, an English visitor to New England, enumerated many fish, including albacore, a tuna species.[8] Others also raved about the seafood, but few made reference to tuna. Tuna just wasn't an important fish in the English diet. Cod was, and it was plentiful not far off the coast of New England. The cod that was not consumed could easily be salted, barreled, and shipped to other colonies, especially the sugar islands in the Caribbean, where salt cod became a core ingredient in slave diets. As for other early European immigrant groups, such as the Dutch in New York, the Swedes in Delaware, the Germans in Pennsylvania, the Huguenots in the Carolinas, and the Scots-Irish in New England, none had any particular appreciation for tuna.

Even if tuna had been in great demand, the fish had irregular migratory patterns, and they might not be found in coastal waters for years. As it was difficult to predict where tuna schools would be at any particular time, a regular supply could not be guaranteed. The exception was Atlantic bluefin, which spawned in the Caribbean and migrated up the east coast of North America in the spring, heading for the waters off Newfoundland and Nova Scotia. Bluefin travel in schools, and large bluefin can weigh up to 1,500 pounds. These voracious carnivores attacked and devoured fish caught in fishermen's nets; when they had their fill, they just crashed through the nets and swam off. Rather than look at bluefin as a desirable fish to catch, fishermen viewed them as predators to be avoided.

Despite their frequent abundance off the east coast, very few references to the fish have been located until the nineteenth century. Timothy Dwight, the president of Yale University in the 1820s, wrote that tuna "formerly frequented this coast in immense numbers, and, in the season, were constantly to be found in the markets (Newport). But about the close of the Revolutionary War they forsook our waters, and have not made their appearance since. They were esteemed a great delicacy, and are the largest of the mackerel species."[9] Tuna returned a few years after

Dwight's account was published, and some fishermen and sailors were surprised by them. Mariners reported "having seen, been chased, or hairbreadth escapes from a—or several—sea-serpents." These monsters were, according to reports, "one hundred or more feet in length, with a body as large as a barrel and a head larger than a horse's." These reports induced one Captain Rich to fit out a vessel with all sorts of instruments to capture the sea monster that had "long terrified the credulous Bostonians." This he accomplished. It was a tuna "measuring nine feet in length, and four or five feet in circumference."[10]

A few intrepid Americans actually ate tuna in the nineteenth century. David Humphreys Storer, a Harvard professor who wrote extensively on zoological matters, reported that a tuna caught near Cape Ann, in northeastern Massachusetts, was fifteen feet long and weighed about a thousand pounds. Storer noted further: "Many of our citizens were enabled to feast themselves on its most delicate meat, resembling much in appearance lean pork, and the best of mackerel in taste." Another tuna became entangled in the seaweed at Provincetown, on Cape Cod, in 1839. According to a contemporary newspaper story, "A large number of the inhabitants were fed from it for several days, sending their children to cut pieces as it lay on the beach."[11] An 1846 account of a tuna stranded near the Beverly Bridge in Massachusetts noted curiously that the flesh "somewhat resembles that of fresh meat."[12] Some tuna tasters managed to even muster a little enthusiasm for the taste of tuna. In 1874, a writer in the *New York Times* confessed to enjoying "pickled tunny," but he was less excited about the fresh fish, which he thought tasted like "fishy veal."[13] Another writer claimed: "In taste, the flesh of the tunny resembles veal."[14]

By the 1860s, fish markets sold tuna, so there must have been some demand for it. Thomas F. Devoe, author of *The Market Assistant* (1867), reported that tuna was rare in markets, but when it was sold, its flesh was "considered good, and some say superior to the sword-fish."[15] P. H. Felker, author of *The Grocer's Manual* (1878), reported that tuna was "eaten both fresh and salted, and is highly esteemed."[16] Writing in the *Grocer's Hand-Book* (1883), Artemas Ward offered high praise for tuna sold in East Coast markets: "Its flesh is considered a delicacy. It yields considerable quantity of oil, twenty gallons being sometimes obtained from a single fish by boiling the head and belly."[17]

COARSE, OILY, SLIMY, SOFT

Few Americans agreed with these overly positive assessments, however, and tuna sales were minimal. The authors of the *New American Cyclopaedia* (1862) agreed that tuna resembled "lean pork," but reported that it was rarely used "except for mackerel bait."[18] The encyclopedia writer Todd S. Goodholme described tuna as "lacking in flavor."[19] In 1885, the New York *Fishing Gazette* reported that a Captain Black caught five hundred tuna "of an average weight of 35 pounds each, and brought them into market and sold them at from 10 to 25 cents each," which made it the least expensive fish in the market. Another ship brought in eight barrels of tuna, which could not be sold. When the fish began to spoil, they were condemned and shipped to Barren Island, off the coast of Brooklyn, which had a fish-rendering plant, where the rotting tuna was converted into fertilizer.[20] Yet another observer reported that the flesh was dark and not particularly attractive.[21]

George Brown Goode, who worked for the U.S. Commission of Fish and Fisheries in the 1880s, reported with surprise: "Although occurring in large numbers and of remarkable size, no effort is made toward their capture; and though not unfrequently taken in weirs and pounds along the coast, they are always allowed to rot on the shore. Occasionally a portion of the flesh may be used as food for chickens, but seldom, if ever, for human consumption."[22] In 1885 the *Fishing Gazette* agreed that tuna was "not a popular fish," but noted that its flesh "resembles lean pork, with a fine mackerel taste." The author then predicted that "the time will probably come when it will form a more important feature of marketable fish."[23]

Negative views continued well into the twentieth century. In 1906 a writer in *Field and Stream* noted: "The flesh of the tuna is oily, and unpalatable to most tastes."[24] David S. Jordan, a leading ichthyologist, admitted that tuna was "valueless" as an article of food.[25] He added to this in *American Food and Game Fishes* (1908), stating that albacore was "coarse and oily," a sentiment echoed by others.[26] Even as late as 1917, when many Americans were buying and eating canned tuna, a magazine writer still referred to tuna as "a huge, slimy, soft fish so repulsive in its natural state that no housewife or cook would buy it and prepare it for the table."[27]

HIGH-END RESTAURANT TUNA

Despite the general lack of enthusiasm for tuna eating, and tuna's generally bad reputation, the fish was offered for sale in some upper-class restaurants. It was included on the menu of Delmonico's, New York's premier restaurant, from 1838. Its *Thon mariné* (pickled tuna) was served as an hors d'oeuvre.[28] The restaurant catered to European visitors and America's wealthy, who likely had traveled in the Mediterranean, so it is not surprising that its customers were familiar with tuna before they dined at the restaurant. The restaurant's two most famous chefs, the Swiss-born Alessandro Filippini and the French-born Charles Ranhofer, both published cookbooks based on the recipes they used at Delmonico's, and both mentioned pickled or oil-packed tuna. Filippini's book, *The Table* (1889), which presented simplified recipes, included one tuna recipe for the hors d'oeuvre "*Thon Mariné*."[29] Ranhofer, Filippini's successor as *chef de cuisine*, published his magnum opus *The Epicurean* (1894), which makes two references to "Tunny fish." In one the tuna is sprinkled with oil and garnished "with chopped parsley, capers, sliced lemon or Séville oranges." It was served with slices of butter. Ranhofer also supplies a recipe for fried tuna with an arrowroot mayonnaise sauce.[30]

Other European chefs who immigrated to the United States also offered a few tuna dishes on their menus and recipes in their cookbooks. Pierre Blot, a French chef who came to the United States around 1855 to lecture on the culinary arts, included three recipes for tunny in his *Hand-Book of Practical Cookery* (1867). In one of these recipes he recommended that the fish be boiled and "served cold in *vinaigrette*." He also included a recipe for "Omelet with Tunny." As for fresh tuna, Blot recommended preparing it "like sturgeon," but warned: "This is not a good fish fresh." He did mention that canned or bottled tuna, imported from Holland, Italy, or the South of France, should be served on a small plate "like every other *hors-d'oeuvre*."[31] Felix Déliée, a French émigré chef at the New York Club, the Union Club, and the Manhattan Club, published recipes for "Tunny à la St. Augustin" (a four-pound chunk of fresh tuna boiled for forty minutes with vegetables and spices) and "Tunny Steak, sauce Robert" (marinated and broiled tuna steak with sauce) in his *Franco-American Cookery Book* (1884).[32]

The tuna served at high-end restaurants was probably not caught or packed by Americans. It was likely imported from Europe, where it had been caught, and salted or pickled for decades. French canned tuna reached the United States by 1865.[33] Canned tuna from Portugal won an award at the Centennial Exposition in Philadelphia in 1876.[34] At the same exposition, the American Fish Culturists' Association met and dined on fifty-eight varieties of seafood, including imported "tunny" from France.[35] By 1885, Sprague, Warner & Co. in Chicago distributed imported canned tuna,[36] and the following year the luxury food merchant S.S. Pierce & Company of Boston had begun importing *Thon mariné* from Philippe & Canaud, located in Nantes, France.[37] Two other French firms, Teyssoneau and Dandicolle & Gaudin, exported tuna to the United States by the early 1900s.[38]

FOOD FOR CHICKENS

As important as imported tuna may have been for America's upper class and the occasional traveler to the Mediterranean, most Americans did not eat tuna and had little interest in doing so. The exceptions were immigrants, such as those from southern Europe, especially those from Italy. In 1850, the census noted fewer than 4,000 people of Italian heritage living in the United States. After the American Civil War, however, greater numbers of Italians immigrated in search of economic opportunities. By the 1880 census, the total number of Italians in America was 44,000, and this was only the beginning. During the next quarter century, Italians immigrated to America en masse, reaching 4.2 million by 1920. Many settled in urban areas, such as the North End in Boston, Ninth Street in Philadelphia, North Beach in San Francisco, and Little Italy in New York and Chicago. Most Italian immigrants were familiar with tuna, and, unlike native-born Americans, they were delighted to find it at local fish markets, especially since this luxury was priced so low that they could afford it.

In the autumn of 1897, the *New York Times* published the saga of an Italian fishmonger who bought a 900-pound tuna for $9 at Fulton Market. The *Times* continued: "About his store that night a changing group made up of old women, old men, young girls, and small boys with bulging eyes worshipped at the shrine. The old people spoke of fish in their day in far-off Italy, and revealed the secret of the wonderful sauce. To this last the young girls paid careful attention."[39] The Italian communities in Boston and Philadelphia also provided a ready market for tuna, which was sold occasionally in those cities' fish markets by 1900.[40]

The small Italian communities on the West Coast ate fresh tuna whenever they could get it. In 1895, the *San Francisco Examiner* reported that Captains Valancola and Gusti caught a tuna in Monterey Bay "after a desperate fight." The fish was frequently plentiful in Southern California waters, although there was little evidence that commercial fishermen were particularly interested in catching it. Even Italian fishermen in Monterey bitterly complained that tuna fish destroyed their fishing nets.[41]

By the beginning of the twentieth century, fresh and salted tuna occasionally were sold in Southern California fish markets, but sales were limited to a few immigrant customers—mostly Japanese and Italians—and the poor, who could not afford more desirable fish.

It was neither the few haute-cuisine aficionados nor tuna-loving immigrants, however, who jolted mainstream Americans into eating this fish. Rather, it was sportfishermen, who loved battling a fighting tuna on the line, although paradoxically few of these fishermen, who would shift American eating habits, actually ate what they caught.

PART ONE The Rise

ONE Angling for a Big Fish

Charles Holder, an East Coast naturalist, first visited Santa Catalina Island, off the Southern California coast, in 1886. Hoping to catch one of the large tuna known to frequent the island's shores during the summer months, he brought along his freshwater rod and reel. There were plenty of fishermen on the island, and they caught plenty of tuna, but they did so using thick hand-lines with multiple hooks. They tied the lines to boats or piers and dropped them into the water. When fish hit the hooks, the fishermen waited until they were exhausted fighting against the line, and then just pulled them in, which usually took a few minutes. Holder proclaimed this method to be unsportsmanlike; he believed that rods and reels gave the fish a fighting chance.

In Catalina, Holder met José Felice Presiado ("Mexican Joe"), the only professional boatman on the island at the time. Presiado had arrived in Catalina at the age of seven from Sonora, Mexico, about 1851. By the 1880s he owned a broad-beamed yawl that he used to take fishermen around the island. Holder hired Presiado to row him to places where he could fish with his rod and reel. Holder and Presiado encountered a school of "leaping tuna," as Holder called them. The tuna weren't leaping out of the water for the fun of it. They were chasing flying fish that jumped into the air as they tried to escape the pursuing tuna. Flying fish have large pectoral fins that allow them to glide more than 150 feet over the surface of the water. The much heavier and less aerodynamic tuna could leap 10 to 15 feet in the air before crashing back into the ocean. Holder vividly described the scene: "Down the Santa Catalina channel they came like a cyclone, turning the quiet waters into foam, in and out of which the big fishes darted like animated arrows or torpedoes, while the air was filled with flocks of flying fishes fleeing in every direction like grasshoppers." Holder and Mexican Joe followed the school for several miles, and Holder cast into the leaping tuna with his rod and reel. He lost every line he cast and didn't catch a fish. This came as no surprise to Presiado, who couldn't imagine why Holder—or anyone else for that matter—would want to catch tuna with a rod and reel; fishermen using hand lines always caught as many as they wanted with very little effort.[1]

Holder's initial failure did not discourage him. He came back season after season, and he even convinced others to go after tuna with rods and reels. Despite all the skill of some of the world's best and most experienced anglers, the results were always the same: the tuna inevitably won, breaking fish lines, often absconding with the rods and reels and occasionally pulling fishermen overboard, as the tuna swam off into the channel.

In 1898, Holder acquired the latest fishing gear with a stronger rod and reel. This worked. He finally succeeded in his twelve-year quest when he landed a 183-pound tuna on June 1. Two weeks later he convened a meeting of sportfishermen at the Hotel Metropole in Avalon, Catalina's largest community. These men, who enjoyed the challenge of fishing for tuna with rod and reel, created the Tuna Club, thereby inventing American saltwater sportfishing. The exploits of sportfishermen and some women alerted the American public to this most unusual fish, and consequently, the largely unknown tuna fish would soon be upgraded from a trash fish to an aquatic celebrity in the American imagination.

FISH WITH CHARACTER

Catalina's Tuna Club was not the first fishing club in America. Sportfishing, an upper-class British tradition brought to America in colonial times, developed a broader social base in nineteenth-century America as railroads made once-remote streams, rivers, and lakes more accessible. Accompanying these shifts were changing views toward nature, a recognition of the disappearance of the natural wonders of America, and an increasing yearning to preserve wilderness areas. As America urbanized in the nineteenth century, many well-to-do Americans took up outdoor leisure activities, such as camping, hunting, and fishing. After the Civil War many Americans began to enjoy sportfishing.[2]

Sportfishing differed considerably from traditional commercial or subsistence fishing where the most efficient methods—hand lines, nets, spears, guns, or on occasion dynamite—were employed to acquire as many fish as possible in the shortest period of time to generate the maximum amount of money with the least effort. Sportfishing was a leisure activity with a very different mind-set. It required a set of gentlemanly practices designed to pit the fisherman's skill against a cunning fish. Fishing clubs, such as the Schuylkill Fishing Company in Philadelphia, were organized to provide upper-class men with an escape from their everyday world. By the early nineteenth century, angling clubs had emerged in many American cities. The purpose of these clubs was primarily social, with a little fishing on the side (although not always with a rod and reel). From these upper-class clubs evolved organizations that would establish the rules for angling using hooks, lines, flies, lures, rods, and reels. As the century progressed, American manufacturers began making and marketing proper fishing gear that had formerly been imported from England. By the end of the century, magazines such as *Forest and Stream* and *American Angler,* and more than 100 books, exalted the art of freshwater sportfishing.[3]

Angling clubs, fishing magazines, and sportfishing books promoted particular methods of fishing and a code of proper conduct for fishermen. Particular fish, especially those with "character" that could put up a fight, were identified as "game" fish. Anglers were encouraged to catch them, while other fish were classified as "rough" or "coarse," and not worth a genteel angler's time. These methods and guidelines helped distinguish upper- and middle-class anglers from the subsistence or working-class fishermen, as well as reducing the sportfishing catch and helping to prevent depletion of fish populations.[4] In many states, laws were passed to regulate fishing—shooting fish, dynamiting ponds, and using nets for fishing became illegal. Licenses were required, and other restrictions were developed. These rules and regulations applied to freshwater fishing in inland lakes and streams, and not to ocean fishing, which remained a commercial activity.

State governments showed an interest in fisheries after the Civil War. Massachusetts became the first state to establish a commission on fish, in 1865, and several other states followed. It wasn't until 1871 that the federal government began to regulate freshwater fishing, but at the time no one considered saltwater fishing a sport.

A VERY GAMY FISH

Some nineteenth-century sportsmen did fish for tuna. As Dr. Pierre Fortin, the Canadian magistrate for the Gulf of St. Lawrence, observed, fishing for tuna was "quite exciting, although tiresome and requiring a good deal of skill, as in the efforts of these fish to escape they pull with such violence as to endanger the lives of the fishermen by dragging them overboard." The few fishermen who were interested in catching tuna employed baited hand-lines with multiple hooks connected by small ropes attached firmly to their boats or docks.[5] When the tuna took the bait, the fishermen just let the fish struggle until exhausted, and then easily hauled them in.

Tuna was common off New Brunswick, Canada, reported an observer in 1844, but it was "rarely taken, because its flesh is not prized for food."[6]

In the same year, British visitor Philip Tocque was surprised to find that few fishermen in Newfoundland were aware that tuna "constitutes a sumptuous article of food, or that it is even fit to eat."[7] Off Cape Cod, bluefin were common during the summer months, and large fish were occasionally harpooned for oil: an average-sized tuna yielded about twenty-four gallons.[8] Fish oil was used primarily for commercial purposes, such as making soap and paints and tanning hides.

In the 1870s, Congress approved budgets that included a study of saltwater fish in American coastal waters. Spencer Fullerton Baird, the commissioner of the U.S. Commission of Fish and Fisheries, asked David Starr Jordan, one of the foremost naturalists of the day and then a professor at Indiana University, to conduct a study of the Pacific coast fisheries. Jordan selected one of his brightest students, Charles H. Gilbert, to assist him in this investigation. They surveyed the West Coast from British Columbia to Baja California.[9] Virtually the entire survey was conducted within a few miles of shore, as their small boats were "too frail to face the dangers of the open sea," as Jordan later put it. Jordan and Gilbert did not locate any tuna, which they expected to find near San Clemente Island, off the coast of Southern California, but they did find albacore, then scientifically considered a genus separate from tuna. Albacore, they pointed out in their report, was caught chiefly for sport, and it was "little valued as a food-fish" as it was "a very gamy fish." Large fish sold for about twenty-five cents apiece.[10]

At the time of their visit, West Coast fishing was conducted by a wild collection of fishermen, whose vessels included "Chinese junks, lateen-rigged Italian boats and New England whale boats."[11] Some did fish for tuna, but they were recently arrived immigrants, especially from Italy, Portugal, Japan, and the Azores, who had eaten tuna in their homelands. In San Diego, some fishermen launched a business, catching, and then salting and pickling albacore, which was abundant in the bay and within a few miles of the coast. It was sold to Japanese immigrant field laborers in California and Hawaii.[12] This business was the exception: most fishermen who caught tuna dumped them overboard far out at sea so they wouldn't foul the beaches, or took them into port where the carcasses were converted into fertilizer or fish oil.

Writing toward the end of the nineteenth century, George Brown Goode, who became U.S. Fish Commissioner when Baird died, observed that despite tuna's excellent reputation in the Old World and its abundance in American waters, it was hardly ever eaten by Americans— although oil from tuna was used for lamps.[13]

LEAPING TUNA

American saltwater sportfishing was transformed by one man: Charles Frederick Holder, a naturalist who spent years working with his father, Joseph Bassett Holder, curator of invertebrate zoology at the American Museum of Natural History in New York. The father-and-son team spent five years studying the growth of coral reefs off the coast of Florida. Charles Holder subsequently served as a consultant to the New York Aquarium in 1875 and then devoted his life to writing books for adolescents.

Charles Holder already had exposure to tuna before he arrived in Southern California in 1885. When he was young, his father had acquired and mounted an 8-foot-long, 1,000-pound bluefin at the Lynn Museum in Massachusetts. Then Holder heard about the tuna averaging 1,000 pounds each that had been captured in Gloucester harbor. During the 1870s, he came across another 9-foot bluefin, which he estimated weighed about 1,200 pounds, in New York's Fulton Market. He carefully measured that fish and published his findings in *Scientific American*. Holder began to wonder what it would be like to catch one of these monsters with a rod and reel. For a time he fished for tuna off the coast of Maine's Boon Island. But in two seasons, he never even saw one.[14]

Holder's only son died at the age of five months in 1885. He and his wife moved from New York to Pasadena, California, to distract themselves from their loss.[15] At the time, Southern California's natural habitat was still relatively pristine and largely unexplored from botanical and zoological standpoints. Taking his rod and reel with him, Holder began exploring the state's mountains, rivers, and coastal waters. He was particularly enthralled with Southern California's coastal areas, where he found "an amazing spectacle in the abundance of fishes, shellfish and crustaceans." Holder also explored the Channel Islands, off the coast of Southern California. Santa Catalina was the easiest to visit, and Holder went there for the first time in 1886. Here, he found a real "fisherman's paradise."[16]

In the very small community of Avalon, Holder found tuna bones in an Indian mound on the beach.[17] Catalina had been occupied intermittently by various American Indian groups, including the Gabrieleño in prehistoric times. Europeans had first visited the island in 1542 and sporadically thereafter. By the mid-nineteenth century, the island was largely deserted. George Shatto, a real estate speculator, purchased the island, established a very small community that would become Avalon, and began building a resort. He built Avalon's pier, making it possible for passenger ships to dock, and started construction on a hotel on the site of the Indian mound that Holder had explored on his first visit to the island. The hotel was initially a modest place for visitors to spend the night, but during the following decade it was upgraded to luxury status.

Early on, the Hotel Metropole was the only commercial hotel in Avalon, and visiting fishermen congregated there. Holder convinced some to go after tuna with rods and reels. As it turned out, it was usually the fish who caught the rods and reels, frequently pulling them overboard. Fishing for tuna this way was dangerous, and the Metropole garnered the nickname "Tuna Hospital" because of all the injured and bandaged fishermen who stayed there during tuna season.[18]

A decade after Holder had first tried to catch a tuna, he reported in *Cosmopolitan* magazine that no one had yet succeeded. It was the fish that had "harvested the rods, reels, and lines."[19] The problem was that the equipment of the time just wasn't strong enough to withstand the tremendous pulling power of large tuna. When Holder finally caught a 183-pound tuna in 1898, he immediately informed the press, and newspapers heralded this astounding feat the following day, reporting that Holder's tuna had been landed after a struggle lasting three hours and forty-five minutes. The *Pasadena Daily News*, Holder's hometown paper, proclaimed that in landing the mighty fish, "the Professor eclipsed all previous achievements in the line of angling."[20]

Despite this nice story, perhaps written by Holder himself, he was not the first to catch a large tuna with a rod and reel. That honor went to Colonel Clinton P. Morehouse, also of Pasadena, who did so during the summer of 1896. During the 1897 season, fourteen more large tuna were caught by other anglers.[21] But it was Holder's catch the following year that proved to be the turning point, for shortly thereafter Holder called a meeting of the sportfishermen then in Avalon. When the group convened, at the Metropole, they inaugurated the Tuna Club. As Holder later wrote, "Among the observers were reporters and correspondents, and I later saw myself pictured playing this leaping tuna forty feet at least in air. Another account in a magazine showed me calmly swimming and playing the tuna, the caption suggesting that I rather preferred that method. The Associated Press telegraphed the story to England, and the members of the peaceful Sea Anglers' Association in London received the account the next morning in the papers, and doubtless marveled at the big things in America."[22] Holder later explained his reasons for founding the Tuna Club:

> The splendid fishes of the region, yellowtail, white sea bass and others, were being slaughtered by the ton. I had seen boats go out with five or six hand lines rigged out astern, to return with forty or more fish, none less than fifteen pounds, and running up to twenty-five, each with the game qualities of a forty-pound salmon. It was a depressing sight, as most of these fishes were fed to the sea lions and sharks. How to stop it was the question, and I conceived the idea of an appeal to the innate sense of fair play that is found among nearly all anglers.[23]

At the club's subsequent meeting on August 22, 1898, Holder wanted five pounds added to the weight of his trophy catch to compensate for blood and fluids lost by the tuna as it fought on the line, and that its weight should therefore be listed as 188 pounds. The *Los Angeles Daily Times* (again with Holder as the likely source) dutifully passed on this claim as well.[24] The feats of these tuna fishermen—and occasionally women— were news at the turn of the twentieth century, and an unlikely fish that few Americans had ever heard of began to be bandied about in newspapers—often with front-page coverage—and magazines across

America, Canada, and Great Britain. These reports were often abetted by Holder and other club members, who were not opposed to gaining a little visibility for themselves, but their main interest was to promote their sportsmanlike approach to saltwater fishing with rods and reels in hopes of stopping the massive slaughter of fish along the coast of Southern California by sportfishermen who caught thousands of fish with hand lines, only to toss the tuna overboard. This is not to say that the sportsfishermen did much more with their tuna when caught, for there's little evidence during the early years that club members actually ate the fish—they usually just had their photo taken with the largest fish they caught, or they stuffed it and shipped it home.

Due to these promotional activities, anglers around the country flocked to Catalina and joined the movement. The club was composed of "gentleman and ladies who have by their skill and perseverance suc-ceeded in taking with rod and reel in the waters of this State and with a line not stronger than 24-thread, one leaping tuna of not less than 100 pounds weight."[25] The purpose of the club would later be defined "to prevent the slaughter of game fish with hand lines, to elevate the standard of sport on the Pacific Coast," and "in every legitimate way to set an example of the highest possible sportsmanship."[26] By the end of July 1898, twenty-four anglers had landed a tuna weighing 100 pounds or more following the club's rules. To those who had achieved this feat, the club awarded a blue button, which was worn—then, as now—with pride. The following year, Holder caught a 196-pound tuna; he was so happy that he sent his catch for mounting by Charles B. Parker in Avalon. As for Holder's record tuna, it was short-lived; it was surpassed a few days later by Colonel Morehouse, who reeled in a 251-pound tuna.[27]

The club's constitution and bylaws permitted the use of fishing lines "up to twenty-four thread only and light rods, with the condition that every angler must land his own fish."[28] Even with improved rods and reels, Holder reported, 50 percent of the fish got away. Thus, he con-cluded, "overfishing is practically impossible, and much finer sport with the rod is obtained. The result is, that to-day the waste of these fine game fishes is practically stopped." To popularize the new sport, Holder cre-ated an "annual angling tournament, to begin May first and end October first, during which valuable prizes of rods and tackle, medals and cups in various classes were offered to anglers who took the largest fishes of various kinds with the light rods and fine lines specified by the by-laws of the Tuna Club." He proudly proclaimed that "Nowhere in the world does a higher standard of sport prevail than on the tuna grounds of Southern California."[29] America's first sportfishing club specializing in saltwater fish was up and running, and it would soon help create the sport of saltwater fishing that would be enjoyed by fishermen throughout the world.

KITES AND BALLOONS

Club rules had to be followed by sportsfishermen, but there was still plenty of room for creativity. When tuna became leery of boats and would not go near them, fishermen invented new ways of catching them. In 1909 Captain George Farnsworth, a boatman and experienced fisherman, developed the creative idea of catching tuna by flying a kite several hundred feet from the boat; a baited fisherman's line was attached to the kite, from which it was dangled vertically into the water. Undisturbed by the close proximity of a boat, the tuna would go after the baited fishing line. When one was hooked, the line broke off from the kite, and the fisherman then was pitted against the tuna. The boatman then reeled in the kite. Farnsworth extracted a solemn pledge from the fishermen who hired him not to divulge his secret, but two years later, word leaked out; within a few years, the kite fishing was in general use. Other anglers used a small "sled" that performed a similar function except that it skimmed across the surface of the water leaving almost no wake. Bait was attached to the sled on a string that was also attached to the fisherman's reel. When the fish was hooked, the bait line broke, leaving the fisherman to reel in the fish while the boatman pulled in the sled.[30]

By far the most unusual idea for catching tuna was proposed by a Dr. B. F. Alder from San Francisco, who planned to use hot air balloons to catch tuna. The fishermen would just hover over the surface of the sea in the balloon, dangling bait into the water. Although balloons were discussed and apparently used, no evidence has surfaced that anyone in a balloon ever caught a tuna.[31] But it was a creative idea.

WHAT DOES RAW TUNA TASTE LIKE?

The publicity that tuna fishing generated attracted some of world's finest anglers and writers during the early twentieth century. Members of the Tuna Club included many prominent Americans. In his youth, the future World War II general, George S. Patton, spent considerable time in Catalina and became a member of the club.[32] Honorary members included President Theodore Roosevelt, who was elected to the club in 1898, when he was governor of New York; Grover Cleveland, former president of the United States; Charles Hallock, founder of *Forest and Stream*; David S. Jordan, the ichthyologist who had examined the fish of California in 1880; and many other luminaries.[33] Fishermen came from around the world to catch the big tuna mentioned in so many articles and books.

Another visitor to Avalon was a writer, born Pearl Zane Gray in Zanesville, Ohio, in 1872. His family changed the spelling of their last name to "Grey," and Pearl later dropped his first name and became known simply as Zane Grey. Trained as a dentist, he began writing fiction in 1902. He published his first western novel—a huge success—in 1910; his subsequent books made him a very wealthy man. One of his hobbies was fishing. He had caught tuna off the New Jersey shore before visiting Catalina for the first time in August 1914. He failed to catch a big tuna that season, but he came back year after year to try again. Zane Grey liked Southern California and settled his family in Altadena, a Los Angeles suburb, in 1918. The following year he finally caught a big tuna at Catalina and later wrote: "The event was so thrilling that I had to write to my fisherman friends about it."[34] He also told the whole world about his "giant tuna" in his *Tales of Fish*, which was written and published shortly after he caught the fish. Grey received his blue button from the Tuna Club and was later elected its president.

Unfortunately, the large tuna disappeared from the Channel Islands, but Grey continued to fish and to write about his experiences. Some weighty tuna continued to be caught by Zane Grey, but those fish were pulled out of the Atlantic near Nova Scotia or the South Pacific off Australia.[35] In 1924, for instance, Grey caught a bluefin weighing 758 pounds—a record at the time—off the coast of Nova Scotia. What pleased Grey most was his ten-year-old son's reaction: "Sure is some fish! Biggest ever caught on a rod, by anybody, any kind of game fish. . . . And I was here to see you lick him, dad!"[36]

Another writer who was drawn to tuna fishing was Ernest Hemingway, and he too wrote about his exploits. In an article for the *Toronto Star* in 1922, Hemingway described catching tuna in Vigo, Spain. Years later Hemingway fished near Bimini and Cat Cay in the Caribbean, and in 1935 caught two large bluefin, which he called "the king of all fish."[37] In hisPulitzer Prize–winning book, *The Old Man and the Sea*, Hemingway is a bit confusing about the kind of fish the old man caught: on one page he says that it's an albacore, on another page it's a tuna, and on yet another page, a bonito.[38] But Hemingway does mention eating raw tuna, something very usual at the time: "What does raw tuna taste like? You'll have to taste real raw tuna to find out." He continues: "It would not be bad to eat with a little lime or with lemon or with salt."[39]

Despite the vast numbers of tuna that were caught, few fishermen actually tasted tuna until the early twentieth century. Even at Tuna Club banquets, tuna was not on the early menus.[40] While most Americans did not eat it, some ethnic groups were happy to feast on a fish they considered a delicacy. Immigrants from Mexico and Japan, for instance, ate tuna, as did those from the Mediterranean region, where people had eaten tuna for millennia. Fishermen from these ethnic groups engaged in commercial tuna fishing, but they sold their small catches only to members of their own communities. Some of the fish were dumped "out a mile from shore as no one with good judgment ate tuna fish."[41] Holder reported in 1908 that nearly all the tuna caught with rod and reel were mounted by Chas. C. Parker, the Avalon taxidermist, "who has sent them all over this country and to England as trophies."[42] By 1914, however, things had changed, and Holder finally reported that young, "meaty and rich" albacore were actually served at the "banquets of the Tuna Club."[43]

CONSERVATION

Holder was not just interested in catching fish in a sportsmanlike fashion; he was also interested in protecting "the game fishes of Southern California."[44] He and other members of the Tuna Club engaged in efforts to preserve the fisheries adjacent to the Channel Islands. Yet tuna began to disappear—partly because of changing migratory patterns, but mainly because of massive commercial canning of albacore, which began in 1903. Holder was not at all happy about this. The most menacing danger, he proclaimed in 1912, was the commercial fishermen who used nets to catch game and market fish, as well as the food that these fish ate.[45] Without sardines and other fish that tuna preyed on, the big fish moved on to more hospitable waters. By 1914, few big tuna were caught off the Catalina shores. Sportsfishermen and newspapers blamed commercial fishermen who operated out of San Pedro. They were extremely efficient and caught tens of thousands of tons of albacore annually for the canneries.[46]

The Tuna Club lobbied for legislation prohibiting commercial fishing around the Channel Islands. A three-mile limit around Catalina was designated as a conservation zone where only sportsfishermen could catch fish. This was found to be discriminatory to commercial fishermen, and it was declared unconstitutional in 1915. The California legislature rushed through new legislation in 1915.[47] When the albacore began to disappear from the channel in 1918, commercial fishermen began intruding into protected areas around the Channel Islands. When the boats were charged with violating the ban, boat owners filed an injunction to prevent the state from enforcing the law. The Catalina ban was upheld, but tuna boats continued intruding into the conservation zone; when caught, owners paid small fines.[48]

Sportfishermen began fishing elsewhere. Zane Grey lamented that the swordfish, white sea bass, yellowtail, and albacore were doomed because the "Japs, the Austrians, the round-haul nets, the canneries and the fertilizer-plants—that is to say, foreigners and markets, greed and war, have cast their dark shadow over beautiful Avalon."[49]

A MONSTROUS TUNA

Ironically, the early sportfishermen who initially turned up their palates at tuna laid the groundwork for a shift in the public's perception of tuna from repulsive bottom-feeder to tasty, inexpensive food. Newspapers and magazines published articles about the exploits of sportfishermen, and writers such a Charles Holder and Zane Grey popularized the fish in their works. At last, mainstream Americans—few of whom were even aware of the existence of tuna prior to 1900—soon became big fans of the canned fish they would find on their grocers' shelves during the following decades.

Fishermen who came to Catalina during the early twentieth century would be instrumental in turning canned tuna into a household staple. One was Wilbur F. Wood, the superintendent of the California Fish Company, a sardine cannery in San Pedro. Wood went fishing near Catalina in 1902 and caught "a monstrous tuna," estimated at 600 pounds, which he fought for seven hours before handing his rod over to his boatman, "who continued for seven and a quarter hours further before it was landed." At the last minute, as so often happened, the line broke; the gaffs couldn't hold the fish, and the dead tuna slipped to the bottom of the sea.[50] Two other sportfishermen who would follow in Wilbur Wood's footsteps were Frank Van Camp and his son Gilbert, who came to Catalina on a fishing trip in 1910. They stayed at the Metropole and agreed to follow the rules of the Tuna Club for catching fish. They made a deal with other fisherman staying at the Metropole to give a can of their "Pork and Beans" to the fisherman who caught the biggest tuna.[51] Wood and the Van Camps would subsequently help create the California tuna-canning industry.

POSTSCRIPT

Charles Holder founded the Pasadena Academy of Sciences in 1888 and became a trustee of Throop University, later renamed the California Institute of Technology. He wrote dozens of articles that promoted the Avalon Tuna Club and sportfishing. He also published more than twenty books, many of which included chapters on tuna. These include *Angling* (1897); *Santa Catalina: Its Sports and Antiquities* (1897); *The Big Game Fishes of the United States* (1903); *The Log of a Sea Angler* (1906); and *The Channel Islands of California: A Book for the Angler, Sportsman, and Tourist* (1910). With David S. Jordan, he coauthored *Fish Stories*, which was published in

1909. Charles Holder died in 1915. For his work in sportfishing, he was inducted into the International Game Fish Association Hall of Fame in 1998.

David S. Jordan became president of Stanford University in 1891; he retired in 1926 after serving twenty-two years in that capacity and three years as chancellor. He opposed American involvement in World War I. He authored or coauthored more than 200 books and reports on various subjects, including one on evolution, and he was called as an expert witness for the defense in the Scopes trial in 1925. A few months before his death in 1931, *Time* magazine selected him for its cover.

Charles H. Gilbert, who had conducted the survey of California fish with Jordan in 1880, became one of America's most important ichthyologists and fishery biologists. He wrote or coauthored more than 200 books and reports on American fish before his death in 1928.

Using Catalina's Tuna Club as a model, other saltwater fishing clubs appeared. The Southern California Tuna Club, founded in 1925, currently boasts 200 to 250 anglers as members. The Atlantic Tuna Club was incorporated in October 1914 on Block Island; it was later moved to Snug Harbor, Rhode Island.[52] The Hawaii Tuna Club was formed in 1914.[53] Anglers founded tuna clubs in many other places, including New York, New Jersey, and Northern California.[54] Overseas clubs included the Tuna Club of Tasmania and the Bimini Marlin-Tuna Club.

Zane Grey continued to write—a total of eighty-nine books—and he continued to fish for tuna. In 1936 he visited Australia, where he fished and wrote about his adventures in *An American Angler in Australia* (1937). He died two years later.

The Avalon Tuna Club survives today, although the bluefin tuna virtually disappeared from the coastal area around the Channel Islands decades ago. In 1908, the club erected a building in Avalon to serve as its permanent home. This modest structure burned to the ground (along with much of Avalon) in 1915. But a new clubhouse—a far more imposing one—was built the following year, and it remains one of the most impressive structures on the beach today.[55]

TWO Looks Like Chicken

Albert P. Halfhill, a heavyset man with a cowcatcher mustache, opened a can and offered its contents to Sig Seeman, a food wholesaler and distributor in New York. Halfhill was one of the founders of the California Fish Company, a small cannery in East San Pedro, not far from Los Angeles. Halfhill had never met Seeman; it was a cold call. Halfhill was making the rounds of East Coast distributors to promote a new product: albacore. It was a tough sell in 1908, because few Americans had heard of the fish, and those who had, disliked it. Some considered albacore a scavenger fish and bottom feeder. Others thought the meat was too oily, and its brown color, when cooked, was unappetizing. Then again the California Fish Company's previous attempts at canning albacore had ended up with fish blood in the cans, which was yet another turnoff for potential consumers.

To avoid these problems, the California Fish Company had experimented for five years, improving the process, and figured out how to make the canned product very light-colored. It called its product "Blue Sea Brand Tuna." Some Americans knew something about tuna, but that fish was not generally consumed either. Seeman looked into the open can and asked: "What's this?" Halfhill responded with a question: "What do you think it is?" To which Seeman purportedly answered: "I don't know what it is, but it looks like chicken."[1]

Seeman liked the California Fish Company's canned albacore, and he became its New York distributor. Sales the first year were good, but in 1909, no one wanted it. Seeman had sold 150 cases to a New York wholesale grocer, Austin, Nichols and Co., which was unable to sell any. All cases were returned. Seeman then gave a free case of tuna to his customers when they bought bags of coffee. Even then, some customers still sent back the free cases. He met with other distributors, such as Carl Trieste of Haas, Baruch Company, who told Seeman that he wasn't crazy enough to try to sell canned albacore. But Seeman was intrigued, and he believed that the canned fish was a winner. He traveled to Los Angeles and proposed a partnership with the California Fish Company. It never materialized, but Seeman was right—canned tuna was ready to take off.[2]

ABUNDANCE OF AVAILABLE FISH

The California Fish Company was not the first seafood cannery in America. Fish had been canned on the East Coast since 1819, when Ezra Dagget and his son-in-law, Thomas Kensett, began using tin cans to pack salmon, lobsters, and oysters in New York City. Edward Wright of Baltimore is said to have packed oysters soon after 1830. In 1839 Upham S. Treat, of Eastport, Maine, began packing salmon at St. Johns, New Brunswick.[3] By the 1840s the canning of seafood was an important East Coast industry.

When gold was discovered in California, William Hume, a fisherman from Augusta, Maine, headed for the Pacific coast. When the gold petered out, Hume looked for another way to make a living. A closer look at the rivers of Northern California convinced him that their true "gold" was not to be found in nuggets, but in the salmon in those rivers. Salmon were easy to catch in quantity when millions migrated upriver to spawn each year. But salmon is fatty, so it spoils quickly. Hume's solution was to salt and smoke the fish, but he had trouble maintaining consistent flavor and quality. In 1864 he solved that problem by establishing a cannery on a barge in the Sacramento River. Soon others began catching and canning salmon from California rivers, and it wasn't long before the salmon were fished out.[4] Hume headed for Astoria, Oregon, where salmon were still plentiful. Other canners followed his lead to the Columbia River, eventually forming the Columbia River Packers Association, which would sell its canned salmon under the brand name "Bumble Bee."

Meanwhile, back in California, the Golden Gate Packing Company was launched in San Francisco in 1889 as a sardine cannery. When sardines were fished out of San Francisco Bay, about four years later, the company sold its canning equipment to the newly formed California Fish Company in San Pedro.[5]

WHITE MEAT

The California Fish Company had been organized by Robert David Wade and Albert P. Halfhill in 1892. It was an unusual decision for them. Neither Wade nor Halfhill had enough cash to build a factory or buy all the equipment needed—and for that matter neither man knew anything about canning. Halfhill was a recent arrival in Southern California. Previously, he had owned a small grocery store in Van Wert, Ohio; he then went into the wholesale grocery business in Mankato, Minnesota, where he was one of the founders of a wholesale firm, Patterson, Halfhill & Zimmerman. He moved to California for his wife's health in 1892.[6] Robert Wade had moved to Los Angeles in 1878, where he became a merchant, served on the Los Angeles Board of Education, and became the county's deputy tax collector. To help fund their operation, Wade and Halfhill approached Joseph H. Lapham, a wealthy merchant who visited Los Angeles in 1892 and liked what he saw; Lapham was also an avid fisherman. Lapham agreed to invest in the new company and became its major stockholder and its president. He moved from Marietta, Ohio, to California in February 1893. A two-story factory with a salting house was constructed on Terminal Island—a four-square-mile, largely manmade island in San Pedro Bay.

San Pedro was a good location for a fish cannery. The waters off the Southern California coast teemed with fish and seafood. A thriving fishing industry had developed in the area, and its products were distributed throughout the western states by railroad, steamship, and the Wells Fargo Company's express service, which employed horse-drawn wagons. The California Fish Company hoped to capitalize on the abundance of available fish, especially sardines, and the existing distribution system to sell its canned fish. In December 1893 the California Fish Company began canning sardines and mackerel.[7]

The cannery owned only one fishing boat, the *Alpha*, with a seven-man crew. The boat had a small gasoline engine but proceeded under sail when on the hunt for fish. It operated only during the day, when the fish could be spotted on the surface. The *Alpha*'s main fishing ground was initially San Pedro Bay; when this was fished out, the *Alpha* plied the waters between the coast and Catalina Island. The fishermen used nets, which scooped up sardines, mackerel, yellowtail, barracuda, and white sea bass. The cans were made in San Pedro. As was typical at the time, the cans were hand cut from sheets of tin and hand soldered. The company would not automate the canning process until the early twentieth century.[8]

Albert Halfhill's main role was to promote and sell the California Fish Company's canned goods. In Los Angeles, he established a good relationship with Harris Newmark, an immigrant from Prussia, who had arrived in San Pedro in 1853 and opened one of Los Angeles's first dry-goods stores; Newmark later branched out into groceries. Another of Halfhill's customers was Hans Jevne, a Norwegian immigrant who moved to Los Angeles in 1882 and established a wholesale and retail grocery store that quickly became one of the city's premier food purveyors. Halfhill was a good salesman, and sardine sales were good. In 1894, the California Fish Company put up 4,000 cases of fish; within four years it was packing 19,000 cases. It was a truly local industry: the fish were caught in the bay; California olive oil was used to pack the sardines; and the products were mainly marketed in the Los Angeles area.

The company's technical ability to can fish was improved by the hiring of two professionals. Wilbur F. Wood, a young canner who had worked for two years at the Brawn Packing Company in Portland, Oregon, was hired in 1898 and two years later became superintendent of the cannery. James McMann, an experienced canner from Maine, was hired as an assistant superintendent in 1902.[9] The following year, the company faced its most serious challenge: sardines disappeared off the Southern California coast.

Rather than close the cannery until the sardines returned at some unknown future date, the company decided to experiment with canning other fish that could be easily caught in San Pedro Bay. Rock cod was plentiful; halibut was less so, but fresh fetched a greater price, so perhaps canned halibut would as well. Halfhill suggested canning tuna—he had seen an expensive can of imported Italian tunny on his travels while selling sardines.[10] Tuna was a high-end product that had been canned in Europe for decades, and there was plenty of tuna off the Southern California coast, but there was little demand for it, and no American canner had ever canned it. But it was worth a try.

So in 1903 the California Fish Company packed 1,500 cases of rock cod, 500 cases of halibut, and 700 cases of tuna. Canned rock cod and halibut were not successful and were discontinued. Sales of tuna weren't that great either, but Wood, McMann, and Lapham were intrigued enough to continue canning it after the sardines returned to the bay in 1904. Over the next few years they perfected their canning method.[11] The Los Angeles grocers Hans Jevne Company and M. A. Newmark & Company purchased a few cases, but two years after selling them, Halfhill walked in their stores and found cans from the original order still sitting on their shelves.[12] The canned tuna was just too oily, strong tasting, and it was an off-putting dark brown color.

Rather than give up on tuna, Wood tried canning albacore, a related species (*Germo*) then considered separate from tuna (*Thunnus*). Albacore is a big fish that is about a quarter "white meat."[13] Local fishermen had some experience catching albacore, which were frequently abundant in the waters off San Pedro during the summer months. Some albacore was sold fresh or salted to Italian, Portuguese, Japanese, and other immigrants, but this was a very small trade. When albacore were caught, fishermen cleaned and hung them on the pier, which drained out much of the fish's blood and some of its oil. The result was a fish with plenty of white flesh that might be attractive to mainstream Americans.[14]

Several technical problems needed to be overcome before albacore could be canned and sold successfully, however. The first problem was how to catch the fish. There were about fifty small boats engaged in commercial fishing in the harbor at the time, and most were operated by Italians, who used purse seines (nets that closed like a purse around a school of fish).[15] Mackerels, sardines, and other fish were caught this way without any problems, but albacore struggled to get out of the nets, damaging their flesh in the process; the result was that canned fish ended up with blood spots. In this condition, canned albacore wasn't very appetizing, so the fish had to be caught with hand lines or poles. The one group of fishermen familiar with catching albacore was the Japanese, a small community of whom had just moved to Terminal Island. They readily consented to catch albacore with poles rather than nets.

The canning process presented more difficult challenges. The California Fish Company began experimenting with ways to make albacore lighter in color, less oily, and milder in flavor. The canners drained the blood from the fish, then cut the flesh in various ways; they tried smoking it; and they tried using just the fatty part of the fish's belly, but nothing worked. Albacore was just too oily. Finally, the canners devised a way to force out the oil by long, slow steaming, which left the meat white with a relatively mild taste. With the theoretical issues solved, the problem now was how to operationalize the process in the cannery.

What emerged was a relatively efficient operation. The fish were initially brought to the cannery "in the round," which meant that they had not been cleaned. These fish were skinned, the heads, tails, and guts were removed, and the blood was drained. Workers placed the trimmed fish on wire trays, which were stacked on rolling racks that were placed in large steamers where the fish cooked for four to six hours. This initial cooking made it easier to debone the fish and separate dark meat from white meat. Workers cut the white meat—roughly one-third of the fish—and put it in cans, which were then filled with olive oil. This gave the albacore a mild, pleasant flavor; olive oil was expensive, however, and was later replaced by cheaper cottonseed oil. The cans were sealed and heated in retorts (large pressure cookers). This permitted the oil and the fish to cook together. When the cans were removed from the cooker, they were swollen due to steam that had built up inside them. Workers punctured the cans with sharp instruments, permitting the steam to escape, and then soldered the holes to prevent the tuna in the can from being exposed to air. The outside of the cans were then cleaned and labeled, and the cans were packed into cases.[16] This method produced a mild-tasting white-meat product that was attractive to consumers, and unlike canned sardines or salmon at that time, canned albacore was solid and did not leave any debris—skin or small pieces—in the can.

Once the company resolved technical production issues, it confronted its marketing problem: how could it sell albacore if no one knew what it was? Then someone at the California Fish Company had an idea: why not just call it "tunny"? Americans were familiar with the fish because of the high visibility of sportfishing off the Southern California coast. But it was a brazen move, for the term *tunny* and its Americanized form *tuna* commonly referred to bluefin, yellowfin, and bigeye tuna, not albacore.

With the name set, Halfhill was responsible for figuring out how to convince consumers to buy a product that they had never tasted. His solution was the time-honored one: give it away. Halfhill displayed the company's tunny at the Los Angeles County Fair in Pomona and other events, and passersby were offered a complimentary taste. The tuna received enough positive reviews from samplers that Halfhill concluded that he should try to interest Los Angeles grocers in it. But most grocers in the early twentieth century were small, and they were just not excited about taking up limited shelf space with an unproven product for which there was no demand.[17] Halfhill hit the road to educate grocers outside of Los Angeles and found a more receptive audience in San Francisco: the Italian community there took to California albacore because it was similar to imported tuna but was much cheaper.

The company's largest sale outside of California was to a wholesaler in Boston in 1907. From here tuna was distributed to other East Coast locations, including the Frank E. Davis Fish Company in Gloucester, Massachusetts.[18] In December 1907, the company published an advertisement for a novelty "Tunny Fish" in *Good Housekeeping*, noting that the fish was "entirely free from bones and skin, packed in fine olive oil. The flavor slightly resembles the white meat of chicken and it also resembles chicken in appearance."[19] Some cans were sold in Vermont, where they were tested by the State Board of Health, which found the tuna to be "good quality, boneless fish, packed in Olive Oil."[20] The Boston sale convinced the California Fish Company that there was a potential market for its canned tuna on the East Coast.

After five years of experimentation the California Fish Company's executives finally concluded that they had a decent product that could attract mainstream Americans. In 1908 they gave their "Tunny Fish" a complete makeover: it was renamed "Blue Sea Brand Tuna," and a new, attractive label was placed on the cans. The company acquired automated can-making equipment to streamline its operation. These were costly changes made in hopes that sales would pick up. Then Halfhill headed east to educate distributors about Blue Sea Brand Tuna.

BONANZA YEARS

Halfhill was good at his job. Sales picked up. In 1910, the California Fish Company packed 6,000 cases of albacore and generated a little more than $32,000 in income—a phenomenal amount for a small canning operation.[21] The company then made another crucial decision: it was time to promote Blue Sea Brand Tuna directly to the public through demonstrations, signs in streetcars, billboards, and advertisements in magazines and newspapers. Advertising paid off. In 1911 the company packed 14,000 cases.[22]

Soaring sales encouraged competition, which materialized overnight. The Columbia River Packers Association of Astoria, Oregon, mainly canned salmon. When albacore were found off the Oregon coast in 1910, it began canning small quantities of the fish, packed under the company's brand name "Bumble Bee." The Pacific Tuna Canning Company set up shop in San Diego, producing 6,000 cases of tuna in 1911.[23] Its "Catalina Brand Tuna" was served at Los Angeles's premier Alexandria Hotel. The restaurant at the hotel purportedly substituted tuna for chicken in its "chicken sandwiches," and not one of its customers "ever knows the difference," reported an article in the *Los Angeles Times*.[24] Catalina Brand Tuna was also sold on the East Coast, where it was promoted as a Lenten food for Catholics and other religious groups who fasted during this time.[25] Within a few years, Catalina Brand Tuna was being sold throughout the United States, and even in Australia.[26]

The White Star Canning Company, under the direction of Warren J. King, began canning White Star Brand Tuna in August 1912. On the can's label was the phrase "Chicken of the Sea."[27] White Star applied for a trademark on the phrase, and it was granted.[28] By that time, the phrase appeared in cookbooks, magazines, newspapers, and even government reports.[29] Other similar phrases appearing in print were "sea chicken," "looks like chicken," "mistaken for chicken," and "tastes like chicken."[30]

While other companies avoided White Star's trademarked phrase, they continued to associate tuna with chicken.[31] South Coast Canning Company in Long Beach began selling "Avalon Brand Tuna" a few months after the White Star Canning Company began offering tuna. South Coast Canning hired the Van-Thomas Company to promote and sell its product, and Avalon Tuna became the first brand to be advertised nationally. Advertising copy for Avalon Tuna stated that the "delicately flavored Tuna meat looks and tastes like breast of chicken, and can be served either as a fish or a meat." The company also used the slogan "Chicken of the Sea," which is the first located use of this phrase referring to tuna. Another advertisement proclaimed that "Avalon Brand Tuna is so delicately flavored—so white and tender that there is little to choose between this 'chicken of the sea' and the two-legged kind."[32]

In 1912, California canners put up a total of 80,000 cases of albacore.[33] Spectacular sales encouraged even more companies to begin canning albacore. The Los Angeles Tuna Canning Company in Long Beach began selling "Panama Brand" tuna, and the "DeLux" brand was canned by the Monarch Canning Company in Wilmington, California. Canneries also packed tuna for other labels: the F. E. Booth Company contracted with the Pacific Tuna Canning Company in San Diego to produce "Booth's Crescent Brand Tuna."[34] C. E. Pierce, a fish broker in San Francisco, began marketing "Pierce's Brand California Tunny," which was packed by the California Tunny Canning Company.[35] In 1913, nine companies put up 128,000 cases of tuna, and those who had been in the tuna business for a few years made small fortunes, reported the *Los Angeles Times*.[36]

With plenty of competition, canners vied for market share. Demonstrations were given in department stores, and signs were displayed in trolley cars.[37] Canners also took to the road to hawk their goods. Halfhill traveled around the United States in an automobile—an unusual activity at the time—drumming up business.[38] Likewise, C. E. Pierce crisscrossed the country promoting "Pierce's California Tunny." His travels earned him the sobriquet "The Tunny Man."[39]

Just as the California Fish Company began to generate sizeable profits, it confronted internal crises. Its first president, Joseph H. Lapham, died in 1909, and Robert David Wade became president. On June 11, 1911, the California Fish Company sold its assets to the newly created Southern California Fish Company. Then Wade died in 1913, and Wiley Ambrose, who had married Wade's daughter in 1907, became president.[40] This distressed Albert Halfhill, who allowed himself to be bought out by Ambrose and other investors. Halfhill and his two sons then formed the Halfhill Tuna Packing Company.[41] Wilbur Wood was not happy with these transitions either, and he partnered with Paul Eachus, who had previously sold fresh fish in San Pedro. They named their new operation the California Tunny Canning Company.[42] Despite these shifts, the Southern California Fish Company managed to stay ahead of the competition, mainly because of its generous advertising budget. In 1911 the company generated sales of $69,000. The following year, sales reached almost $100,000, and by 1914, sales reached more than $248,000, a phenomenal increase by any standard.[43]

The Italian community in San Francisco was an ideal market for canned tuna. Eugene O'Neill (no relation to the playwright), a representative of the Southern California Fish Company, hosted "tuna demonstrations" for several months in that city featuring the firm's "Blue Sea Brand" at Washington Market. According to the *Pacific Fisherman*, the main West Coast fishermen's periodical, six months later these demonstrations were "still showing good results." From San Francisco, the company sent representatives to work the trade in the surrounding areas.[44] Other tuna companies began marketing their products in San Francisco.[45] Despite all these efforts, Italian Americans in the Bay Area preferred imported Italian tuna. It would not be until World War I, which reduced imports from Italy, that canned California tuna began to dominate the San Francisco market.

FULL SWING

Albert Halfhill, now with his own company, bought or constructed seventeen boats. Many were sold on time payments to fishermen, who in turn agreed to supply his cannery with fish. One new boat, named the *Theo-Hy*, was a top-of-the-line 70-footer with an 80-horsepower engine. It could travel farther and bring back a larger catch. Halfhill began experimenting with purse seines to catch tuna species other than albacore. The *Theo-Hy*'s purse seine was 1,500 feet long and 160 feet deep.[46]

Another tuna company was launched by two midwesterners. Indianapolis pork-and-beans canner Frank Van Camp and his son Gilbert first came to California to fish in 1910. A decade earlier, Frank Van Camp and two other canners had tried to corner the American tomato market in order to run up the price. Supported by bankers and brokers, they formed a syndicate and tried for two years, but both years saw bumper crops of tomatoes, and the syndicate failed. Van Camp had used his company as collateral, and the banks finally foreclosed. Frank Van Camp was forced out, although the company retained the Van Camp family name. After all the debts were paid, Frank Van Camp, once a multimillionaire, was down to his last $100,000.

With no family business to go into, Gilbert moved to Southern California where he worked as an engineer at the California Gypsum Tile Company in the Mojave Desert. But Gilbert was from a long line of canners and was interested in reviving the family fortune. He met with canning executives in Southern California, and found out that tuna canning was the growth industry in Los Angeles. Gilbert evaluated its spectacular rise during the previous few years and concluded that it could be revolutionized by applying the latest canning technologies. Gilbert convinced his father to head west and go into tuna canning.[47]

Rather than start from scratch in an industry they knew little about, the Van Camps assembled another group of investors and, with $200,000 in capital, purchased the California Tunny Canning Company from Wilbur Wood and Paul Eachus. In April 1914 the company was relaunched as the Van Camp Sea Food Company.[48] Wood continued to run their plant, but the Van Camps also brought in technical assistance from their formerly owned Indiana canning facilities. Gilbert set about modernizing the plant, and Frank launched a high-powered advertising campaign, outspending all other tuna canners. Within a decade, the company's advertising budget would be $750,000 a year, an astronomical amount for the fish canning business at the time.[49] As the Van Camps ramped up their promotions, sales soared, and other companies followed suit.[50] As one observer noted about tuna, "not until enterprising packers" began "advertising it did the people appreciate it."[51]

Again, advertising paid off. Tuna canners in Southern California increased production and sales to 325,000 cases in 1914.[52] Along with the promotion was a makeover of the fish's image. In September 1914, the *Los Angeles Times* concluded that "excellent"-tasting canned tuna was "one of the best nourishers of the human system, in no way inferior to the best beef steaks or lamb chops." The thriving tuna industry, predicted the *Times*, had a "big future."[53] The tuna canning industry was in "full swing," reported the *Long Beach Daily Telegram*.[54]

EAT MORE FISH

It is hard to imagine that the Southern California tuna industry in 1914 could be affected by an event thousands of miles away in a small city in the Austro-Hungarian Empire, but after the assassination of an Austrian archduke in Sarajevo in 1914, World War I broke out, and the Southern Californian tuna industry was never the same. At first the industry just lost some fishermen: a few European-born tuna fishermen returned home to fight for their countries, but they were promptly replaced by experienced Japanese fishermen who flocked to Southern California.[55] Then, almost overnight, European nations began ordering shipments of canned food from the United States on an unprecedented scale. Canned tuna was cheaper than any other protein source, so sales leaped forward. California tuna was sent in bulk to the United Kingdom, where it was repacked as "Jack Tar Tuna Fish." Its flavor was "like the breast of chicken," so British advertisements proclaimed, and it required no cooking. It was an "absolute treasure in War-time," reported English consumers.[56]

Simultaneously orders poured in from grocers across America, thanks to massive advertising by canners. Prices rose accordingly, yielding hefty profits for all connected with the industry. Canners responded by plowing their profits back into operations. Expansion happened everywhere. Canners enlarged their facilities with the intent of doubling their output, and new canners entered the field.[57] Larger boats were constructed, and canneries sold them to fishermen on credit. Everyone wanted in. "Orange growers, bank clerks, carpenters, and men in various other occupations," reported the Long Beach Press, were "all trying to get into the tuna game."[58] By 1915, twelve canneries employed 1,800 workers, contracted 1,200 fishermen on 400 boats, and packed an estimated 350,000 cases of tuna.[59]

But the industry had expanded too quickly. Canneries had invested too much in new boat construction and new facilities, and competition was severe. Small canners could not afford to compete with the massive advertising campaigns of the large companies. Several joined together to promote tuna through collective advertising. Big canners refused to join the effort, because they believed collective advertising was an attempt by their competitors to gain market share at their expense. Instead, big companies lowered prices for their tuna to pressure other canners to give up the joint advertising venture. All this did was start a price war with their competitors. The price for a case of wholesale tuna dropped from $5 to $3.25, and then below $3, finally bottoming out at $2.20, which was less than the cost of production. It was a financial disaster for small canneries, two of which were sold at rock-bottom prices, but it was a great boon for consumers—and eventually for the tuna industry as a whole, as low prices meant many new customers. Demand for cheap tuna shot up, and canned tuna sales outpaced salmon production in California for the first time.[60]

The financial disaster turned around in 1916, when canners figured out that price wars had harmed them all. The war in Europe dragged on, so sales continued to be robust, and profits for the canneries returned. Soon the problem was supply. Canneries paid fishermen between $35 and $40 per ton for tuna at the beginning of the season, but when demand for tuna skyrocketed, canneries just doubled the price for their canned tuna. The price hit $5 and then $7 per case as the year progressed. The good times were back, and the profits rolled in.[61]

When the United States entered World War I in April 1917, the price of tuna advanced even higher. Beef and other meats were rationed, and the government encouraged Americans to observe "meatless days" to help the war effort. Tuna, which was not rationed, was presented as a fine alternative to meat. It was also promoted as a healthful food and a good source of protein and vitamins. Tuna remained relatively inexpensive, and canning companies continued to promote their brands. Sales soared when the U.S. Bureau of Fisheries launched a campaign to encourage the American public to "Eat More Fish,"[62] and the federal government placed large orders for tuna for the military.[63] The demand for tuna, and its price, skyrocketed even further, and more new companies jumped into tuna canning, constructing even more facilities and tuna boats. At the beginning of 1917 twenty-two tuna canneries dotted the Southern California coast. By the end of the year there were thirty-six canneries selling all they could. Their total output that year was 700,000 cases of tuna—double what it had been two years before.[64]

One new tuna canning company was launched by Martin J. Bogdanovich, a Croatian immigrant from the island of Vis, who arrived in the United States in 1908. Two years later he bought a boat and began fishing for sardines. During World War I his operation flourished, and in 1917 he and five partners launched the French Sardine Company in San Pedro; the company started packing tuna the following year. With the help of investors, Bogdanovich was able to build a canning company on Terminal Island. Despite its name, about half the company's output was canned tuna, which it sold to the government. One hot summer day, the tuna began to spoil, and Bogdanovich had an idea: why not take ice on board to keep the tuna cold and reduce spoilage? Bogdanovich was not the first fisherman to do this, but he often receives the credit for it.[65]

The albacore catch peaked at 34 million pounds in 1917; the following year, the catch nose-dived by three-fourths. This shift was due to overfishing as well as the unpredictable migratory patterns of albacore. At this time the United States was embroiled in the war, and orders for tuna poured in from the U.S. government as well as from allied countries. The canneries could not stand idle, so American fishermen headed south into Mexican waters searching for albacore. What they found instead was yellowfin and skipjack. The good news was that they were plentiful and they could be caught with purse seines, which meant that they were much easier to catch than albacore. The bad news was that the white meat of the skipjack and yellowfin was just not as white as the meat of the albacore. But the public was already hooked on tuna, and with a slight name change to "fancy tuna" or "light tuna," buyers hardly knew the difference, and as canned yellowfin and skipjack cost less, the public eagerly purchased them. By the end of the 1917 season, only 23 percent of the tuna packed was albacore.

A specific problem with skipjack (*Katsuwonus pelamis*) was that it was not a tuna species, yet it was packed as "tuna." By the time the Food and Drug Administration got around to examining the labeling, it concluded that commercial names did not have to follow scientific nomenclature. Other canners also canned bonito (*Sarda chiliensis*) and called it tuna, and there were reports of mackerel and yellowtail (*Seriola dorsalis*) also being canned as tuna. The Food and Drug Administration would eventually define albacore and skipjack as tuna, but exclude bonito, mackerel, and yellowtail.[66]

TUNA CAPITAL OF THE WORLD

When the California Fish Company in East San Pedro began canning albacore in 1903, the fish were caught within a few miles of the shore by small trollers (or jig boats), which were 25 to 35 feet long with a top speed of 5 or 6 miles per hour. As the albacore close to shore were fished out, fishermen ventured into the channel between the mainland and Catalina. When these areas were also fished out, fishermen acquired bigger boats upgraded with 15-horsepower gasoline engines. By 1910, their fishing grounds extended from San Clemente Island to St. Toma, south of San Diego, and bigger boats with 45-horsepower engines were needed to make the round-trip.[67] But there was only a limited number of tuna in this area as well. American fishermen, especially those from San Diego, began moving south of the international border between the United States and Mexico, and then to Central America.

As American tuna fishing moved southward, the canning industry gravitated to San Diego, which was geographically closer to the fishing grounds. Historically, San Diego Bay and nearby coastal waters teemed with fish, shellfish, and sea mammals. American Indians, Spanish explorers, and Mexicans had all fished in the bay and surrounding ocean. Whales were processed in San Diego in the 1830s. During the 1860s, two Portuguese fishermen launched a commercial fishing operation in San Diego, but few San Diegans were buying commercial fish, and the business soon went under. Other Portuguese came in the early 1890s and began fishing for yellowtail, bonito, and albacore, which were pickled and sent to Hawaii. Portuguese flocked to San Diego during the early twentieth century, and they became the largest group of foreign-born fishermen in the city.[68]

Opening in 1911, the Pacific Packing Company was San Diego's first tuna cannery. The Premier Packing Company opened the following year. Other canneries set up shop in San Diego: the Neptune Sea Foods Company and Wheeler-Chase in 1915, the Steele Packing Company in 1916, Knut Hovden in 1917, and Arrow Packing in 1918. But the canneries could not keep up with wartime demand, and three of them merged in the interest of increasing efficiency. The Pacific Packing Company, the Premier Packing Company, and the San Pedro Canning Company merged to create the International Packing Corporation, headquartered in San Diego.[69]

When World War I ended in November 1918, orders for tuna slackened and then dried up. The federal government stopped pumping money into the economy, and a recession set in throughout the nation. European nations began producing their own food, and international orders for tuna dried up. For an industry that had been enjoying boom years for a decade the bust years were a shock. Canneries closed. Employment in California's fish canning industry fell 55 percent from 1919 to 1921.[70]

Mergers were again proposed in hopes of creating economies of scale; discussions had been under way among the large companies since the end of World War I, but no agreement could be reached. As tuna sales continued to plummet, serious merger talks began in early 1922. On June 1, 1922, four companies—Nielsen & Kittle, International Packing, White Star, and Van Camp Sea Food—consolidated as the Van Camp Sea Food Company, with Frank Van Camp as president. The new company operated four canneries in San Pedro and two in San Diego.[71] Frank Van Camp concluded this was the time to diversify, and the company began packing grapefruit, tomatoes, spinach, and olives. This venture failed, and the entire company went into receivership. Just when things looked bleakest for Van Camp, sardines showed up en masse off the San Pedro coast, and the company was able to pay off its debts, and he reacquired the presidency.[72]

Other struggling canneries were sold. In 1920, Wheeler-Chase was sold, and the new owners changed its name to the Sun Harbor Company. It would later merge with Westgate Sea Products Company. Westgate had started out as Arrow Packing Company; like Wheeler-Chase, it faltered in the aftermath of World War I, and in 1921 it was sold to Wiley Ambrose, an experienced tuna canner from Los Angeles. Ambrose had moved with his family to Los Angeles from Urbana, Ohio. At the age of eighteen, he began working at Union Hardware & Metal Company, where he remained for the next fifteen years. Ambrose worked his way up to the position of head salesman, and he did business with the California Fish Company, producers of Blue Sea Brand Tuna. In 1911, the company was reorganized under a new corporation and renamed the Southern California Fish Company. The following year, Ambrose became the firm's president—a position he held for four years. When the International Packing Corporation was formed in San Diego in 1918, Ambrose joined the board of directors and became a manager in the company. But he wanted a cannery of his own, so he bought one and named it the Westgate Sea Products Company.[73] In 1923, he acquired the Old Mission Packing Corporation and added canned fruits and vegetables to the list of products produced by Westgate.[74] In 1926, the company brought out its "Breast O' Chicken" tuna, which quickly became one of the most popular brands in America.[75]

To supply the tuna canneries, San Diego fishermen began building bigger boats that could travel farther south. Manuel O. Medina, a Portuguese immigrant from the Azores, built a 102-foot tuna boat. People thought he was crazy—it was bigger than other tuna boats of the time. The boat, named the *Atlantic*, cost an unprecedented $55,000; it had a 300-horsepower engine, $5,000 worth of refrigeration equipment, and a cork-insulated hold that could accommodate 110 tons of iced tuna. The *Atlantic* also had a large bait tank and fishing racks on which fishermen stood in the stern, just a few feet above the water—features that would become standard on tuna boats.[76] In the fall of 1926 the *Atlantic* left San Diego harbor and headed south. When the clipper returned to San Diego two months later, the catch grossed more than $105,000. Suddenly Medina didn't seem so crazy after all. The *Atlantic* became the prototype for transoceanic "tuna clippers," and the *Atlantic*'s success persuaded others to build large boats that extended their fishing grounds thousands of miles from the United States.[77]

When the *Atlantic* was launched, there were already several tuna boats longer than 90 feet—big enough to hold sufficient bait, water, and fuel for long voyages. They could easily operate up and down the length of Baja California. Their holds were well insulated, and their refrigeration systems maintained cold temperatures to protect the catch.[78] Others soon built even larger and more sophisticated tuna boats that could travel farther and bring back more frozen tuna to California canneries. American tuna boats started fishing off the coast of Central America. By 1929, American tuna boats began visiting the Galápagos Islands, 500 miles west of Ecuador and 2,400 miles south of San Diego. Medina made his first visit in the spring of 1929, taking four sister vessels with him. There was plenty of albacore south of the equator, and profits were stupendous.[79] Tuna fishing off the west coast of the United States was dwarfed by the industry south of the international boundary line between Mexico and the United States.[80]

San Diego's tuna fishing and canning industries surpassed San Pedro's in importance, and the city acquired the sobriquet "Tuna Capital of the World." At its peak, the tuna industry employed more than 40,000 people, ranking as the city's third largest employer (after aircraft construction and the U.S. Navy).[81]

POSTSCRIPT

C.E. Pierce died in 1915, and Pierce's Brand California Tunny soon disappeared.[82]

The F.E. Booth Company began canning sardines in 1903. The company switched to packing tuna, and it continued to do so until 1965, when it closed its San Francisco tuna cannery.[83]

Wilbur F. Wood, who had helped figure out how to can albacore at the California Fish Company in 1903, continued in various tuna canning companies for the following two decades. He became the president and general manager of the Southern California Fish Company in May 1924 and remained in that position for the next twenty-six years. He died in San Pedro on November 8, 1975, at the age of ninety-six.[84]

Albert P. Halfhill was an excellent promoter and an even better self-promoter. He became a correspondent of the *Pacific Fisherman*, the main journal of the West Coast fishing community, and he credited himself with launching the American tuna industry. Other writers picked up his claim, and he was frequently referred to as the "Father of Tuna Canning." He retired from the Halfhill Tuna Packing Company in 1922, handing over the reins to his sons, Charles P. and H.J. Halfhill. Two years later Albert Halfhill died.[85]

The Columbia River Packers Association continued canning small quantities of Bumble Bee tuna until the 1930s when it ramped up its tuna canning operation. In 1937 it packed 1.5 million pounds. The following year, albacore was found in large schools off the Oregon coast, and 10 million pounds of tuna were canned, and production continued to increase.

In 1942 the tuna cannery launched by Martin J. Bogdanovich first used the brand name "StarKist." Martin J. Bogdanovich died at the age of sixty-one in 1944. His son Joseph Bogdanovich took over the company, which, under his leadership, became the largest tuna canner in the world, a position the brand retains today.

Frank Van Camp remained president of the Van Camp Sea Food Company until his death in 1937. He was occasionally identified as "the father of the tuna industry in Southern California."[86]

Gilbert van Camp, who had encouraged his father to start Van Camp Sea Food Company, sold the company to Ralston Purina in 1963. He died in San Pedro in 1978.[87]

Wiley Ambrose stayed on as president of Westgate until his death in 1939. In 1949 Westgate merged with Sun Harbor to form the Westgate-Sun Harbor Company.

Manuel Medina, the pioneer of "tuna clippers," died at the age of ninety-three in 1986 at Point Loma, a seaside community in San Diego. His nephew, Harold Medina, invented the Medina Panel, which has reduced the number of dolphins that become entangled in tuna fishing nets.

THREE Enemy Aliens

The most important reason for the pre–World War II success of tuna fishing in California was the involvement of Japanese-born fishermen. Their involvement in the industry started almost by accident. One Sunday in March 1901, twelve Japanese men who worked as cleaners and carpenters in the Southern Pacific Railroad yard in Los Angeles hopped a train to San Pedro. As they strolled along the beach, so the story goes, they spotted the large, unmistakable shells of abalone, a large mollusk whose meat was a highly prized delicacy in Japan, but not appreciated by most Americans. Japanese and Chinese divers all along the California coast had been catching, drying, and shipping abalone to Japan and China for years, and the railroad workers knew that the small but growing Japanese community in Los Angeles would welcome a supply of fresh abalone. They rented a small stretch of beach at White Point, four miles northwest of San Pedro, put up a shed, and bought an old boat, named *Columbia*. They dived for abalone during the day, cooked it at night, and sold it to the Asia Company, which ran a department store serving the Japanese community in Los Angeles. The abalone business did well, and the men supplemented their income by canning abalone and shrimp, which they sold mainly to two American buyers in San Pedro. These buyers, in turn, sold the canned seafood to the larger Japanese community in San Francisco and found a market for the beautiful shells in the shops of Catalina Island, off the Southern California coast.[1] While diving for abalone, the enterprising fishermen of San Pedro Bay noticed schools of albacore just a few hundred yards offshore. The abalone gatherers didn't think much about their discovery, for there was little demand for albacore.

When abalone began disappearing along the California coast, the state legislature passed a law, in 1905, limiting the number and size of the shellfish that could be harvested. The California Board of Fish and Game Commissioners proclaimed that the law was really aimed at Japanese and Chinese immigrants, "who were taking them by the ton without regard to size by the aid of diving suits, removing the meat from the shell in the water, bringing it ashore, where it was dried and shipped either to China or Japan."[2]

In the face of these restrictions, the Japanese abalone gatherers at White Point decided to sell their business.[3] They told Riyojiro Hamashita, owner of a candy store in Los Angeles, about the albacore in San Pedro Bay. Albacore was an important fish in Japan, and Hamashita, who had been a fisherman in Japan, thought this sounded promising. He sold his store and bought the abalone gatherers' boat. He constructed a house on the isolated northeastern tip of Terminal Island, which was then separated from the mainland by a channel about a hundred yards wide. In May 1906, he began catching albacore and other fish, which he sold to markets in the San Pedro area. As few nonimmigrant Americans ate albacore—indeed relatively few Southern Californians ate fish of any kind—this was not a lucrative business, and Hamashita initially made only $3 or $4 a day, but he was doing what he wanted to do—fish.[4]

Hamashita was joined by several others who had worked as gardeners in Los Angeles, but who also preferred to fish for a living. They built their own boats with 5- to 10-horsepower engines and fished in San Pedro Bay. They also built wharves and wooden houses on stilts on top of the breakwater. Their community came to be called "East San Pedro." These squatters sold albacore and other seafood to markets along the coast, and some of their catch was transported by railroad to places as distant as Utah. Still, the albacore was not a big seller, and it brought them only two or three cents a pound, but this was about to change.[5]

THE YELLOW RACE

The naturalization statute passed by the United States Congress in 1790 limited citizenship to "a free white person." After the Civil War, this was modified to include people of "African nativity or descent." As Asians were considered neither white nor of African descent, they were excluded from American citizenship.[6] This provision did not exclude Asians from living in the United States, and their children who were born in the United States automatically became citizens.

Chinese immigrants arrived in California within a few months of the discovery of gold in 1848, and immigration from China continued well after the gold petered out. Chinese immigrated to California and other parts of the West Coast for the next three decades. By 1880 an estimated 105,000 Americans of Chinese descent lived in the United States. Nativist Californians were strongly opposed to Asian immigration in general and Chinese in particular. They pressured the U.S. Congress to pass the Chinese Exclusion Acts in 1882, which greatly restricted further immigration. It wasn't just the Chinese who were targeted by this legislation, but anyone identified specifically as a member of "the yellow race." This included Japanese.

At the time Japan was a rapidly industrializing and modernizing nation, and its leaders wanted their country to be honored and respected as an equal internationally. The Japanese leaders took issue with the immigration ban, which they believed was an insult to their nation. The United States was interested in expanding trade relations with this up-

and-coming Asian nation, and there were few Japanese in the United States anyway, so in 1894 the United States and Japan signed a treaty that assured free movement of citizens between the two countries. Japanese immigration to the American mainland picked up; after 1900 it veered upward, and then it turned into a flood.

Most immigrants came directly from Japan, but others came from Hawaii. Before 1898, Hawaii was an independent island nation. Japanese immigration to Hawaii had been under way since 1865, when Eugene M. Van Reed, Hawaii's consul in Japan, arranged to send 149 Japanese men to Hawaii; many more soon followed. At the time Hawaii faced a serious labor shortage; few native Hawaiians wanted to work on the rapidly expanding sugar plantations, so the owners began looking abroad for cheap labor. In 1875, when Hawaii and the United States signed a Reciprocity Treaty permitting duty-free importation of Hawaiian sugar into the United States, a surge of Japanese immigrants arrived in Hawaii to work the cane fields. When the United States annexed Hawaii in 1898, Japanese immigration to the islands increased, and many Japanese in Hawaii migrated to the mainland.

By 1900, 24,000 Japanese lived on the U.S. mainland. Most were men hoping to find jobs, earn some money, and return to Japan; some did, but most stayed. By 1905, 41,000 Japanese immigrants lived in California— mainly in San Francisco and elsewhere in Northern California. About 4,000—laborers and gardeners—had moved to the Los Angeles area, where they worked for the Southern Pacific Railroad or engaged in gardening and farming.[7]

ALBACORE

When the California Fish Company began canning albacore, the small group of Japanese fishermen on Terminal Island happened to be in the right place at the right time. They knew how to catch the fish easily and efficiently, which was precisely what the cannery needed. The small community expanded as Japanese fishermen flocked to the seaport during the summer albacore season. During the off-season many engaged in other jobs, but those who wanted to fish could do so year-round by shifting to sardines, mackerel, barracuda, and other fish when tuna were not available.[8]

The only way to reach the Japanese community was by boat or by walking a mile and a half from the village of Terminal, a rapidly growing beach resort on the island. In the years that followed, other canneries were constructed on the island and the surrounding California coast, and they all wanted albacore. It was an all-male community at first. A few married fishermen brought their wives, and a dozen women cooked for all the men, who took turns eating in a single room. As more women arrived, they took jobs in shops on Terminal Island. Others worked in the canneries. When loaded boats came in—day or night—horns would sound, and the women would leave their homes to work in the canneries for as long as it took to process the catch. Within a few years, the Japanese population on the island reached 600.[9]

BATHS AND ALL MODERN CONVENIENCES

When Los Angeles annexed San Pedro in 1908, Terminal Island was expanded into the bay, and a "Fish Harbor" was built near where the Japanese lived. Eight new canneries, as well as fish oil and fish meal plants, were built on the north side of the harbor. As the canneries grew, even more fishermen—mainly Japanese—came to the island.[10]

As the canneries considered the Japanese to be the "best fishermen," they vied "with one another in providing attractive living quarters close to their plants," reported the *Pacific Fisherman*.[11] On reclaimed land, the canneries constructed barracks and apartments and rented them to tuna boat captains, who in turn sublet apartments to their crews. Canneries sometimes offered free rent and bonuses ranging from $100 to $200 to Japanese fishermen as inducements to sign contracts to fish for the company during the tuna season. Some residences were luxurious by the standards of the time, complete with "baths and all modern conveniences."[12] As another inducement, canneries advanced money to Japanese fishermen to build or buy boats. A typical arrangement was that the loan was to be paid off over five years and buyers agreed to fish only for the cannery that lent them the money. This was a successful model. Loans were repaid, and Japanese-owned boats dominated albacore fishing.

The thriving Japanese community on Terminal Island was just one of several Japanese fishing villages in California. The Santa Monica community began in 1899. By 1909 it was thriving with 300 residents and thirty boats. When it burned down in 1916, it was demolished, and most residents moved to Terminal Island.[13] California's Alien Land Laws, passed in 1913 and 1921, prevented Japanese nationals or corporations controlled by them from buying, leasing, transferring, or renting land.[14] Facing discrimination elsewhere in the state, and as the demand for canned albacore increased, more Japanese moved to Terminal Island. It was eventually home to more than 4,000 Issei (American residents who were born in Japan) and Nisei (children of the Issei who were born in the United States and were American citizens).

Of all the Japanese communities in California, Terminal Islanders were the most isolated and the least Americanized. An elementary school was built on the island, and all children were required to speak English at school. "We used to catch hell from the schoolteachers for speaking Japanese," recalled Lilian Takahashi Hoffecker, who grew up on Terminal Island. The students immediately slipped back into Japanese once outside school. A night school for adults was opened. Japanese-run businesses were established to serve the community. Riyojiro Hamashita, who had started fishing for albacore, gave up fishing and went back to shopkeeping; he ran a grocery store that stocked Japanese products. Other grocery stores, pool halls, hardware stores, restaurants, barber shops, soda fountains, a dry goods store, and a meat market set up shop; a Shinto shrine and a Baptist mission also arrived on the scene. Virtually all signs and conversations in the village were in Japanese, but over time English words crept in, giving the community a language all its own. Residents ate Japanese foods and celebrated Japanese holidays. They often wore traditional Japanese clothes. Their houses featured tiny goldfish ponds, and they grew vegetables and cured "fish on screen frames hung from tall poles above the house tops," reported one observer. The commercial section was a quarter mile long, and most of the businesses were operated by Japanese. Businesses included a gas station, fish inspection facilities, tackle shops, and cafés that served "Oriental meals" night and day.[15] As one Japanese resident said in the 1930s, "I never thought I was in America. Everything was the same as in my small home in Japan."[16]

JAP POLES

Japanese were the most experienced fishermen when it came to albacore. Their "cane poles" or "Jap poles"—slender bamboo rods—were the only way to catch the fish.[17] Here is how it was done:

> A short, unyielding bamboo pole is employed with a line slightly longer than the pole itself. A live sardine is hooked through the back and so held with this pole and line that it swims about on the surface of the water. The pole is supported by one hand with its butt against the body. With the other they scatter splashing drops of water around the swimming bait, with a cup shaped bamboo paddle tied at the end of a short springy piece of bamboo. This is supposed to make the one sardine look like a whole school. If the fisherman is alert he will check the albacore as soon as it seizes the bait and before it gets started down with it, and lifting it bodily from the water, swings it into the boat in one mighty heave. When the albacore are coming fast this is the favorite method of fishing, for it is much faster. With the hand lines a gaff has to be used to lift the fish into the boat.[18]

Fishermen could handle bringing in small albacore by themselves, but two, three, or four men with a common hook were required to bring in larger fish. There were no barbs on the end of the lines; tuna bit into the lures and when the fish were in midair, they let go of the lure and fell onto the deck, where they thrashed around until they were thrown into the ice.[19]

In addition to the bamboo pole, the Japanese introduced other innovations. The first was the use of blanket nets to capture bait, and Japanese fishermen were credited with introducing "chumming"—throwing live baitfish into the water to attract large schools of tuna.[20]

Before starting on a trip the fishermen prepare a quantity of bait for chumming by chopping up sardines and other small fish common in the local waters. When the fishermen are on the way to the fishing grounds they catch sardines for bait by seining alongside the boat; the sardines are placed in a tank on board, and the water is renewed frequently to keep the bait in good condition. To test the ground, a live sardine is placed on a trolling line and the boat proceeds slowly. When a strike is made, indicating the presence of a school, the engine is stopped and the chopped bait is thrown overboard to keep the school about the boat. The hand lines are then baited with live sardines; and if the fish are running well they can be taken almost as fast as the lines can be cast and hauled. It is reported that two men have taken a ton of tuna by this method in less than an hour.[21]

Japanese boats had bait tanks, and fishermen constantly poured salt water into them to keep the bait alive. When they ran into a school of albacore, "live bait was thrown into the water near the boat. The fish seemed to go into a feeding frenzy and would strike at anything in the water, including the artificial lures the Japanese slapped the water with. The live bait method spread through the fishing fleet and a new and apparently inexhaustible source of fish was added to the varieties of white fish and sardines already being gathered."[22] The artificial lures were made of leather topped with deer horn; hooks were concealed and were barbless.[23] These innovations soon became standard for albacore fishing.

Other fishermen learned from the Japanese, but the Japanese continued to dominate the industry.[24] The fishery expert Norman B. Scofield reported in 1917: "Half of the tuna fishermen are Japanese and this one-half catches 85 per cent of the fish."[25] In 1920, only 488,180 pounds of albacore were caught by "white fishermen," while Japanese hauled in more than 12 million pounds, or 89 percent of the total catch. The Japanese were "more persistent" than the "white fishermen," claimed an article in the *Pacific Fisherman*. The Japanese fishermen routinely worked twelve- to fifteen-hour days.[26]

Another reason for the success of the Japanese fishermen was their scientific knowledge about tuna. Japan was an island nation with little arable land and limited food supplies. The Japanese government looked to the ocean as a major food source and subsidized and supported

Japanese fishermen. Japan had the largest fishing fleet in the world. In 1905 the Japanese Diet passed the "Pelagic Fishery Encouragement Act," which gave aid to fishermen and boat owners and established fishery schools and research vessels. This ongoing effort meant that equipment and techniques were improved constantly. This information about the best tuna-fishing techniques, the latest technology for locating and packing tuna, and the best boat construction methods was disseminated to Japanese fishermen in the United States via immigrants, journals, and Japanese associations in America.[27]

A $10 BONUS

In 1909, the Terminal Island men created the San Pedro Japanese Fishermen's Association to handle community affairs and negotiate with other communities. It lasted only three years, but its successor organization, the Southern California Japanese Fishermen's Association, was much more powerful. It oversaw working conditions, negotiated prices for raw tuna with canneries, established a welfare program for its members, and created an apprentice system.[28] Fishermen worked long hours and were paid on a profit-sharing basis according to how much fish all of the boats brought in. The Japanese fishermen sold albacore to the canneries for $30 per ton.[29]

The association opened a small office in the White Star Cannery Company on Terminal Island,[30] and soon afterward built "Fishermen's Hall," a modest building that became the community center for the Japanese. Members paid annual dues of $10—a considerable amount of money at the time for immigrant fishermen. A secretary was hired to handle the association's business, and a fund was established to help members who got sick or were injured (fishing was, and continues to be, one of America's most deadly occupations). In addition, the association bargained with the canners to establish a price for the tuna that they caught. In 1914 when Croatian and other fishermen went on strike asking for more money for the fish they sold to the canneries, the Japanese fishermen undercut them and agreed to the price the canneries offered. The

Croatian fishermen quickly caved in and went back to work once the Japanese fishermen had broken the strike.[31] The Japanese fishermen's strike breaking did not endear them to other fishermen, and it would lead to trouble.

When albacore sales skyrocketed in 1915, Japanese fishermen demanded $35 per ton for tuna—$5 more than the previous year. Cannery owners refused and decided to break the power of the Japanese Fishermen's Association. They contracted with other fishermen in San Pedro and imported "white fishermen" from Northern California and the Pacific Northwest to break the Japanese control of albacore fishing. Japanese fishermen gave up and agreed to the $30 figure. This was the first of a series of bitter wage battles.[32]

As it turned out, the "white fishermen" were not successful at catching albacore, and they returned to their home ports empty-handed as the season wore on. The canneries paid $35 per ton by the end of the season, as demand for albacore exceeded supply. Perhaps in retaliation for the canners' attempt to undercut their power the previous season, the Japanese Fishermen's Association demanded $80 per ton as their minimum price for albacore in 1916.[33] The cannery owners balked, and the Japanese fishermen refused to fish. The strike was finally settled for a lower price than the Japanese had demanded, but as the season wore on canneries bumped up the pay to $70 to $80 per ton just to keep up with the orders that were pouring in.[34]

Other fishermen saw that the Japanese Fishermen's Association was effective, and formed their own associations, including the American Fishermen's Protective Association. This included two main groups— non-Japanese tuna boat owners and fishermen. In the rapidly expanding market of 1917, it was in everyone's interest to come to a quick agreement, which was reached early in the season. The year was financially rewarding for the fishermen, but even more so for the canners, as the United States had entered World War I, and the orders for tuna skyrocketed, and profits soared.

By the time the 1918 season rolled around, the fishermen wanted their share of the profits. Once again they failed to reach an agreement, and a strike ensued. But this time there were two important differences—first, albacore had largely disappeared from the coastal waters off Southern California, and second, the United States was at war with Germany, and maximum production of food was needed for the war effort. Captain W. C. Crandall, the Southern California director of the U.S. Fish Administration, met with the Japanese fishermen on April 28. The fishermen reported that after expenses they netted only $100 per month during the very short albacore season, and there weren't many albacore to catch; they wanted more money. Crandall refused their request. The fishermen appealed to Herbert Hoover, then the U.S. Food Administrator in Washington. Crandall upped the price that canners paid the fishermen to $95 per ton. Other fishermen accepted the offer, but the Japanese fishermen demanded $150 per ton. The canners refused. The Japanese fishermen continued their strike, and their wives quit working for the canneries. The Federal Wage Adjustment Board stepped in and offered the fishermen $100 per ton. American, Italian, and Portuguese fishermen accepted the offer, but only Japanese fishermen could catch albacore in the quantities that were needed by the canneries. As little albacore was coming in, canneries reduced wages for their workers, and then the cannery workers went on strike. The Japanese fishermen demanded $120 per ton and continued their strike. By July—four months after the strike had begun—Crandall had had enough. The United States was at war, and the nation and its allies needed all the high-protein food that they could get. He told the Japanese fishermen that if they continued their strike, they would be considered "disloyal" and "unpatriotic." Their fishing licenses would be revoked, and their boats would be confiscated. It was a hollow threat, and the Japanese fishermen called his bluff. Boat owners announced that they had quit fishing and planned to go into gardening. They put their boats up for sale. Crandall backtracked and granted the Japanese fishermen a $10 bonus for albacore beyond $100 per ton. This worked; the Japanese fishermen and their wives returned to work.[35]

While the strike was under way, other fishermen caught a great many bluefin, skipjack, and yellowfin using purse seines, so the total amount of tuna caught during the season was not much lower than previous years. This success enticed salmon purse seiners from the Puget Sound and Oregon to come south to fish.[36] The following year, the canneries and the Japanese Fishermen's Association, the Italian Fishermen's Association, and the American Fisherman's Protective Association agreed on a price.[37] By 1920, 65 percent of the tuna fishermen were of Japanese heritage, compared with only 13 percent American, 11 percent Slav, and 6 percent Italian.[38]

Despite the Japanese-led strikes, the canneries continued to support Japanese fishermen and opposed any legal restrictions on them.[39] "There is no doubt," reported a correspondent to the *Pacific Fisherman*, "that most, if not all, the Southern California canners would heartily favor American fishermen on an even basis, but the packers are in business for profit and not sentiment. The packers are entirely dependent on the Japanese hook and line fishermen for the albacore supply, and it would be absolute suicide for them to aid in eliminating the Japanese when there is no proved source of supply to replace them." In times past, "numerous white men have attempted to fish for albacore," the correspondent warned, "but only a few succeeded and the rest became discouraged and turned their boats back on the canners at a tremendous loss to the latter."[40] Not everyone, however, was happy with the Japanese fishermen.

YELLOW PERIL

By the time Japanese began migrating en masse to the United States, there had already been four decades of anti-Oriental hysteria in California. Nativists saw little difference between the Chinese and the Japanese. Anti-Asian sentiment died down in the late nineteenth century, and Japanese immigrants might not have ended up as targets of nativists had it not been for the increased immigration of Japanese and the Russo-Japanese War, which broke out in 1904. Much to the surprise of Europeans and Americans, the Japanese navy sank the Russian fleet, and the Japanese army captured several strategic ports in the Russian Far East. This was the first time that an Asian power had decisively defeated a European nation, and many Americans were shocked and fearful: Japan could easily menace the Philippines (then a recently acquired American possession), Hawaii, or even the lightly populated West Coast of the

United States. Concern about Japanese power in the Pacific raised fears about the national loyalties of Japanese immigrants. Organizations and newspapers called for the end of Japanese immigration. The San Francisco *Chronicle* ran Japanese-bashing articles beginning in 1905. William Randolph Hearst, publisher of several California newspapers, launched a vicious anti-Japanese campaign, labeling Japanese immigration "The Yellow Peril." Hearst's campaign would last thirty-five years. His newspapers fabricated stories about Japanese immigrants really being soldiers who were infiltrating America. Japanese fishermen engaged in spying for their home country, Hearst papers claimed, and the Japanese were planning an imminent attack on the West Coast.[41]

This relentless verbal assault had its desired effect: the California legislature identified Japanese laborers as "transients" and "undesirables" because they worked for lower wages than did "white" laborers. The legislature called on the U.S. Congress to "limit and diminish further immigration of Japanese."[42] In 1907, by executive order, President Theodore Roosevelt barred Japanese immigration to the mainland from Hawaii, Canada, and Mexico.[43] The Japanese government felt that Japan would lose face if the United States officially prohibited Japanese immigration, so in 1908 the two governments concluded a "Gentleman's Agreement" in which the United States would not officially halt Japanese immigration, but the Japanese government would deny visas to laborers who wanted to go to the United States or Hawaii.

Japanese immigration declined, but it did not end. As Japanese men were forbidden by California state law to marry white women, and there were few unmarried Japanese women in the United States, Issei began selecting picture brides from Japan or accepted marriages arranged by their families back home.[44] As the "Gentlemen's Agreement" did not bar Japanese women from immigrating to America, they began arriving in large numbers, and the Japanese population again veered upward. As this happened, anti-Japanese sentiment in California also increased. In 1913, the California legislature passed the Alien Land Law, which excluded "aliens ineligible for citizenship"—a roundabout way of specifying the Japanese—from owning land in California. But there was an obvious loophole: since all children of Japanese parents born in the

United States were automatically citizens, ownership could simply be changed to their names. Likewise, companies were established with a 51 percent white ownership, which in fact were run by Japanese.[45]

When Europe became embroiled in war in July 1914, Japan quickly joined the Allies—almost three years before the United States. Japanese naval ships assisted in the destruction of German naval forces in the Pacific and Indian Oceans. Japan also secured German-held territories in China and German-held islands in the Pacific. Throughout the war, German propaganda in the United States constantly hammered home the idea that Japan—not Germany—was America's real enemy, and many Americans agreed.[46] One was James D. Phelan, a former mayor of San Francisco who successfully ran for the U.S. Senate in 1915 with the slogan "Keep California White." Phelan claimed that Japanese-owned boats violated registry laws, and that the real purpose of the fishing fleet was espionage and illegal smuggling of Japanese laborers into the United States.[47] Legislation had been proposed in California to exclude Japanese from owning fishing boats, but it had not passed, mainly because the Japanese in the Los Angeles area were well integrated into the business community.[48] Beginning in 1919, however, Pacific coast states passed a series of restrictive laws intended to restrain the activities of Japanese fishermen from California to Alaska. Nativists urged legislation prohibiting aliens from owning fishing boats. The fish canners complained that these laws, if passed, would wipe out their industry.[49]

The *Pacific Fisherman* had editorialized against the Japanese fishermen since 1908, when the editor proclaimed that the West Coast needed to "be protected against immigration of the 'Yellow Race.'" In 1920 it again campaigned against Japanese fishermen. According to the *Pacific Fisherman*, Japanese fishermen refused to "Americanize" their way of life, as other immigrants had, and white men were shut out of the fishing trade because Japanese fishermen worked for lower pay. This last point in the editorial ran counter to fact: Japanese fishermen constantly demanded more money from canners, and it was non-Japanese fishermen who fished and made money while the Japanese were on strike for higher wages.[50]

At the beginning of 1923, the canneries and the Japanese Fishermen's

Association again failed to agree, and yet another strike began. The strike was not resolved until the end of June, when the California State Commissioner of Fish and Game mediated between the two sides. Newspapers ran articles opposing the Japanese-led strike, and nativist groups supported a bill introduced into the California legislature that prohibited "aliens" from engaging in fishing. The bill was not passed after the canneries testified that they could not find white fishermen to catch albacore.[51]

As a result of such agitation, however, the United States Congress passed the Immigration Quota Act, which ended all immigration in 1924. This caused a serious labor problem in Hawaii, where more than 200,000 Japanese lived, and most ate fish.[52] Few Hawaiians wanted to engage in the labor-intensive fishing industry, and virtually all commercial fishing in Hawaiian waters was conducted by Japanese fishermen, and they needed regular replacements. To sustain the Hawaiian fishing industry, Japanese fishermen were permitted to immigrate to Hawaii well after the cessation of Japanese immigration to the United States.[53]

THOUSANDS OF JAPANESE

Masaharu Kondo, a member of the Board of Commissioners of the Imperial Fisheries Institute of Tokyo, had been commissioned to investigate fishing technology outside of Japan. In 1908 he visited Los Angeles, where he met Mexican-born Aurelio Sandoval, who had moved to the United States in 1904. Sandoval had acquired an exclusive concession from the Mexican government, led by Porfirio Diaz, for all the fisheries on "the west coast of Mexico from Guaymas north to the mouth of the Colorado River, and to all the water that surrounds the Baja California peninsula."[54] Sandoval needed financial help to develop the concession, so he created the International Fisheries Company in Los Angeles. French investors were interested, and Sandoval began construction of a small cannery on Margarita Island in Magdalena Bay, the best natural harbor on the west coast of Mexico. He also needed technical assistance on fishing techniques and canning methods. At Kondo's suggestion,

Sandoval hired a Japanese expert named Tatsunosuke Takasaki, a chemist who had worked at a sardine canning operation in Japan. Takasaki visited Magdalena Bay in April 1912, and Sandoval placed him in charge of the cannery. Takasaki hired six Japanese, a similar number of Chinese, and ninety-plus Mexican workers and began packing abalone.[55] It was salted, dried, and shipped to Hawaii or Japan.[56]

While negotiations between Sandoval and Kondo were under way, the Hearst newspapers caught wind of them and proclaimed that Japan was trying to purchase Magdalena Bay. The *Los Angeles Examiner*, a Hearst paper, announced on April 1, 1912, that there were plans for a large Japanese colony at Magdalena Bay. Two days later the *San Francisco Examiner*, another Hearst paper, claimed that 75,000 Japanese, mainly soldiers, were already in place in the bay. William Randolph Hearst himself chartered a ship to visit the bay, where he found only two Japanese men, but that didn't stop his anti-Japanese rhetoric. Hearst's reporters interviewed Takasaki, who, according to the story they wrote, was planning for 100,000 Japanese colonists. When the story was published, Takasaki and Sandoval denied it,[57] as did Japanese and Mexican leaders, but the powerful Hearst papers paid no attention and continued to harp on the Japanese menace in Baja California.

About the time that Sandoval's cannery on Margarita Island went into operation, Mexico erupted in revolution. Mexican president Porfirio Diaz fled to Europe, while the victorious Francisco Madero proclaimed that any concessions granted by the Diaz government were null and void. Sandoval supported the side that lost, and he continued to support opponents of the Madero government. He was charged in U.S. courts with trying to overthrow the government of Mexico and promptly disappeared from public view.

Kondo acquired Sandoval's fishing concessions from the Madero government and created the Mexican Industrial Department, based in San Diego, to harvest the fish in Baja California, and he started the Lower California Fisheries Company, which was incorporated in Delaware, probably because the state was a tax haven, but also because Delaware had no restrictions on Japanese citizens owning corporations.[58] Kondo expanded the cannery at Magdalena Bay and also began shipping iced and later frozen tuna to San Diego for canning. Tatsunosuke Takasaki, formerly the superintendent of Sandoval's cannery, became an employee of the Lower California Fisheries Company.

WORLD WAR I

In January 1915, a Japanese battle cruiser operating in conjunction with a British squadron hunting German raiders ran aground in Turtle Bay in Baja California, 300 miles south of San Diego. Hearst and others claimed that the cruiser was on a mission to establish a secret Japanese base. Newspapers reported that 150,000 veteran Japanese soldiers were in Mexico, preparing to invade the United States. Despite widespread coverage, no evidence has ever shown that the incident was anything other than an accident. That didn't stop Hearst, who continued to harp on the Japanese menace.[59] The Hearst-controlled International Film Service Corporation released a film called *Patria*, which spun a yarn about the Japanese conquest of the United States with the assistance of Mexico.[60] In 1917, Hearst papers published yet another report of "thousands of Japanese" who manned fishing boats in the morning and drilled with rifles in the afternoon.[61] None of these reports had any foundation, but they did sell newspapers, which encouraged Hearst's and other newspapers to regularly fabricate such stories for more than two decades.

When the United States entered World War I in 1917, beef and other meats were rationed, and the government encouraged Americans to eat more fish. Kondo expanded his fishing operation; he recruited more Japanese workers and moved his operation to Turtle Bay, where living conditions were primitive, but fish and shellfish were abundant. The fishing trips usually lasted only a day or two. The boat brought the fish back to Turtle Bay, where they were transferred to a larger tender for shipment to a cannery in San Diego. Kondo tried refrigerating the tuna with dry ice, but it proved expensive, and dry ice was too cold and harmed the tuna when it came in direct contact with the flesh. Working cooperatively with San Diego canneries, Kondo acquired two large, top-of-the-line refrigeration ships from Himuro Mumi in Yokohama, Japan.

These ships picked up fish in Baja California, froze them, and brought them into San Diego for processing.[62] The ships were revolutionary: with them tuna boats could travel great distances from canneries and transfer their catch to large mother ships, which returned regularly to canneries without much spoilage. Refrigerator ships would soon become standard throughout the industry.

Throughout the war, the United States government was concerned about both German and Japanese activities in Mexico. Inflammatory newspaper accounts about Kondo's operation in Baja California alerted the Office of Naval Intelligence (ONI), which kept a dossier on Kondo's Magdalena activities. William H. Van Antwerp, the director of the San Francisco branch of the ONI, believed that Kondo was a Japanese agent and that his operations in San Diego and Baja California were part of a plot by the Japanese to take over Mexico. In one cable Van Antwerp reported that Kondo was constructing a chain of packing houses and wharves along the Baja California coast that would "give this Japanese Company stations at practically every big point on the Lower California peninsula."[63] No evidence then or since supported Van Antwerp's beliefs that Kondo was a Japanese agent or engaged in anything other than trying to make money by fishing.

THE SPY CURB LAW

Even after the war ended, attacks against the Issei and Nisei in America continued unabated. These were generally engineered by nativists, who opposed all "aliens," particularly those who posed an economic threat. Organized labor also opposed Japanese workers, who toiled industriously for low wages, or so labor claimed. The Depression exacerbated tensions: eleven bills were introduced into the California legislature to deny commercial fishing licenses to anyone who was not a United States citizen. As people born in Japan were unable to become American citizens, these bills were directly aimed at Japanese fishermen who had been granted licenses since the state began issuing them in 1909. One bill passed in 1933. It amended the California Fish and Game Commission code to exclude commercial licenses for anyone who had not been a resident of California for at least a year. Intent on testing the law, Tokunosuke Abe, the president of Taiyo Sangyo Gaisha in San Diego, hired a group of Japanese fishermen who had not resided in the United States for a year, and sent them to fish off the California coast beyond the three-mile territorial limit. When the boat, *The Osprey,* brought its catch into San Diego harbor, the California Fish and Game Commission stopped the catch from being unloaded, as it had violated the new state law. Abe took the commission to court to test the validity of the law. On September 18, 1934, the Superior Court found that the code violated the equal protection clause of the Fourteenth Amendment of the United States Constitution and was therefore void. The decision was appealed to the California Supreme Court, which upheld the lower court ruling. Japanese-born fishermen could bring fish caught in Mexican waters into the United States without restriction.[64]

Japanese fishermen looked at this as a great victory, but it made little difference to those agitating against them. Nativists just moved to new arenas. In 1934, Lail Kane, a marine surveyor, former Naval Reserve officer, and an officer of the American Legion, appeared before a Special Committee on Un-American Activities of the U.S. House of Representatives and charged that "Japanese fishing vessels then operating out of San Diego and San Pedro could easily be converted into mine layers and torpedo boats within from three to six hours, and then be utilized to hinder the operation of the United States Pacific Fleet."[65] It would have been impossible to convert the relatively slow-moving tuna clippers into high-speed torpedo boats, but again contrary factual information was simply ignored.[66]

John Dockweiler, a congressman from Los Angeles, announced that Japanese fishing vessels were captained by Japanese naval officers, who were constantly replaced at sea by officers from Japan.[67] This was patently absurd, as it was pointed out at the time, because Nisei commercial fishermen had been in the United States for decades before the time that the accusation was made. In accordance with U.S. immigration law, no Japanese could immigrate to the United States after 1924. For the charge to be true, it would mean that the Japanese navy had sent these men decades before to spy on America.[68] Yet another myth claimed that the tuna boats were resupplying Japanese submarines with gasoline at sea. No evidence was ever produced then or since that any of these stories were true. But at the time this possibility was given some credence by the United States Navy, which put a restriction on tuna boats in 1940 that they could not carry extra tanks of gasoline on their decks. These stories were frequently repeated without any supporting evidence, but the repetition convinced many non-Japanese Americans that the stories were true.

California politicians found it politically advantageous to attack Japanese Americans, most of whom were not American citizens or were younger than twenty-one years old and therefore couldn't vote. Sam Yorty, then a California assemblyman from Los Angeles and later the city's mayor, proposed that aliens not be permitted to acquire fishing licenses. That measure failed, but within months the California state legislature passed the "Spy Curb" law, which required registration of all alien commercial fishermen.[69]

The anti-Japanese campaigns and spy scares continued right up to World War II. In March 1939, Benjamin Harrison, the U.S. Attorney for Southern California and an active member of the Native Sons of the Golden West, launched a series of charges against Japanese fishermen. He proclaimed that "Japanese operating out of our ports know every foot of the coast of North and South America, including where cables are located and mines could be laid." When the San Diego tuna fisherman Tokunosuke Abe sent tuna boats into the Caribbean to catch tuna, Harrison claimed that these Japanese-controlled tuna boats were really in the Caribbean to observe naval maneuvers. Abe's denial was ignored.[70]

John L. Spivak, a muckraking reporter, interviewed Tokunosuke Abe and was convinced that Abe's fishing and canning facilities in Baja California were a front for Japanese espionage. Spivak's book, *Honorable Spy*, contributed to anti-Japanese hysteria in the United States.[71] Congressional hearings on these charges were conducted by Martin Dies, the chairman of the House Committee on Un-American Activities. On August 1941, Dies repeated the espionage charges against Issei and Nisei fishermen on Terminal Island. Dies favored rounding up all Japanese fishermen in America to restrict their activities.[72] The fishermen were charged specifically with mapping and plotting channels in harbors and the West Coast. As was pointed out at the time, all this information was readily available on publicly available topographical maps that sold for a few dollars. These facts, however, fell on deaf ears, as did the pathetic Nisei "efforts to convince whites of their loyalty," as one historian later described their response.[73]

TERMINAL JAPANESE TUNA

When the United States entered World War I in 1917, the navy began constructing a base in San Pedro. When it was completed two years later, President Woodrow Wilson based several ships there. When Japan invaded Manchuria in 1931 and China six years later, American opinion went strongly against Japan, and the U.S. government was deeply concerned.[74] More naval ships—including all of America's battleships—were transferred from the Atlantic to San Pedro. With tensions mounting in the Pacific, President Franklin Roosevelt sent the battleships based in San Pedro to Pearl Harbor, in Hawaii, on April 1, 1940. The Japanese considered this deployment a threat—as the American government intended—but they also viewed it as an opportunity: it was these battleships that Japanese naval forces attacked and sank in Pearl Harbor on December 7, 1941.

Within hours of the attack, the FBI arrived on Terminal Island and arrested Issei boat owners and community leaders, including those running organizations, Japanese language teachers, martial arts instructors, and others on a watch list.[75] Issei and Nisei fishermen were prevented from sailing. Those boats that were at sea at the time of the attack were directed by radio to return to the closest U.S. naval facility, and as they arrived, they were stopped and boarded by the Coast Guard, which took into custody all Issei fishermen. The homes of other community leaders and fishermen were searched, and contraband, including "radios, cameras, pictures of Japan, even kitchen knives," was confiscated. Soldiers in jeeps with machine guns patrolled the streets twenty-four hours a day. On February 9, 1942, all Issei with commercial fishing licenses still on

Terminal Island were picked up, and many were sent to a prisoner-of-war camp in North Dakota.

This was only the beginning. In January the Los Angeles Board of Supervisors called for the eviction of all "enemy aliens" from San Pedro harbor. On February 19, President Roosevelt signed Executive Order 9066, authorizing military commanders to exclude anyone from military areas. Six days later, Terminal Island was declared a restricted military area, and all civilians were ordered to leave within forty-eight hours. Many Nisei moved in with relatives and friends in the Los Angeles area. A few months later all Issei and Nisei living on the West Coast—110,000 people, many of whom were American citizens—were ordered to internment camps. Most Terminal Islanders ended up at Manzanar Relocation Camp in California. Within two months of the evacuation from Terminal Island, the Japanese village there was bulldozed by the U.S. Navy.[76] As a result of these actions, Issei and Nisei lost an estimated $130 million in property—real estate, businesses, homes, inventories, boats, and personal possessions—which was confiscated or otherwise sold far below market value.[77]

While the Japanese were in jail or camps, the navy requisitioned some of their tuna boats and used them with minimal upkeep and repairs for more than three years. When the Japanese fishermen returned from the internment camps in 1945, they found the surviving boats leaking badly and in need of complete restoration. The navy paid token compensation for the use of the tuna boats during the war, but the fishermen's attorneys billed the Japanese owners $10,000 per boat, claiming that they had negotiated on behalf of the Japanese while they were in the internment camps.[78] To build new boats was virtually impossible for the penniless Japanese Americans who just emerged from the camps. Due to technological advancements, tuna boats were even more expensive, and the canneries were less willing to assist fishermen with loans to construct multimillion-dollar boats.

Even if the Issei fishermen had had boats, they could not have fished legally. In 1943 the California legislature had finally passed a law stating: "A commercial fishing license may be issued to any person other than an alien Japanese."[79] The law was clearly intended to prevent resident Japanese from returning to their fishing jobs when the war ended.

Fearing that the statute would be declared unconstitutional, in 1945 the legislature amended the code, removing the term "alien Japanese" and replacing it with a reference to any alien who was "ineligible to citizenship." By 1945, Congress had included most Asiatic groups, such as the Chinese, Filipinos, and Indians, in the list of those who were eligible for citizenship—the Japanese were the notable exception. Hence the amended code intentionally tried to prevent resident Japanese from reentering the tuna fishing industry.

When this and other discriminatory measures were passed by the California legislature, Japanese Americans were in internment camps and were unable to fight back, as they had so often done before the war. In 1947, one fisherman, Torao Takahashi, tested the law by requesting a commercial fishing license from the California Fish and Game Commission; he was denied it because he was born in Japan and was therefore an "alien ineligible for citizenship." Takahashi had lived in the United States since 1907, and fishing was the only trade he knew. He became the captain of a tuna boat in 1915, and he routinely applied for and received a commercial fishing license until 1942, when he was incarcerated. With the help of the American Civil Liberties Union and other organizations, Takahashi took the Fish and Game Commission to court. He won his case in Los Angeles Superior Court but lost in the California Supreme Court. His case was then appealed to the United States Supreme Court. The Washington lawyer and future secretary of state Dean G. Acheson presented Takahashi's case to the Supreme Court. The court, almost unanimously, declared the California law unconstitutional in 1948. Takahashi returned to fishing for a few years before his death in 1954, but most other Issei and Nisei who had been fishing for tuna before the war never reentered the trade.[80] Many ended up working as gardeners.

POSTSCRIPT

In 1922 Masaharu Kondo's success in his operations in San Diego and Baja California earned him the nickname "the Fish magnate of

California" from the *Pacific Fisherman*.[81] In Mexico, he was named "El Pescador más Grande del Mundo."[82] And some Japanese-American historians regard Kondo, not Albert Halfhill, as the "father of the Southern California fishing industry."[83] When the Depression hit in 1929, Kondo's company suffered financial difficulties, and it went bankrupt in 1931. Its assets were acquired by Abe Tokunosuke, who died in January 1941. His company's twenty tuna boats were confiscated by the U.S. Navy during World War II.

No Japanese fishermen from Los Angeles or San Diego were ever charged with espionage or spying for Japan.[84]

During World War II, 33,300 Nisei and their children served in the American armed forces. The 442nd Regimental Combat Team, composed mainly of Nisei, became the most highly decorated unit in the U.S. Army.[85]

Takasaki Tatsunosuke returned to Japan, where he became president of Toyo Canning Company. He survived World War II and after the war served as the Japanese minister of international trade and industry.[86]

A bronze sculpture was erected at Fish Harbor on Terminal Island honoring the Japanese village. A 1970 reunion of Terminal Islanders drew 1,000 former islanders and their families.

South of the fishing pier on Shelter Island in San Diego stands a 16-foot-tall bronze sculpture by Franco Vianello depicting Portuguese, Italian, and Japanese fishermen reeling in a tuna.

FOUR This Delicious Fish

By the beginning of the twentieth century, tuna had been popularized by magazine and newspaper stories detailing the exploits of sportsfishermen, and their astounding catches. Most Americans, however, were unaware that tuna was also a delicious, nutritious food, and the few who were willing to try it had no clue how to prepare and serve it. This was a very serious problem for canners and grocers: how do you sell a food product if potential consumers have no idea how to eat it?

Early tuna canners ran small operations, even by the standards of the day, and they simply didn't have the expertise, time, or money to invest much in advertising campaigns. The South Coast Canning Company of Long Beach, packer of Avalon Brand Tuna, hired C. E. Van Landingham, co-owner of the Van-Thomas Company in Los Angeles, to help promote its product. Van Landingham concluded that the main obstacle to selling tuna was that most homemakers had no idea how to serve it. He had previously promoted other food products by developing recipe booklets, such as *Van's Pure California Honey* (1911), produced for beekeepers in Southern California,[1] and he thought the concept might work with tuna, too. Van Landingham collected a few tuna recipes and printed them in a booklet, which he distributed free to grocers who sold Avalon Tuna, and to anyone else who requested one by mail. The booklet, released in 1912, was the largest compendium of published tuna recipes at that time.

Armed with the booklet, Van Landingham then launched stage two of his promotional campaign—a series of advertisements in the *Boston Cooking-School Magazine*, the single most influential cookery magazine in America at the time. Each ad included a few recipes, and readers were encouraged to send away for a free "Tuna Recipe Booklet."[2] Other tuna canners followed Van Landingham's lead, and consumers were soon barraged with tuna recipes in booklets distributed by grocers and through the mail. Thanks in part to these booklets, tuna was on its way to becoming one of America's favorite foods.

WHET THE CONSUMER'S APPETITE

Van Landingham did not invent the use of recipes for promotional purposes. Since the mid-nineteenth century, companies had used recipes to sell products. At first, the recipes were incidental to the products advertised. Publishers hoped that the recipes would capture the interest of readers, who would then notice and buy the advertised product. As the century progressed, advertisers became much more sophisticated; the recipes clearly featured commercial products, which were listed by their full brand names in the ingredient line ("1 cup Pillsbury's Best," "2 cups of Haxall Flour"). These recipes, in turn, were often reprinted with slight revision in newspapers, magazines, and cookbooks.

When the U.S. Patent Office began registering trademarks and slogans, in 1870, memorable brand names and eye-catching labels proliferated. Around the same time, a drop in the price of paper and the invention of the rotary press made high-speed, low-cost printing possible. Coupled with major advances in color lithography and photography in the late 1800s, these developments allowed food companies to advertise nationally through magazines and by publishing promotional pamphlets. These pamphlets encouraged customers to demand particular brand-name products at local grocery stores rather than accept unbranded bulk goods. Local stores, in turn, were encouraged to purchase the products directly from the manufacturer. This eliminated the need for middlemen or brokers and reduced the price for retailers and customers.

Many food products that arrived in stores around the turn of the twentieth century were new creations that had no generic equivalents and no precedent in the kitchen. Manufacturers had to create a demand for these products by showing homemakers how to use them. The Shredded Wheat Company addressed the issue in a series of advertising cookbooklets provocatively titled *The Vital Question* (1899), featuring dozens of creative uses for Shredded Wheat, interspersed with completely unrelated pictures of American battleships, which had been popularized by their successes in the Spanish-American War. The thought behind this was that people would acquire or save the booklet for the photos, and it would be a regular reminder to buy Shredded Wheat and use the recipes. At about the same time, the Genesee Pure Food Company distributed spectacularly colorful booklets featuring a wide variety of recipes made with its revolutionary new product, Jell-O.

Some companies gave away recipe booklets with their products by inserting them in the package. Cookbooks issued by makers of kitchen equipment, such as stoves, refrigerators, and choppers, took the form of instruction booklets, with recipes as a bonus. Others supplied the booklets to grocers, who in turn gave them to customers. Another common method of distribution was to offer the booklet in a magazine advertisement or on the product package: a recipe booklet would be sent to the customers free, or for the price of a stamp. This allowed the manufacturer to develop mailing lists for future advertising.

Cookbooklets were intended to be enticing; they usually featured illustrations of the product (or the full product line), pictures of prepared dishes, awards the product had won at fairs and expositions, and sometimes a depiction of the corporate headquarters or factory, demonstrating modernity and cleanliness. Early booklets were relatively simple black-and-white affairs devoid of artwork. Later, cookbooklets became more colorful, elaborate, and attractive, filled with anecdotes, jokes, or riddles, helpful advice, and florid testimonials. The booklets introduced new color-processing techniques in illustration and photography. Full-color artwork was an irresistible eye-catcher in the early twentieth century designed to whet the consumer's appetite.[3]

HUNDREDS OF WAYS TO SERVE WHITE STAR BRAND TUNA

Unlike boxed or bagged foods, which had plenty of room for recipes on the package surface or tucked inside, canned foods offered limited space on their labels, and the small tuna cans had even less label space than did soup or vegetable cans. Around 1906 the Alaska Packers Association, a San Francisco–based salmon cannery published booklets on ways to prepare canned salmon.[4] This idea for using cookbooklets (and even some of the recipes slightly revised) to promote products would soon be borrowed by the fast-growing tuna industry in Southern California.

The goal of early tuna recipes was to add tuna or replace another fish or meat ingredient with tuna in existing recipes. Americans were familiar with salads, croquettes, cutlets, and meat loaf, so the Van-Thomas Company's 1912 booklet for Avalon Brand Tuna included recipes for each of these with tuna as the main ingredient.[5] The same year the Avalon recipe booklet appeared, the C. E. Pierce Company in San Francisco distributed a booklet promoting Pierce's Brand California Tunny, and it too included common recipes for fritters, sandwiches, and stuffed tomatoes.[6] White Star Canning Company's recipe booklet advised consumers that tuna was "Good for Breakfast, Luncheon and Dinner or Supper. There are a hundred ways to serve White Star Brand Tuna. Can be used in place of Chicken, Crab or Lobster."[7] Other tuna packers followed similar paths but increased the number of recipes. The Los Angeles Tuna Canning Company's booklet contained thirty-one tuna recipes for its

Panama Brand Tuna, including the first located one for creamed tuna served on toast.[8]

The Southern California Fish Company took a thriftier approach to promoting its products: it printed recipes right on the can labels. A recipe for tuna salad, for instance, was printed on the front of the can: "Prepared Ready to Eat for a Delicious Salad add to this tin of tuna fish one-half cup celery chopped fine with equal parts salad dressing and cream or condensed milk."[9] A single recipe, however, was unlikely to convince homemakers of tuna's versatility. Then someone had a brainstorm: why not put more recipes on the blank reverse side of the label? All customers had to do to get free recipes was remove the label from the can. Today, many food companies do this, but at the time it was an original idea.

The Southern California Fish Company printed three different labels, with different recipes on the back of each. The hope was that these recipes would encourage consumers to buy at least three cans of Blue Sea Brand Tuna. One unusual recipe, for "Tuna Chowder—California," consisted of onion, bacon, salt pork, butter, tuna, milk, and diced potatoes. The company proclaimed that this was "better chowder than clam."[10] The company followed up with a small brochure, which included the recipes previously printed on the labels.[11]

SPREADING THE WORD

Cookbooklets helped consumers develop a culinary repertoire using tuna, and had a secondary influence through newspapers, magazines, and cookbooks. The *Boston Cooking-School Magazine* discovered tuna in 1913, when Avalon Brand Tuna began advertising. The magazine offered additional recipes for tuna, such as one for hollowed-out tomatoes that were filled with a mixture of tuna, hard-boiled eggs, onions, parsley, and mayonnaise.[12] A few months later the magazine printed a recipe for tuna salad,[13] in close proximity to ads for Avalon Brand Tuna that also contained tuna recipes. In 1914 it went all out with eleven recipes.[14] The following year, the magazine recommended canned tuna for "any of the ways in which leftover fish is used: croquettes, creamed, plain, or au gratin, in tomato sauce, deviled, in fish-balls, fish-cakes, curried fish, in omelets or in salad."[15]

Newspapers discovered tuna about the same time. The *Brooklyn Eagle* suggested tuna as a "Lenten Food."[16] The *New York Tribune* proclaimed that tuna was ideal for "the Buffet Lunch,"[17] "the Tea Hours,"[18] a "Seasonable Out of Doors Salad,"[19] and even "Easter Dinner."[20] The *Aberdeen Daily News* identified tuna as "this delicious fish" and offered recipes for Deviled Tuna Fish, Tuna Fish Salad, and Tuna Fish au Gratin.[21]

In February 1913, the *Christian Science Monitor* reported that in California tuna was being "introduced generally in the best restaurants, not only because it is new, but because people are beginning to value it for what it is."[22] Indeed, Los Angeles's ritzy Alexandria Hotel served tuna in its dining room, and in 1913 its chef published two tuna recipes—one for Tuna Salad à la Catalina and one for Catalina Tuna en Surprise—in a salad cookbook.[23] A Baltimore chef published a recipe for Tunny Canapé the following year in another cookery booklet.[24] San Francisco's fashionable Hotel St. Francis had Tuna Salad, aka Salade Thon Mariné, on its menu.[25] Jean Vulpat, chef at the Hotel del Coronado, in Coronado, California, prepared tuna dishes for the hotel's restaurant.[26] Other tuna recipes—many cribbed directly from promotional materials—began showing up in American cookbooks around 1914.[27]

When the United States entered World War I in 1917, tuna became a mainstay substitute for rationed foods.[28] By the 1920s, tuna was a staple in American households. Following the stock market crash in 1929, tuna sales declined, but as the Depression deepened, there was a surge in canned tuna sales—tuna was a cheap protein source that could be eaten, if necessary, right out of the can. During World War II, when other protein sources were again rationed, tuna again took center stage in the American diet. When the war was over, and beef was back on the table, tuna continued to shine. It was the perfect inexpensive food for families. In fact, for the first time, tuna sales topped those of salmon, and tuna became America's most popular fish, an honor it has retained ever since.

From the first, ways of using canned tuna were surprisingly diverse: there were recipes for tuna canapés, cakes, salads, soufflés, loaves, rolls, balls, melts, pies, croquettes, omelets, and puddings, and for creamed tuna on toast, and, of course, tuna sandwiches. Tuna was combined with a variety of vegetables, fruits, and starches, including tomatoes, celery, peppers, corn, peas, squash, rice, spaghetti, macaroni, and apples. By the 1930s every major cookbook with a fish section had tuna recipes.

A few dominant uses of tuna emerged from this diversity: salads, sandwiches, soups and chowders. And—destined for greatness—the tuna noodle casserole debuted during the 1930s, became emblematic of American foodways in the 1950s, and has recently reemerged as comfort food.

POPULARITY OF CANNED TUNA FOR SALADS

Since ancient times, humans have enjoyed a variety of dishes made with raw vegetables similar to present-day salad ingredients, such as lettuce, cabbage, and cucumbers. European colonists brought the concept of salads to the New World, and most colonial kitchen gardens included salad ingredients such as lettuce, cabbage, watercress, kale, cucumbers, carrots, parsley, shallots, onions, spinach, and chives. By the early twentieth century, salad making was an art form. The first reference to Tunny Salad appears in a 1907 advertisement for tuna, which was "very dainty served cold as taken from the can and makes an excellent salad."[29] In 1909, Myrtle Reed, who published a series of cookbooks under the nom de plume "Olive Green," included a Tonno Salad in her *One Thousand Salads*. She noted that "Tonno comes in small cans and can be had at any Italian grocery."[30] A 1910 fund-raising cookbook from Tenafly, New Jersey, offered another early recipe for Tunny Fish Salad. The directions say to cut canned tuna into "small pieces and mix thoroughly with the oil of the fish and with mayonnaise dressing. Serve on crisp lettuce leaves."[31] In a 1912 cookbook published in Chicago, a Mrs. A. C. Christy of Glen View, Illinois, improved the basic formula by adding "3 tomatoes, peeled, and sliced, and 3 green peppers, seeded and cut into rings. Serve on lettuce and mix with French dressing, using cider vinegar."[32] A. C. Hoff's *Salads and Salad Dressings by the World Famous Chefs* (1913) contains a tuna salad recipe from the chef of the Alexandria Hotel in Los Angeles. The salad is made with fresh raw tuna—the first mention of raw tuna in any published American source.[33]

Virtually all tuna cookbooklets included one or more salad recipes.[34] The booklet prepared by Premier Packing Company in San Diego included four. The Los Angeles Tuna Canning Company proposed a recipe for Tuna Asparagus Salad: "Marinate cold boiled asparagus in French dressing and place on top of Panama Brand Tuna. Serve with mayonnaise dressing."[35] Recipes for Waldorf Tuna Salad were common. It began as a combination of apple, celery, and mayonnaise (walnuts were added later); its 1896 invention is credited to Oscar Tschirky, maître d' at the famed restaurant in the Waldorf Astoria Hotel in New York. The Southern California Fish Company's recipe for Waldorf Tuna Salad was the same recipe, only with tuna added.[36]

By 1914, dozens of tuna salad recipes had been published.[37] The *Los Angeles Times* reported that "the popularity of canned tuna for salads has attracted the attention of packers and jobbers all over America."[38] Increasingly, canned tuna was promoted as an economical substitute for chicken. Elizabeth Condit and Jessie A. Long, in *How to Cook and Why* (1914), wrote: "Tuna-fish is coming more into popularity for salad, and so delicious do many people find it when combined with celery that they have named it 'mock-chicken.'"[39] For a cookbook published in 1916 by the Daughters of the American Revolution, Irene H. Childs, of the Bunker Hill Chapter, supplied a tuna recipe for what she called "Mock Chicken Salad."[40]

Yet another tuna dish—Salade Niçoise—is said to have originated in Nice, France, where it started out as a summer salad made from whatever ingredients were available. When it arrived in the United States during the 1950s, the recipe was converted into one consisting of tuna or anchovies (but never both), diced potatoes, tomatoes, hard-boiled eggs, green beans, olives, and other ingredients.[41] It is usually dressed with a vinaigrette of oil, vinegar, salt, pepper, mustard, and occasionally garlic and herbs. It remains a popular restaurant menu item today.

Simpler tuna salads became standards on American menus beginning in the 1960s for reasons other than tuna's taste. Tuna is high in protein and vitamins and relatively low in calories, so tuna salad became stereotypical dieters' luncheon food, and it has remained so ever since.

WILL MAKE FORTY SANDWICHES

The Fourth Earl of Sandwich was probably not the first person to place food between two pieces of bread and eat it out of his hand, but his doing so launched a culinary revolution that has gained momentum ever since. Sandwich aficionados experimented with serving different foods in this way, such as ham, cheese, and shrimp. Recipes for sandwiches appeared in cookbooks by the 1770s. The British immigrants and cookbooks introduced sandwiches into the United States, where sandwich fillings included cheese, meat, fish, poultry, and seafood. Tuna fish sandwiches first appeared in print beginning in 1893. American cookbook author Dell Montjoy Bradley offered two tuna sandwich recipes in *Beverages and Sandwiches for Your Husband's Friends* (1893): Botargo Sandwiches, made with tuna roe, and Tonno or Thon Mariné Sandwiches, made with imported Pretto's Italian Tonno.[42]

Some tuna sandwich recipes were complex. The Blue Sea Tuna recipe for a multilayered Tuna Club Sandwich consisted of three slices of toast: one with crisp lettuce and mayonnaise, the next with more lettuce and flakes of tuna, and the third topped with three slices of broiled bacon and thinly sliced pickles. It was garnished with parsley and olives.[43] Tuna sandwiches caught on quickly because they were inexpensive yet tasted "like chicken." As one cookbook writer observed, "A fifteen-cent can of tuna fish and a ten-cent bunch of celery will make forty sandwiches, and are often mistaken for chicken sandwiches."[44]

When the United States entered World War I in 1917, Americans were urged not to eat bread because of wheat shortages, and while many tuna recipes were published during the war, sandwiches were not featured. When the war ended, and bread was readily available, drugstore soda fountain operators were urged by a trade publication to serve tuna salad sandwiches: all they had to do was use the same recipe for tuna salad and put it between two slices of bread or toast.[45]

The tuna melt is a latecomer to the tuna sandwich world. It was most likely invented by Kraft in an attempt to promote Velveeta, a Kraft processed-cheese product. Tuna melts appeared on restaurant menus in the 1960s, but it was Kraft that popularized them by including a recipe in an advertisement: "Good old Velveeta. Good in so many ways." One of the ways was to "slice it on your tuna, bake and you'll see what we mean." Processed cheese does melt easily and it remains a favorite for those making tuna melts, but they can be made with any kind of cheese.[46]

THE MOST DEPENDABLE QUICK DINNER DISH

Oven-baked one-pot meals are found in all traditional cuisines, but during the late nineteenth century the casserole was a favorite focus of culinary creativity in America. Casseroles were thrifty, sustaining one-dish meals in which leftovers could easily be incorporated. A cup or two of diced chicken, for instance, could be augmented with potatoes, noodles, or rice, all bathed in a creamy sauce. Canned tuna made a novel substitute for chicken, and tuna casseroles became popular during World War I. Reah Jeannette Lynch's *"Win the War" Cookbook* (1918) includes a recipe for Baked Tuna Fish: the tuna is layered with crackers in a casserole dish.[47] Those who devised these dishes often called their concoctions Mock Chicken Casserole.[48] Many other tuna casserole recipes have been developed, including Sour Cream Tuna Casserole, Tuna-Swiss Casserole and Green Bean Tuna Casserole.[49]

The most famous tuna casserole, however, is the Tuna Noodle Casserole. Recipes for this popular concoction began appearing in print during the Depression.[50] Many tuna noodle casseroles contained mushrooms and cream or a cream sauce, while others called for canned mushroom soup. The Campbell Soup Company saw its opportunity and began publishing recipes that incorporated a can of Campbell's Cream of Mushroom Soup. The first of these, called Company Casserole, appeared in 1941; it was pretty much a standardization of the already popular formula.[51] It wasn't until 1947 that Campbell's tuna casserole acquired its iconic topping of crumbled potato chips and somewhere along the way incorporated peas.[52] Campbell continued to popularize tuna casseroles, and they became a touchstone of American home cooking in the 1950s. Cookbook author Nell Beaubien Nichols wrote in 1952: "The tuna-noodle-mushroom soup casserole, often topped with crushed potato chips, takes the blue ribbons as the most dependable quick supper dish."[53] The dish slowly faded into obscurity toward the end of the twentieth century only to reemerge for periodic revivals as retro "comfort food."

Another special tuna casserole was the Tuna Surprise. Recipes so titled were published from 1913, but they became popular during the 1930s. Lily Haxworth Wallace, a leader in the domestic science movement and a prolific food writer during the first half of the twentieth century, published a recipe for "Tuna Surprise" in 1931 that became the basis for subsequent recipes.[54] Variations on the Tuna Surprise have been published ever since, including recipes for Tuna Surprise Balls, Tuna Surprise Croquettes, Cheese-Tuna Surprise (a sandwich), and una Surprise Salad.[55] During Lent in 1964, StarKist and Kellogg's Corn Flakes entered into an alliance to advertise "Crusty Tuna Surprise," with full-page ads in *Ladies Home Journal, Good Housekeeping, Better Homes & Gardens,* and *Life* magazines. It comes as no surprise that these recipes contained both StarKist tuna and Kellogg's Corn Flakes.[56]

UNUSUAL RECIPES

Cookbooks, cookbooklets, newspapers, and magazines strove to be innovative, and this meant that they came up with many unusual recipes for canned tuna; most disappeared after a brief flurry of popularity. "Deviled" foods were originally named because of a spiciness usually created with hot pepper or mustard. But Fannie Farmer's *Boston Cooking School Cookbook* (1896) demonstrates the "white saucing" of American food in the late nineteenth century. The Devilled Oysters and Devilled Scallops have just "a few grains of cayenne," but Devilled Crabs are dressed with a sauce seasoned with nothing more piquant than black pepper. White Star Canning Company's recipe for Deviled Tuna Baked in Shells, published about 1914, is similarly devoid of heat.[57]

A dish prepared *au gratin* is covered with a nicely browned topping; for savory dishes, the topping is usually grated cheese and/or bread-crumbs. Fish au gratin was common in the nineteenth century, and Pierce's Tunny again offered a tuna equivalent.[58] Lobster à la Newberg, created at the fashionable Delmonico's restaurant in New York about 1876, was the epitome of elegant eating. Recipes for the dish were widely circulated, and toward the end of the century, cookbook authors began to substitute other seafood for the lobster, hence such dishes as Clams or Terrapin à la Newberg. Several tuna canneries offered Tuna à la Newburg recipes in their cookbooklets. These bore little resemblance to the ever-popular Delmonico's dish but were presumably intended to give tuna an aura of elegance.[59]

The Premier Packing Company's cookbooklet included several unique recipes, some attributed to Jean Vulpat, the chef at the famous Hotel del Coronado in San Diego. The cookbooklet features a recipe for Tuna en Rémoulade—rémoulade being mayonnaise made piquant with mustard, herbs, and chopped capers or pickles. Vulpat's Tuna Eggs was a simple variation on deviled eggs, which lack any hint of heat.[60] This booklet also included a recipe for Tuna Pudding, recommended especially for children—probably because of its soft, custardlike texture.[61]

Yet another unusual recipe was Chop Suey with Tuna, published in the *Boston Cooking-School Magazine*. Chop suey had been invented in California late in the nineteenth century by Chinese restaurant cooks who needed something minimally "exotic" to offer their non-Chinese customers. In 1889, Chicago chef and cookbook author Jessup Whitehead wrote that "chop soly" was a savory ragout: "Its main components are pork, bacon, chicken, mushrooms, bamboo shoots, onions, and pep-per."[62] Within a few years, there were more than 100 chop suey restau-rants in New York. By the late 1890s, hundreds more had opened in New York, San Francisco, Philadelphia, Chicago, and other cities.[63] The *Boston Cooking-School Magazine's* recipe with tuna, however, bears no resem-blance to any known Chinese dish.[64]

"Cutlets" made from minced beef, poultry, or seafood are a time-honored way of dressing up leftovers. Many early tuna cookbooklets included recipes like the Van-Thomas Company's recipes for Tuna Cutlets, in which tuna and other ingredients were molded into a cutlet shape and were fried in oil.[65]

TUNA COOKBOOKS

Tuna canneries continued to publish advertising cookbooklets through the 1920s and 1930s and beyond. The booklets became larger and more sophisticated, replete with enticing color graphics. During World War II no booklets were offered, because tuna was in such great demand that advertising was unnecessary. But after the war, tuna companies once again began producing cookbooklets, often featuring television celebrities, such as Arthur Godfrey, the host of a popular 1950s television show, and Hopalong Cassidy, a popular movie and television cowboy.[66] The latter seems to represent the first recognition that children were an important target for tuna advertising.

More substantial tuna booklets emerged in the 1950s. The 1956 *Coral Tuna Cookbook*, from Hawaiian Tuna Packers in Honolulu, included "104 delicious dishes with Hawaiian Tuna." The recipes were written by Miriam J. Emery, a home economist, and featured several "Coral" products, including Smoked Tuna and Mid-Pacific Tuna Flakes. The "hors d'oeuvres, canapés and cocktails" section includes unusual recipes such as Tuna-Avocado Dunkum, Tuna Crisp Wun Tun, and Smoked Tuna Spread. The soups include Tuna Bouillabaisse, Tuna-Noodle Soup, and Tuna Minestrone, as well as New England Tuna Chowder. Entrees include recipes for Barazushi ("Scattered" sushi served over a bed of Vinegared Rice), Smoked Tuna and Corn Custard, Tuna Chow Mein, Tuna Egg Foo Young, and Tuna Welsh Rabbit. Salads include Smoked Tuna Aspic, Tuna Roni Salad, and Frozen Tuna Salad. Creative tuna sandwiches include Tunafurters and Three Decker on Rye. Ms. Emery offered menu suggestions for a TV supper, an "Our Gang" luncheon, presumably inspired by the pre–World War II children's movie series (later shown on television), and "Tuna Sandwiches for 100."[67]

The first noncommercial cookbook devoted exclusively to tuna was *The Tuna Cookbook* (1972) by Sheila Metcalf, which groups recipes into entrées, salads, sandwiches, soups, and "tidbits."[68] A quasi-corporate cookbook, Tracy Seaman's *The Tuna Fish Gourmet* (1994), had a relationship with Chicken of the Sea, which is featured on the cover. Other tuna cookbooks include Andy Black's *A Can of Tuna* (1995)[69] and Joie and Drew Warner's *Joie Warner's Take a Tin of Tuna* (2004), which includes recipes for every meal.[70]

StarKist introduced tuna "pouches" in 2000, and other companies followed with similar products a few years later. They take the convenience of canned tuna to the extreme, with large chunks or flakes of fish packed in foil pouches. The tuna comes marinated or mixed with other ingredients (onions, herbs, or sun-dried tomatoes, for instance), ready to be mixed into a salad or casserole, and the package requires no can opener and no draining. The pouches cost twice as much as canned tuna, but many consumers seem to appreciate the convenience. Today, about 3 percent of retail tuna consumption is pouched.[71]

Yet another development has been the marketing of "vegetarian tuna," and vegan cookbooks for Tuna Friendly Tuna. The latter is a frozen tuna-like product, made from soybean protein, whey protein, and other products for vegetarians, who like the taste of tuna and want to enjoy traditional sandwiches and casseroles. In appearance, texture, and taste it comes pretty close to the real thing.[72] There are also recipes in vegetarian and vegan cookbooks for "Tuna Friendly Tuna," made from a number of vegetable products.

Perhaps the most significant new development is tuna on the Internet. Most tuna companies have developed an online presence with plenty of recipes on their websites. The hugely popular website epicurious.com, owned by Condé Nast (publishers of *Bon Appétit* and, formerly, of *Gourmet*), offers blogs, videos, articles, and an archive of more than 100,000 recipes. During the past few years epicurious has attracted more than 5 million visitors every month. The website currently lists nearly 600 tuna recipes, sourced either from its publications or from reader-contributors. The Chicken of the Sea website has 238 recipes. Recipezaar.com, which boasts more than 400,000 member-contributed recipes, provides more than 1,900 for tuna.

Few Americans ate tuna before the twentieth century. This changed mainly due to the promotional efforts of tuna canners. Their recipes, which were published in pamphlets, magazines, newspapers, and cookbooks, greatly encouraged Americans to use tuna. The tuna recipe booklets achieved their purpose, although the diversity of the early recipes didn't survive into the post–World II period, when Americans settled down to just a few traditional ways of consuming tuna—sandwiches, salads, and casseroles. The early diverse recipes, however, helped increase the consumption of tuna. One of the ways that mainstream Americans in the 1950s did not consume tuna was raw. But this was about to change.

POSTSCRIPT

The Alaska Packers Association, which published a salmon cookery book in 1906, merged with the California Packing Corporation in 1916. That company later changed its name to its popular Del Monte brand, which would later acquire the company that canned StarKist tuna.

Within a few years of his successful advertising efforts on behalf of Avalon Brand Tuna, C. E. Van Landingham established a firm to promote canned tuna for other companies. By 1917, he represented many small canneries.[73]

FIVE

Caucasians Who Have Tasted
and Liked This Speciality

West Coast cities, especially San Francisco and Los Angeles, with significant Japanese-American populations, had many Japanese restaurants,
a few dating to the nineteenth century. New York, on the other hand,
had a very small Japanese community. The few Japanese restaurants
established there before World War II catered almost exclusively to
Japanese expatriates and visiting tourists from Japan. To attract a wider
clientele, Japanese restaurateurs offered sukiyaki, tempura, and other
Americanized dishes.[1] During the early 1950s, this began to change as
Japanese markets in New York began to sell raw fish for sashimi and
sushi to resident Japanese nationals, and raw fish was also bought
by some "Caucasians who have tasted and liked this speciality," as a
Japanese market owner reported in 1954.[2]

By the late 1950s, Japan had recovered from the devastation of World
War II, and its economy was booming. At the time, many American

corporations were headquartered in New York City, and Japanese businessmen flocked there, opening offices managed by Japanese nationals. These professionals demanded authentic, high-quality Japanese food, not the made-up American dishes identified as "Japanese," and they could afford it. Japanese chefs and sushi masters were imported to feed their compatriots. New restaurants opened, manned by sushi professionals, and their Japanese customers invited their American counterparts to share in Japanese food. Japanese cuisine is complex and subtle, but what received the most attention from the Americans were sashimi—sliced filets of raw fish—and sushi—vinegared rice topped with raw fish (among other things). The most commonly used raw fish is tuna, and the most expensive is the fatty portion of bluefin.

Mainstream Americans just did not eat raw fish, and it seemed unlikely that most would ever sit down to a meal of raw seafood—the beautifully crafted sushi and sashimi that hold such an honored place in Japanese dining. But this began to change during the early 1960s, and Craig Claiborne, the *New York Times*'s restaurant reviewer, chronicled the shift. Classically trained, Claiborne was at home with French cookery and haute cuisine. He didn't discover Japanese food until 1961, when he reviewed the Kabuki Restaurant in the Wall Street area. "Not all of these dishes will appeal to American palates," he wrote; "Count among these sashimi or raw fish." But, Claiborne continued, "for those who have never tried it, dining on raw fish can be an interesting experience."[3]

In June 1962 Claiborne visited Japan and was introduced to the wide world of sushi and sashimi, as well as myriad other Japanese dishes.[4] Claiborne would make several more trips to Japan during the following two decades, and he frequently mentioned sashimi and sushi in his columns. When he reviewed the New York City restaurant Nippon in 1963, he noted that raw fish was the specialty. The restaurant had a sushi bar, perhaps the first in America to have one, and it offered "fillets of tuna, halibut, squid and abalone." Claiborne cautioned that raw fish was probably still "a trifle too 'far out' for many American palates."[5]

American palates, however, were changing, at least in New York. Three years after Claiborne first mentioned sushi in print, he described New York City as "a metropolis with a growing public enthusiasm for the Japanese raw fish specialties, sashimi and sushi."[6] Two years later, he noted that "gastronomically there has been no phenomenon in recent years to equal the proliferation of Japanese restaurants, East Side, West Side and up and down the town."[7] By 1970, Claiborne proclaimed sushi and sashimi haute cuisine in their own right, and he noted that New Yorkers had taken to them "with what could be regarded as passion."[8] In less than ten years, raw tuna had emerged from an unimportant exotic ethnic niche and had landed smack in the mainstream of American cuisine.

THE JAPS GROW STRONG, EVEN FIERCE, ON RAW FISH!

Although the Japanese sushi chefs get the credit for introducing most Americans to eating raw fish, the tradition was common throughout the Pacific. Polynesians were great sailors and excellent fishermen, and archaeological remains on many islands inhabited by Polynesians attest to the importance of tuna in their diet. Polynesian voyagers reached Hawaii about 600 CE, and it has been determined that they ate *aku* (skipjack) and *ahi* (yellowfin, bigeye and albacore) there. The earliest located reference to *native* Hawaiians eating raw fish—with no specific mention of tuna—appeared in a 1904 publication, which described the fish as being chopped up, combined with a few other ingredients, and eaten as a salad.[9] *Nahu-pu* (raw mullet) and *lomi-lomi* (raw salmon, cod, or mackerel) were common, and raw fish was frequently served at luaus.[10]

Hawaiians' taste for raw fish was strengthened by the arrival of thousands of Japanese immigrants during the late nineteenth century. Many Japanese immigrants became fishermen in the islands, and they ate raw tuna, when available, in their homes as well as in restaurants catering to them. Raw tuna sales increased in Hawaii during the twentieth century, and raw fish began to appear in Hawaiian cookbooks. Katherine Bazore's *Hawaiian and Pacific Foods* (1940) included a recipe for sashimi.[11] After World War II, the Honolulu Chamber of Commerce invited Dr. Aya Kagawa, the president of the Kagawa Nutrition College in Tokyo, to lecture on Japanese cooking and give practical demonstrations. As a text she used the translation of her *Japanese Cookbook,* first published by the Japanese Tourist Board in 1949. "Vinegared Rice Ovals with Tunny" was one of many recipes for sushi and sashimi.[12] By 1952 a substantial portion of the Hawaiian tuna catch was consumed fresh. In addition, Hawaiians also began importing tuna from Japan to help meet local demand.[13] On the mainland, mainstream Americans were aware that Japanese ate raw fish, but this caused disgust.[14] Some Americans visited Japan during the early twentieth century; upon returning home, however, they spoke of their experiences eating raw fish. David S. Jordan, the ichthyologist who had studied California fish in 1880, and who had subsequently become president of Stanford University, had noted raw tuna as a valuable consumable on his trip to Japan during the early twentieth century.[15] Another visitor to Japan noted that of the fish eaten raw the tuna was "by far the most highly prized."[16]

Many Japanese moved to California, especially San Francisco, during the late nineteenth and early twentieth centuries. California's Japanese restaurants proliferated dramatically during the early twentieth century. Clarence Edwords, in his 1914 book *Bohemian San Francisco: Its Restaurants and Their Most Famous Recipes,* described a Japanese restaurant offering "thinly sliced raw fish, served with soy sauce."[17] The Japanese community in Los Angeles also grew during the early twentieth century. The city had only two Japanese-owned restaurants in 1902, but by 1927 there were 103.[18] Those were small establishments whose patrons were mainly of Japanese heritage. They may have served raw tuna, but most offered Americanized versions of Japanese foods, such as *sukiyaki, chawan-mushi* (savory custard), and grilled *tai* (sea bream).[19]

About 1926, Japanese grocers in Los Angeles created the Mutual Trading Company to import Japanese delicacies—sauces, rice, and general groceries—otherwise unobtainable in the United States. These products were sold to Japanese restaurateurs and to the wider Japanese community in Los Angeles.[20] The company soon expanded its market, selling to customers in San Francisco, New York, and other cities. By 1941, the Mutual Trading Company was the nation's dominant wholesale purveyor of Japanese food in America.[21]

Traditional Japanese fare, including sushi and sashimi, was served at least on occasion in some Japanese restaurants prior to World War II.[22] These establishments catered mainly to Japanese Americans or Japanese tourists. With the minor exception of soy sauce, Japanese cuisine had little influence on the mainstream American diet. Americans just didn't eat Japanese delicacies. The first located English-language Japanese cookbook by a Japanese author was Kaneko Tezuka's *Japanese Food* (1936). It was published in Japan for English-speaking tourists, but the book received wide circulation in America. It described the preparation of sashimi (including directions for sliced raw tuna) and told how to prepare sushi, which was identified as a light luncheon or snack.[23] Recipes using raw tuna did appear in a couple of prewar American cookbooks. Pearl V. Metzelthin's *World Wide Cook Book* (1939) notes that sashimi—thin slices of raw fish—was often made from tuna.[24] Justus George Frederick, the president of the Gourmet Society of New York, included a recipe for "Raw Tuna Appetizer, a La Japanese" in his *Long Island Seafood Cook Book* (1939):

> 6 tuna fish steak slices cut about ½ inch thick, 2 inch squares
> ½ cup Shoya Sauce
> 1 tablespoon freshly grated horseradish

> Clean tuna fish slices, wash, rub some salt it, let stand 5 minutes; then wash in another water. Mix the grated horseradish in the Shoya sauce (obtainable at Japanese stores). To eat, spear the tuna fish steak slice on your fork, dip well in the sauce and eat! (Yes, it's good! The Japs grow strong, even fierce, on raw fish!)[25]

CALIFORNIA ROLL

Japanese businesses on the West Coast were devastated by the relocation of Japanese Americans during World War II. All Japanese-owned businesses were closed, and most were sold to non-Japanese. When the war ended, many Japanese Americans from Los Angeles slowly returned to Little Tokyo. The Mutual Trading Company was particularly fortunate: Maryknoll nuns had guarded its warehouse and preserved the supplies and equipment, which were returned to the owners after the war. By the 1950s, the business was thriving again, but its sole market was the Japanese community in Los Angeles.[26]

Meanwhile, in Japan, Noritoshi Kanai, who had served in the Japanese army in Burma during World War II, opened the Tokyo Mutual Trading Company, a subsidiary of the Los Angeles firm. He made his first trip to the United States in 1956.[27] Eight years later Kanai moved to Los Angeles, where he soon took over the parent company, continuing to supply the Japanese community—a very small proportion of the population in the rapidly expanding Los Angeles metropolitan area. Kanai wanted to reach a wider audience. At a fancy food show, he met Harry Wolff Jr., an American food broker, and the two became partners, importing "Harvest Cookies," honey-and-sesame crackers that were new to Americans. In 1966 the two visited Japan, where Wolff fell in love with a sushi bar across the street from their hotel. He was particularly impressed with the performances of sushi chefs, who prepared everything to order right in front of the diner. Wolff became convinced that Americans could get excited about sushi. When Wolff and Kanai returned to the United States, they began to push for sushi bars in Japanese restaurants. The first to take their advice was Kawafuku in Little Tokyo; then a second Japanese restaurant with sushi bars opened in Beverly Hills, and another in Santa Monica. Sushi bars were novelties for most Americans, but eating raw fish was only part of the experience; it was also the rapport between customer and sushi chef that made the meal so memorable. The few professional sushi chefs in America were in great demand, and their incomes reflected their status. As word of their financial success filtered back to Japan, more sushi chefs came to seek their fortunes in the United States.[28]

Young sushi chefs were also delighted to work in the United States because in Japan, becoming a sushi master required a long apprenticeship; but young chefs who emigrated could go right to work and achieve quick success. One such émigré was Shigeo Saito, who worked at Kawafuku. The restaurant had sashimi on its menu in 1950 but had probably served raw fish to its Japanese patrons even before World War II. In 1964 it added a six-seat sushi bar, the first in Los Angeles. Saito built his menu on ingredients imported from Japan combined with local fresh foods, especially fresh fish, including tuna, when available in local fish markets.[29]

Tokyo Kaikan opened in Los Angeles in 1964. At first, the restaurant served "Japanese and Chinese style" food in a Polynesian setting—a takeoff on the then wildly popular Trader Vic's Polynesian restaurant chain that was then expanding throughout the United States. Observing Kawafuku's success, in 1966 Tokyo Kaikan's management changed its decor and added a sushi bar.[30]

For many Californians, raw fish remained a hard sell. Then some Japanese-American chef hit on the idea of creating sushi from ingredients that Californians would accept. The result was the California Roll (also called California Maki): an "inside-out" sushi roll filled with cucumber sticks, crabmeat, and avocado, wrapped in seaweed and rice; the rice forms the outer layer and is rolled in sesame seeds. Ichiro Mashita, the sushi chef at Tokyo Kaikan in Los Angeles, and his assistant, Teruo Imaizumi, have been credited with this invention. Supposedly they created the California Roll because they couldn't rely on the availability and quality of fish in Los Angeles, and they needed something to replace tuna (for instance) when it was out of season.[31] This is a nice story, but it's unlikely to be true. By the 1960s, Los Angeles had plenty of fish markets, and tuna and other sushi fish were brought in year-round.

A much more likely claimant to the title of California Roll inventor is Ken Seusa, master sushi chef at Kin Jo on La Cienega Boulevard near Hollywood. Seusa had been a sushi chef at the famous Fuzsushi Roppongi in Tokyo; in Los Angeles, he was known for a more "creative type of cuisine to appeal to the sophisticated Los Angeles diner." A contemporary newspaper article described Seusa's use of all sorts of non-Japanese ingredients, such as "hot sauce, mayonnaise, yogurt and cream." The California Roll is made with un-Japanese sushi ingredients, such as avocado, and many early recipes include mayonnaise. Seusa was credited, in an Associated Press story, with creating the California Roll, and no one challenged the attribution or offered an alternative until more than twenty years later.[32]

Many Japanese customers were put off by this novel concoction, which differed so much from "authentic" Japanese sushi, but the California Roll was a big hit with non-Japanese diners in Los Angeles.[33] The California Roll gained national visibility when it was mentioned in *Gourmet* in 1980. The *New York Times* mentioned it the following year, when Mimi Sheraton warned New Yorkers against this "misbegotten invention" devised to appeal to American tastes.[34]

Despite Sheraton's warning, the California Roll spread across America and even to Japan itself, where traditionalist sushi masters refused to serve it. For many Americans, the California Roll opened the door to "real" sushi and sashimi, and as it turned out, millions of Americans *did* love to eat raw fish after all. The choicest fish for sushi and sashimi was, and remains, tuna.

SUSHI COMES OF AGE

The Immigration Act of 1965 liberalized United States immigration law, making it easier for professionals to become American citizens. Jet air service between Japan and California made travel easier, swifter, and more affordable. Even more Japanese businessmen came to the United States, and they brought with them an appetite for fine Japanese dining.

Sushi and sashimi quickly spread across America and gained extensive visibility. The Bush Garden restaurant, in Portland, Oregon, was an "excellent establishment," reported Craig Claiborne in 1965. He noted that its raw tuna "was of premier freshness."[35] In Chicago, Kamehachi opened across the street from the Second City comedy club, where comedian John Belushi performed. In 1975 Belushi joined the cast of *Saturday Night Live,* playing a samurai sushi chef with a long sword and a short temper.[36] In Los Angeles, sushi bars expanded from Little Tokyo to other parts of the city.[37] In 1970, Osho opened in Century City, right next to Fox movie studios. Movie actors, such as Yul Brynner, frequented Osho, and their presence added prestige to sushi eating. The restaurant Something's Fishy, in Malibu, California, attracted Hollywood names like Robin Williams, Olivia Newton-John, Neil Diamond, and Barbara Streisand.[38] James Coburn, Cheryl Ladd, Richard Dreyfuss, and Henry

Winkler were also reported to be sushi aficionados.[39] Celebrities added glamour to the sushi scene, and soon sushi restaurants were routinely reviewed in national magazines, such as *Gourmet* and *Esquire*.

Matao Uwate was a Japanese American who moved from Columbus, Ohio, to Los Angeles in 1949 to become the manager of the Japanese Chamber of Commerce. He became a loyal fan of Matsuno Sushi, located near his office. In 1975 Matao Uwate published the first American cookbook solely devoted to making sushi. In it, Uwate highlights tuna as the basic ingredient of "sushi making." It was important to acquire "the best and the freshest" tuna. He announced that "the local bluefins are caught during the summer season, and they are really the best."[40]

The rise in prestige of Japanese cuisine in America is reflected in Mimi Sheraton's reviews. She first reviewed the restaurant Hatsuhana in 1978. Sheraton tasted a number of tuna dishes, including raw tuna from the sushi bar, and found the grilled skewered tuna with shrimp and vegetables "succulent." She particularly liked the "chopped belly of tuna with scallions." Sheraton noted that Hatsuhana's sushi and sashimi merited a three-star rating, but the ordinary dishes were not up to that standard, so she gave the restaurant two stars—still a great review, by New York standards.[41] The following year, Florence Fabricant gave two stars to Tsubo, another Japanese restaurant. She was most impressed with its sushi and sashimi.[42] Sheraton had reviewed Takezushi, where the prize sashimi dish was "fatty tuna."[43] She revisited Takezushi two years later and once again raved about the fatty tuna. In 1983, she reviewed the restaurant a third time, mentioning that the *natto*, an earthy, cheeselike paste of aged soybeans, was wonderful with a white-fleshed fish, tuna, clams, squid, or the most subtly flavored *toro*—fatty tuna. She praised the "sunny yellow vinegar sauce made of lemon juice, bean paste and sake" that is "the basis of nuta, a salad made with plain or fatty tuna," and she also liked the "squares of tuna . . . complemented by a satiny sauce of taro root (called yam here)," noting: "A little soy sauce adds piquancy." This time Sheraton gave Hatsuhana four stars—the first time that the *New York Times* had awarded a Japanese restaurant such an honor.[44] Fabricant's and Sheraton's reviews helped popularize sushi, and more and more Americans were willing to try it. No longer was tuna salad or a tuna fish sandwich the only acceptable way to eat this versatile fish.

There were many reasons for this shift—Japanese businessmen, American travel to Japan, the increased American willingness to try new cuisines, for instance—but one of the most important reasons had to do with television. *Shōgun*, a mini-series based on a James Clavell novel, began airing in 1980, and American interest in everything Japanese, including food, skyrocketed: the sushi boom was on.[45]

THE MAGURO EXPERIENCE

American sushi fans gained sophistication in their appreciation of tuna. Aficionados of tuna (*maguro*) know that different tuna species have different textures and tastes. Northern bluefin (*hon-maguro, kuro-maguro,* or *shibi-maguro*) is the largest of the tunas and has the reddest flesh. It is highly prized and commands a premium price. In 2010, a 513-pound bluefin fetched $170,000.[46] It was purchased by the owners of Kyubei, an upscale sushi restaurant in Tokyo's Ginza district, and Itamae Sushi, a casual, Hong Kong-based chain. This record was topped in January 2011 when a 754-pound tuna was sold at Tokyo's Tsukiji fish market for $396,000, or $526 per pound. It was purchased by the same restaurateurs who had purchased the most expensive tuna in 2010. In 2012, the Sushi-Zanmai restaurant chain purchased a 592-pound bluefin for $736,500, or $1,238 per pound, the largest sum ever paid for a dead animal. The buyers of these fish believed that their purchases were propitious and would give them worldwide visibility.

The flesh of the bluefin is firm and particularly well suited for sushi making. It has more fat in the belly muscle than other tuna species, and a stronger flavor. Bluefin is the tuna species of choice for Japanese restaurants, where it can sell for $24 per piece in high-end restaurants. Southern bluefin (*minami maguro*) are caught in the South Pacific and Indian Oceans. They are smaller than northern bluefin. The quality of their flesh differs depending on where and when they were caught and how they were brought to the market. Southern bluefin lose flavor when frozen, but fish used for sushi is often frozen to ensure that it is less likely to have parasites. Yellowfin (*kihada*) is the second most commonly served tuna in U.S. sushi restaurants. Bigeye tuna (*mebichi*) is usually served in the spring, when its flesh is firmest and most flavorful. Albacore (*shiro-maguro* or *bincho*) is also called "white tuna," but its flesh is actually a pale peach or rose color. The fatty underbelly (*binjo*) of the albacore is prized by sushi aficionados.[47]

When tuna is to be used for sushi, the head and tail are removed, and then two filets, called *toro*, are cut from either side of the backbone. The front of the *toro*, called the *ōtoro*, contains almost 40 percent fat. The *ōtoro* has two parts: the *jabara* (snake's stomach), which is cut from the fish's underbelly; and the *shimofuri* (fallen frost), which comes from the upper belly and is marbled with thin lines of fat. The *shimofuri* is considered the choicest part of the fish. It is also the most expensive, and it is usually unavailable outside of Japan. At the tail end of the fish is the *chūtoro*, which is fatty but not as lush as the *ōtoro*; it, too, is very expensive. Between the *ōtoro* and the *chūtoro* is *akami*, which is the muscle that propels the fish forward in the ocean. It is a leaner red meat, and it is much cheaper than other parts of the fish. *Akami* is the most common cut found in American sushi bars.[48]

The sushi served in inexpensive restaurants and sold in grocery stores is usually made with smoked tuna prepared in Southeast Asia. Smoking preserves the fish, so it can be sold weeks or months later with relatively little deterioration. The smoking also fixes the tuna's bright red color, and it acquires no obvious smell from the process. It was flash-frozen and shipped to the United States in bulk.

In addition to the species and cut of fish, the sushi experience involves other elements: rice, dried seaweed, soy sauce (*shoyu*), and pickled ginger (*gari*). Next to the fish, the rice is the most important ingredient. Short-grain rice, glossy and slightly sticky when cooked, is traditionally used for sushi making. The cooked, cooled rice is mixed with a special rice vinegar (*awase-zu*) and then formed into small, neat portions. A slice of fish is placed on top.

In America, sushi is often served with what is called *wasabi*, which is usually regular horseradish that has been colored green. Technically, wasabi (*Wasabia japonica*) is a specialty high-end condiment not typically found outside of Japan, where it is not usually served with sushi or sashimi.

TUNA FUSION

Beginning in the 1980s, tuna became part of an entirely new cuisine. In Los Angeles, Japanese restaurants proliferated, and sushi bars became the "in" place for Hollywood stars and agents to congregate for lunch. One such establishment was Matsuhisa, on La Cienega near Wilshire Boulevard. Its owner, Nobuyuki Matsuhisa, was a Japanese-born sushi chef who had immigrated first to Peru, where he worked in a restaurant, then to Argentina, and then to Alaska, where he opened a restaurant, only to have it burn down. After nine years of working for others, he finally managed to open his own place in 1987. Matsuhisa selected ingredients from his many experiences in Japan, Peru, Argentina, and America and used them to create new combinations that would later be identified as "fusion food." Matsuhisa's sushi bar served unusual items, such as sashimi sparked with cilantro or garlic. When the restaurant first opened, a customer sent back her sashimi, pleading that she couldn't eat raw fish. Matsuhisa took the plate back into the kitchen and cooked the fish briefly in olive oil. The customer loved the barely cooked fish, and the chef went on to experiment with this new concept, adding sesame oil to the olive oil and arranging "ginger, garlic, chives and sesame seeds on each slice of fish for more complexity."[49]

Among the early fans of Matsuhisa was Robert Ovitz, founder of Creative Artists Agency. He brought many of his clients, including the actor Robert De Niro, into the restaurant. De Niro was so impressed that he offered to enter a partnership with Nobu Matsuhisa on a restaurant in New York. That restaurant, called Nobu, opened in 2001, and that same year Matsuhisa published *Nobu: The Cookbook*.

Nobu Matsuhisa wasn't the only chef experimenting with new ways of preparing tuna. Recipes for tuna steaks had been around for years, but they weren't often found on restaurant menus until the sushi craze hit. *Gourmet* first wrote about tuna steaks in 1980.[50] The restaurant chain Ruby Tuesday began offering tuna steak grilled over mesquite in 1986.[51] Geoffrey Zakarian, chef at Maxwell's Plum in New York, offered a tuna steak "seared at the edge, just warm at the core, served with roasted cloves of garlic, barely wilted spinach and tomatoes slowly roasted to intensify their flavor," reported restaurant critic Gael Greene.[52] In Austin, Texas, a restaurant served tuna steak with *salsa veracruzana,* a Mexican sauce usually paired with red snapper.[53] A small, thick cut of tuna resembling a filet mignon became a mainstay of fine restaurants; it was invariably cooked rare, as Gael Greene described the Maxwell's Plum version. Tuna fillets and steaks, braised or seared, graced the menus of restaurants all over the country, and Americans discovered that tuna was also easy to cook at home.

A more unusual dish that became yet another fad was Tuna Tartare, which may well have been a French import to the United States. The earliest located reference appeared in a *Newsweek* magazine article in 1975 that announced that "Tuna Tartare" was served at the popular Parisian restaurant Le Duc.[54] In the next ten years the dish made its mark in the United States, where it took on a variety of different forms. In 1983, *New York Magazine* ran an ad for American Express that included Chef Michael Fitoussi saying: "I take pride in pleasing the most discriminating palates, with specialties like" Tuna Tartare. The following year, Japanese-born and French-trained Shigefumi Tachibe, then executive chef at Chaya Brasserie in Beverly Hills, diced tuna and added a mayonnaise sauce. Los Angeles's Spago restaurant had a more Asian Tuna Tartare; that at San Francisco's Aqua was more Italian.[55] In 1990, the *Texas Monthly* reported on a version of the dish offered at the Pyramid restaurant at the Fairmont Hotel in Dallas: "A mound of yellowfin tuna tartare with blue and yellow tortilla chips, serrano sour cream, and various exotic condiments was the hub of an edible wheel that was topped with a raw quail egg—a fantastic visual image."[56]

Tuna Carpaccio—like Tuna Tartare, an adaptation of a beef dish— came on the scene in the early 1980s.[57] Carpaccio, shavings of raw beef served with a lemony mayonnaise, is said to have originated at Harry's Bar in Venice. Tuna Carpaccio consisted of thinly sliced raw tuna that had been pounded, with other ingredients, such as lemon. Restaurants in France and Italy also served this dish in the 1980s.[58]

Yet another new gourmet treat is Tuna Poke, a traditional Hawaiian dish composed of marinated slices or cubes of raw fish. Recipes for poke, sometimes using raw tuna, began appearing in Hawaiian cookbooks in the 1970s. Hawaiian master chef and restaurateur Sam Choy hosts a three-day poke tasting contest at the Annual Aloha Festival in September. Contestants from around the Pacific enter their dishes, and seventy-five finalists are selected for judges to taste. Selected recipes from these contests were published in *Sam Choy's Poke: Hawaii's Soul Food* in 1999. Tuna Poke is now served in large hotels and restaurants in Hawaii, and it has recently migrated to the mainland.[59]

The 1960s was a time of ferment in America, with the struggle for civil rights, Vietnam War protests, advocacy of women's rights, and the rise of the hippie or "New Age" movement. It was also a time when America shed its traditional views toward food and began to experiment with new culinary styles. It was in the 1960s that Julia Child, as the French Chef, swept America off its feet, and when hippies experimented with brown rice, sprouts, and food coops. This was the era when many Americans first sampled sushi and sashimi. Eating raw fish would have been unthinkable in the 1950s, yet in the following decade, Americans conquered their fears and learned to love raw tuna. A contemporary writer called sushi a "clean, light food," and it was also promoted as diet fare.[60]

At sushi bars, food preparation emerged from behind the scenes to become a spectator sport, with diners raptly observing the sushi master as he sliced the fish and formed it into sushi and sashimi. The sushi bar, a shared table, permitted conversations among customers and between chef and diners. A new etiquette was required for how to order and communicate with the chef. These sushi cuisine rules slipped as it became more popular, and then disappeared as sushi moved from haute cuisine restaurants into corner delis and green grocers. It isn't just small sellers anymore: Sarku Japan, the largest fast-food sushi restaurant chain in America, now has 200 stores and operates in 37 states.

Sushi bars were a precursor of today's American passion for cooking as entertainment and spectacle—all sorts of restaurants switched to open kitchens so that patrons could watch their food being prepared. The ascendance of sushi and sashimi in the 1960s took tuna out of the can and allowed it to shine in its natural state. These Japanese traditions also freed chefs to experiment with tuna in new ways, and today Americans eat a wide variety of fresh tuna dishes both at home and when dining out. New fusion foods emerged, such as ahi tuna tostadas and sushi tacos.

American demand for fresh tuna grew tremendously toward the end of the twentieth century, and fishermen scoured the seas, searching for the finest tuna. New technology was developed to transport the fish from where it was caught—usually thousands of miles from U.S. shores—and supply lines were set up to ensure that the fish would arrive in prime condition. The need for sushi chefs outpaced the supply, and schools such as the California Sushi Academy were established; other culinary schools offered both professional and recreational classes on sushi and sashimi. The American hunger for tuna seemed to know no limits, and this meant increased fishing, especially for bluefin—the king of fresh tuna.

POSTSCRIPT

Craig Claiborne continued to write about tuna and its various manifestations. He retired from the *New York Times* in 1988 and died in 2000.

Mimi Sheraton remained the *New York Times* restaurant critic until 1983. She has written sixteen books, including her autobiography, *Eating My Words: An Appetite for Life* (2004).

Robert De Niro and Nobu Matsuhisa have since franchised "Nobu" restaurants, and twenty-four have opened in various cities around the world.

Geoffrey Zakarian became one of Manhattan's top chefs. He became executive chef at Patroon, to which Ruth Reichl awarded three stars in her review in the *New York Times* in 1998.[61] He later opened the restaurants Town (2001) and Country (2005) in Manhattan.

In the fall of 2010, students in a genetics class at Nova Southeastern University in Florida tested fish advertised as white tuna from ten sushi restaurants in Broward, Dade, and Palm Beach Counties. All ten were improperly labeled. The restaurants were serving escolar rather than white tuna. When the study was duplicated in 2011, eight out of ten restaurants were serving escolar rather than white tuna.

PART II The Fall

SIX Foreign Tuna

Despite tuna's incredible culinary success in the mid-twentieth century, not all was well in the American tuna industry. A major problem was foreign competition, initially from Japan. Even before Japan attacked the U.S. naval base at Pearl Harbor, the American fishing industry was affected by increasing tensions between the two nations. The U.S. government purchased thirty purse seine vessels that were converted to patrol boats and sent out to guard the Alaskan coast. Tuna boats had to request permission to fish in Central and South American waters. When the war began, the eighty or so tuna vessels then at sea were ordered to go to the nearest port. One captain didn't get the message, and his boat was fired on by American patrol aircraft protecting the Panama Canal, before the boat pulled into a port in Costa Rica.[1]

Within days of the Japanese attack on Pearl Harbor, the U.S. Navy requisitioned forty-nine tuna clippers and converted them into patrol boats.

The navy painted the boats battleship gray, removed their bait tanks and refrigeration systems, and installed depth-charge racks and small guns on their decks. Other boats retained their refrigeration systems and were used to transport food to American troops in the Pacific Islands.[2]

The tuna industry suffered not only the loss of the clippers during the war, but also the loss of its most experienced fishermen—and not just those who joined or were drafted into the military. Italians who were not U.S. citizens could not leave the territorial limits of the United States, even in a fishing boat. More than half of the 1,511 Italian fishermen in California were barred from offshore fishing during the war.[3] Even more devastating was the loss of an estimated 3,500 fishermen of Japanese birth or ancestry who were jailed or interred in relocation camps for the duration of the war.

Total fish production in the United States declined as World War II progressed. This was a serious problem for the war effort, as meat was rationed, and high protein fish was a good substitute. Consequently, the U.S. government sought new sources of fish. This quest led to two programs. The first encouraged the establishment of canneries and fishing fleets in other countries, which could then export fish to the United States during the war. With technical assistance and equipment, friendly countries, such as Costa Rica, Peru, and Ecuador, could develop their fishing and canning capabilities. The idea was good; none of these countries consumed much canned tuna at the time, so virtually all production could be exported to the United States. Canneries were built, and some tuna was shipped to the United States, but most American-assisted operations didn't come on line until the war's end.[4]

The second program increased tuna imports into the United States during the war by lowering tariffs on imported fish. In August 1943 the United States signed a trade agreement with Mexico that sharply lowered tariffs on tuna canned in oil from 45 percent to 22½ percent. The United States also signed a bilateral agreement with Iceland reducing tariffs on fish to 12½ percent. This agreement included tuna canned in brine, even though Iceland did not catch, can, or consume tuna at the time—or later. How and why tuna was placed in the agreement, and why it wasn't subsequently removed, have never been fully explained.[5] Neither agreement did much to increase tuna availability in the United States during the war.

For those who remained engaged in the tuna industry, however, the war years were financially rewarding. Tuna were again abundant along the Southern California and Baja California coasts. Wages were high, and meat rationing meant that more Americans were trying tuna for the first time.[6] Tuna catches dipped during the war mainly due to lack of fishermen and tuna boats. When the Japanese navy was largely destroyed in October 1944, territorial restrictions on American tuna boats were relaxed, and the United States government permitted the construction of new tuna clippers.[7] These larger, faster tuna clippers had steel bottoms and 1,560-horsepower engines and were more than 130 feet in length.[8] The American tuna industry emerged from war as the largest in the world, and American tuna clippers ruled the Pacific.

The tuna industry revived after the war as veterans returned home. Immediately after the war, tuna sales exceeded those of salmon for the first time, making tuna the most popular seafood in America. In a few years, it would become the most heavily consumed fish in the world. American tuna fishermen and canners looked forward to a bright postwar future. This was not to be, however.

Agreements the United States signed with Iceland and Mexico during World War II changed the American tuna industry after the war in important ways. These changes were connected to the "most favored nation" principle, which is that all countries so identified by the United States government would be subject to the same tariffs. Thus any country on the United States' "most favored nation" list would pay the same tariffs on tuna canned in oil as did Mexico, and the same tariffs on tuna canned in brine as did Iceland. Tuna imports from Central and South American countries skyrocketed after the war, and the American tuna industry began to lose out to the competition. Competition from Latin American countries, however, was just the beginning of problems for the American tuna industry.

A PRESIDENTIAL PROCLAMATION

The 1950s was not the first time the American tuna industry had faced serious competition from abroad. In 1924, the supply of albacore fell below demand, so the Halfhill Packing Corporation began importing frozen albacore from Japanese fishing operations in Baja California. When albacore largely disappeared from the west coast waters the following year, American packers imported frozen albacore from Japan.[9] By 1929, 7 percent of the tuna canned on the U.S. mainland (mostly in San Pedro) was imported from Japan and Hawaii.[10] During the Depression, the Japanese yen was devalued, making imported fish even cheaper.[11] California canners were very happy with this turn of events: they were able to import frozen Japanese tuna at a lower price than they would have had to pay American fishermen for the same product, and this meant that they could sell low-cost canned tuna and still make a sizable profit.

Fishermen and tuna-boat owners, however, despaired of their livelihoods; they couldn't compete with cheap imports.[12] In 1930 the American Fishermen's Tunaboat Association, initially composed of owners of thirty-five tuna clippers, was formed to negotiate with the powerful canneries.[13] Nine of the largest canners responded by creating the Tuna Canners Institute to protect and lobby for the industry.[14] This organization was short-lived—there was too much disagreement over basic issues. Canners from the Pacific Northwest acquired virtually all of their tuna from Japan and therefore wanted no duties on frozen tuna. California canners, on the other hand, acquired most of theirs from American tuna boats, and they wanted high tariffs on imported tuna.

Japanese companies began sending canned tuna to the United States in 1931, and because of the low wages paid to Japanese fishermen and cannery workers, even with a 24-percent tariff Japanese canned tuna was still cheaper than the domestic product. By 1933, Japanese imports equaled nearly one-third of the total market. American canners believed that the Japanese were dumping canned tuna on the U.S. market to destroy their businesses. They lobbied for hefty import duties, and Congress passed a 30 percent duty on canned tuna. But the tuna industry wanted more, so the U.S. Tariff Commission was directed to determine whether the tuna industry had been harmed by cheap and unfair Japanese imports. The commission reported that the American tuna industry was in fact being harmed. President Franklin Roosevelt, by proclamation, increased the

tariff on imported canned tuna in oil to 45 percent.[15] Despite these lev-
ies, Japanese tuna continued to be imported and still remained slightly
cheaper at retail than tuna canned in America. Just when things looked
bleakest, the demand for tuna suddenly jumped: inexpensive, versatile,
and highly nutritious, it was just what Americans needed during the
Depression. By 1934, tuna fishing was again profitable, even with the
imports of frozen and canned tuna still flowing in from Japan.

When Japan invaded China in 1937, American media urged a boycott
of all imported Japanese goods, including tuna. Japanese imports slowed
appreciably in 1938 but snapped back the following year. There was still
a strong market for cheap imported tuna, and Japanese imports fell only
slightly over the next few years. But in December 1941, after the Japanese
naval attack on Pearl Harbor, importation of all Japanese goods was
halted and would not be resumed until the late 1940s.[16]

A CONTRIBUTION TO OUR OWN SECURITY

The American tuna industry's postwar prosperity was entirely due to an
unusual circumstance. The American industry's main competitors, the
Japanese, were devastated by World War II; under the rules imposed by
Allied occupation authorities, Japanese fishing was restricted to waters
near Japan, and all the tuna caught by these vessels was to be consumed
in Japan.

Geopolitical considerations would change this. In the war's aftermath,
the United States occupied Japan and spent vast sums of American tax
dollars to reconstruct the Japanese economy and feed its people. Japan
needed almost everything, and during the postwar years, Japan had a
chronic trade deficit with the United States. It made sense for the American occupation forces to grow the Japanese tuna industry. It had been one
of Japan's most important prewar industries, and if it could be revived, it
could easily provide a cheap protein source for a malnourished population. It also employed thousands of people in fishing, canning, trans-
porting, and selling tuna products, and indirectly the Japanese tuna
industry helped employ tens of thousands of others who sold products

and services to the canneries and to the fishermen and their families. As Japan recovered from the war, it rapidly modernized and expanded its depleted fishing fleet and its freezing capacity.

The U.S. State Department also wanted a revived Japan that might serve as a bulwark against rapidly expanding Asian Communism. By the late 1940s, the United States was engaged in a cold war with the Soviet Union and the People's Republic of China, which had been created when the Communists had taken power in 1949. The following year, the United States became enmeshed in a hot war on the Korean peninsula, when North Korean military forces, with Soviet support, attacked South Korea. When it appeared that North Korea would be defeated by the United Nations forces under American command, China intervened on behalf of the North Koreans. At the time Japan had a large and active Communist Party, and the United States needed Japan as a base for its military operations. In addition, America was opposed to Japan trading with the PRC, and the main alternative was trading with the United States. It was in America's financial and geopolitical self-interest, most international relations and military leaders believed, to revive Japanese industries as quickly as possible to create a self-sufficient nation. Permitting Japan to sell tuna to the United States made perfect sense.[17]

It wasn't just because of the "Communist menace" or economic self-interest in the postwar recovery of Japan that America opened up its markets to foreign tuna. Many economists and government officials around the world believed that national protection of industries was, in the long run, inefficient and harmful to the economies of all nations. International trade should be based on comparative advantage, permitting each nation to do what it could do best. Economists and government officials also believed that the best way to revive the world's economy in the postwar period was to increase international trade, and the best way to do that was to decrease tariffs. As the U.S. Tariff Committee stated at the time, "In the longer run, a liberalized American tariff could make a worthwhile contribution to our allies' economic health and military strength . . . and hence a contribution to our own security."[18] This view led to the General Agreement on Tariffs and Trade (GATT), which was formed in 1947 to lower tariffs and increase international trade. Over the next forty-six years GATT was responsible for lowering tariffs on a wide variety of products, including tuna in 1955. As a result of these decisions, world trade dramatically increased, boosting the economies of many nations, including the United States, which at the time exported more to GATT countries than they exported to the United States. This was particularly true of Japan in the late 1940s and early 1950s. Japan needed dollars if it was to revive its industrial might, and tuna exporting was one obvious way to generate money, which would then be used to purchase needed industrial equipment from American companies. This made sense to many American leaders.

While the Japanese ate both fresh and dried tuna, they didn't care much for the canned product, and the majority of their canned tuna could be exported. But in the late 1940s, the only country that consumed large quantities of canned tuna was the United States, which permitted imports of Japanese tuna beginning in 1948. Even with the costs of transportation figured in, it was less expensive for the Japanese to catch tuna, freeze it, and transport it to the United States than it was for American fishermen to supply tuna directly to canneries. An even more serious problem for American tuna developed when a Japanese canner had a stroke of marketing genius. Rather than packing tuna in oil and paying 40 percent tariff, why not pack it in brine and pay just 12½ percent? In 1950, Japan exported about a thousand cans packed in brine per month. This proved financially successful. In fact it was so successful that the following year, Japan exported 100,000 cans packed in brine per month.[19]

Frozen tuna imports from Japan also escalated—from 22 million pounds (7.5 percent of total tuna consumption) in 1947 to 116 million pounds in 1952. The American tuna industry, fighting for its livelihood, urged that tariffs be levied on imported tuna. In 1951, the U.S. House of Representatives voted to impose a duty on frozen tuna, which previously had been admitted free into the United States, but the bill died when the Senate declined to pass it. Both the House and Senate held hearings on imported tuna, and strong political pressure was applied by many in the tuna industry to restrict foreign competition by imposing tariffs.[20]

Congress asked the U.S. Trade Commission to determine whether the American tuna industry had been harmed by this massive importation of tuna canned in brine. While the commission was conducting its year-long investigation, the Japanese concluded that it was in their self-interest to "voluntarily" restrict exports of tuna canned in brine to the United States. As this was only 4 percent of all tuna consumed in the United States, the commission concluded in November 1952 that there had been no injury to the American tuna industry.[21] This finding was hailed by the U.S. secretary of state, John Foster Dulles, who praised the Japanese fishermen for their restraint. American canners were also delighted, but they wanted to make sure that the Japanese continued their restraint in the future. The three big American canners—Chicken of the Sea, Bumble Bee, and StarKist—traveled to Japan and hammered out an agreement with the five big Japanese canners. All it needed was Dulles's approval. But what was good for the big tuna canners was bad for other American canners, and the latter launched a lobbying campaign against the agreement. Those advocating free trade jumped in and also argued against the agreement. Finally, Dulles sided with those who were against the agreement and opposed restricting Japanese imports.[22]

Then the Allied authorities in Japan went one step further. They lifted all restrictions on the movement of Japanese vessels. Their tuna harvesting operations generated a huge surge in exports. Frozen tuna imports into the United States soared, reaching 277 million pounds (46 percent of total consumption) in 1957. All West Coast canneries from Northern California to Washington depended mainly on imported frozen tuna. Likewise, imported canned tuna increased from 13 million pounds in 1951 to 44 million pounds in 1957.[23]

Japan was not the only country exporting tuna to the United States. The tuna industry in Latin America, which had been encouraged by the U.S. government during the war, also wanted to export its products to the United States, which was the only real market for Latin American canned tuna at the time. Canneries had been established in Chile, Peru, Ecuador, Venezuela, Costa Rica, and other countries. Some were offshoots of American canneries. Their exports to America expanded exponentially during the early 1950s.[24] Tuna industry leaders pointed out that while American canneries were paying fishing boats $300 to $400 per ton for tuna, foreign canneries were paying just $20 to $40 per ton. Fishermen in other countries were paid as little as 60 to 90 cents *per day*, compared with the $5,300 average annual wages of American fishermen at the time.[25] Foreign companies could pay all their costs, ship the canned tuna to the United States, pay a 24 percent tariff, undercut American retail prices, and still make a substantial profit.

OPERATING AT ABOUT 25 PERCENT OF CAPACITY

In June 1950, Mexico announced that it would discontinue the fisheries agreement made with the United States in 1943. This agreement had lowered tariffs on imported oil-packed tuna to 24½ percent. According to the agreement, at the end of six months, in January 1951, the tariff would revert to 45 percent. Again due to the most favored nation clause, other countries had been importing tuna into the United States at 24½ rate. Japan, Ecuador, and Peru rushed as much oil-packed tuna into the United States as possible in order to avoid the higher tariff. This rush of imported tuna created a massive glut of the fish in the United States. The American tuna industry—fishing boats as well as canneries—came to a standstill. Tuna boats idled in ports, and canning machinery fell silent.

The American Tunaboat Association (ATA), consisting of owners of many tuna boats in the United States, requested congressional hearings on the situation. The ATA specifically wanted to remove tuna from the trade agreement with Iceland, which would double the American tariff on tuna packed in brine. Others in the industry wanted a levy on frozen tuna. The U.S. House of Representatives considered several bills; the only one that passed, in October 1951, placed a temporary tariff on frozen tuna.[26]

When the Senate considered the House bill in 1952, the tuna industry made the same arguments in favor of the tariff, but by this time, strong opposition to the bill had emerged. Tuna canners on the East Coast and in the Pacific Northwest, as well as small canneries elsewhere, relied on imported frozen tuna, and they strongly opposed placing a tariff on it, which would increase the price of their products. Businesses that exported commodities and other products to those countries also strongly opposed the bill, for it was very likely that if the United States increased tariffs on tuna, other countries would reciprocate with increased tariffs on American imports. This would reduce U.S. exports and harm those companies that produced those goods in America. In addition, the tuna tariff would mean higher prices for tuna in the United States, and this might well have an inflationary effect—or so the U.S. secretary of commerce argued. Bankers said that the tariff might discourage American businesses from investing in other countries. The State Department was opposed to the tariff because it might alienate other nations. The State Department also believed that the Japanese could fund their own economic recovery if they were able to generate monies by exporting tuna. Still others argued that the bill was necessary only because of mismanagement of the tuna industry since the end of World War II. Japanese tuna exporters, of course, strongly opposed the tariff, as did government officials and businessmen from five other tuna-exporting nations, including Peru and Ecuador.[27]

The Senate did not pass the bill, but it did request an investigation. The result was the *Survey of the Domestic Tuna Industry*, completed by the U.S. Fish and Wildlife Services, Department of the Interior. It recommended, among other things, a comprehensive international agreement on tuna.[28] In 1954, the United States proposed a treaty with Japan that would cover fresh, frozen, and canned tuna. This proposed agreement would have *lowered* tariffs on imports from Japan. Hearings were held on the West Coast with representatives of various constituencies of the tuna industry. They were not united in their views. The ATA made a strong case for protecting American fishermen, while canners from the Pacific Northwest, and East Coast packers, opposed any tariff on frozen tuna. Some observers accused the tuna industry of trying to create a monopoly and pointed out that demands for high tariffs harmed American consumers because the price for tuna was kept artificially high. Still others blamed the tuna industry for straining relations with Japan, Ecuador, Peru, and other countries.[29]

During the six-year period from 1948 to 1954, imports of frozen tuna increased from 9 million pounds to 123 million pounds, and imports of canned tuna in oil increased from 8 million pounds to 31 million pounds, while employment on domestic tuna boats decreased by 20 percent, and the domestic share of American canners of the tuna market dropped from 91.4 percent to 65 percent. In the mid-1950s, as a result of the huge volume of imports, the American tuna fleet was operating at about 25 percent of capacity.[30]

William Knowland, California's senior senator and majority leader in the U.S. Senate, and Richard Nixon, U.S. vice president (and a former senator from California), supported the big California tuna canners and pestered President Eisenhower into creating a White House Tuna Task Force to study the matter. In 1955 the task force submitted its report. To the surprise of Nixon and Knowland, it supported the free trade position and opposed increasing tariffs on imported tuna. Eisenhower went along with the task force's recommendations and opposed increasing tariffs to protect California's tuna canners.[31]

FREE TRADE

On June 9, 1955, GATT made the question of tuna tariffs largely moot when the United States gave concessions to Japan and other nations that exported tuna to the United States. These concessions lowered the import tariff on oil-packed tuna from 45 percent to 35 percent. Tuna canned in brine retained its 12½ percent tariff, and no tariff was placed on frozen tuna. This upset many in the American tuna industry, but the tuna-exporting countries were pleased. With the tariff battle lost, many U.S. tuna companies tried to get the government to create or lower quotas on imported tuna, but this proved futile. Many observers believed that the tuna industry was doomed; some industry insiders requested that the federal government give financial assistance to the ailing industry. The Fisheries Act, passed in 1956, offered some financial relief in the form of low-interest (5-percent) loans. This was disappointing to American fishermen, who had hoped for direct assistance or protection via tariffs and import quotas.[32]

The ATA and many large canners lobbied repeatedly for higher tariffs on imported tuna during the succeeding decades. It was a losing battle.

In many cases the tariffs were lowered. The Andean Trade Preference Act was enacted in 1991 to assist four Andean countries (Bolivia, Colombia, Ecuador, and Peru) in their fight against drug production and trafficking by expanding economic alternatives for legitimate businesses. Under this act and its successor, the Andean Trade Promotion and Drug Eradication Act (ATPDEA), some types of tuna processed in these countries were allowed into the United States tariff-free. This resulted in a large increase in imported tuna from Colombia, Peru, and Ecuador. In addition, U.S. tuna companies invested in canneries and other related activities in these countries to take advantage of the low or nonexistent tariffs and the low wages for cannery workers and fishermen. Bumble Bee and StarKist, for instance, opened canneries in Ecuador. A similar agreement was reached in 2000 when the United States Caribbean Basin Initiative established similar relationships with other nations in the Caribbean and Central America.[33]

Yet another significant shift came in 1994 with the creation by the United States, Canada, and Mexico of the North American Free Trade Association (NAFTA). Under this agreement, tuna tariffs were scheduled to decrease so that by 2008 there would be no tariffs on tuna imported from Canada or Mexico. As a result of NAFTA, Mexico became a major supplier of tuna to the United States.

Asian countries, such as the Philippines, South Korea, Taiwan, Indonesia, and Thailand, complained bitterly, as tuna imported from their countries cost more than tuna from ATPDEA and NAFTA countries.[34] One potential solution was to create a free trade zone in the Pacific that would expand the volume of trade by lowering or eliminating tariffs. In December 2009, President Barack Obama proposed creating free trade agreements among Pacific nations. The proposed Trans-Pacific Partnership Trade Agreement is currently under discussion. If approved, the agreement would permit Pacific countries, such as Vietnam, to import tuna into the United States without a tariff. It is the hope of the Obama administration to expand the free trade area to other Pacific nations, such as Ecuador, to join a future date. The tuna companies with the few remaining canneries in the United States and its territories are strongly opposed, claiming that if Ecuador, Vietnam, and other countries can import tariff-free tuna, the few remaining American canneries will not be able to compete because of the low wages in these other countries.[35]

Increased imports from abroad have had a continuing depressing effect on tuna prices. When adjusted for inflation, canned tuna prices declined by about 30 percent from 1948 to 1957.[36] Tuna prices declined 60 percent when adjusted for inflation during the period 1980–2008. Lower prices encouraged American consumers to buy more canned tuna. Perhaps because of its low cost when canned, tuna has remained America's most commonly consumed fish for more than sixty years.[37]

POSTSCRIPT

Senator William Knowland was defeated when he ran for California governor in 1958. He died in 1974.

Richard Nixon was elected president of the United States in 1968 and resigned the presidency in 1975 due to the Watergate scandal. He died in 1994.

In 1993 the General Agreement on Tariff and Trade (GATT) was replaced by the World Trade Organization (WTO).

In 2008, a monument to the "Tuna Fleet Service during World War II" (also called the YP Monument) was dedicated in San Diego's port district, honoring the tuna boats and their crews.

Today, Thailand is the world's leading exporter of canned tuna. It is also a major exporter of tuna loins. Thai companies have developed markets in Japan, the United States, and Europe.[38]

The Andean Trade Promotion and Drug Eradication Act (ATPDEA) expired in February 2011 and has not been renewed.

SEVEN Tuna Wars

On the evening of March 26, 1955, fifteen American vessels were drifting 27 miles off the coast of Ecuador. Two of these, the *Santa Ana*, a small tuna clipper, and the *Arctic Maid*, a 980-ton freezer ship, were approached by an Ecuadorian patrol boat. The *Arctic Maid* was boarded by an Ecuadorian officer and crewman who inspected the ship and interviewed its captain, Homer Kyros. Kyros later complained that he did not understand Spanish, and the officer did not understand English. The Ecuadorian boarding party returned to its patrol boat with the *Arctic Maid's* log and charts. According to Kyros, the patrol boat disappeared into the night. Believing the incident over and wanting to avoid further difficulties, Kyros started the ship's engines and headed west, away from the patrol boat. But minutes later, the patrol boat reappeared, and, without warning, the crew fired machine guns at the *Arctic Maid.*[1]

Kyros turned on the ship's deck lights, but the firing continued. The chief engineer, William Peck, hearing the noise, ran up on deck, where he was shot in the hip and leg. When Kyros reversed the ship's engines, bringing it to a standstill, the patrol boat stopped firing. The Ecuadorian officer demanded that the *Arctic Maid* and the *Santa Ana* proceed to Guayaquil, Ecuador—a trip that would take fifteen hours. Knowing that he could not care for Peck's wounds on board the *Arctic Maid*, Kyros requested medical assistance, but the Ecuadorian officer refused, most likely because he had none to give. Kyros then asked the patrol boat, which was smaller and swifter than the *Arctic Maid*, to take Peck into port, and again the officer refused, presumably because he believed that the *Arctic Maid* would sail off into the sunrise once the patrol boat headed off.[2]

As the two American ships headed for Guayaquil, the patrol boat followed to make sure that both captains did as they had been told. When the *Arctic Maid* arrived in port, Peck was treated at a clinic, where part of a projectile was removed from his hip. Four days later, he was airlifted to the Panama Canal Zone, then a U.S. territory, where he underwent a second operation, and a few days later he was flown to Seattle, his home port. The *Arctic Maid* and the *Santa Ana* and the rest of their crews were placed under guard in Guayaquil. They were released on April 15, 1955, when the captains of the vessels paid $43,481 in fines. The boat owners lost an additional $50,000 in expenses and cargo. The estimated financial loss for Peck—hospital expenses and loss of work for life—was later estimated at $240,000.[3]

Thomas M. Pelly, congressman from Washington State, called for the United States to send naval vessels and airplanes to protect America's tuna fleet.[4] The United States Department of State called in the Ecuadorian ambassador for consultations; Rollin S. Atwood, director of the Office of South American Affairs, and Fred E. Taylor, a foreign affairs specialist, were dispatched to Ecuador to investigate the matter. The State Department described the actions of the Ecuadorians as "an indication of the gravity with which the Department of State views the incident." American tuna fishermen thought the State Department's response inadequate—a belief they would hold for the next three decades about official U.S. actions as numerous other battles took place.[5]

PRELUDE TO WAR

Historically, nations recognized a three-mile offshore limit to their sovereignty.[6] When American tuna boats began fishing off the coast of Mexico, the Mexican government established regulations for fishing in its territorial waters and charged a fee.[7] Mexican regulations changed regularly and required that 70 percent of the crew be Mexican nationals. Then the Mexican government required every boat to stop in Ensenada for inspection, which meant that fishermen would lose a full day on their return trip if they obeyed the law. What was worse, regulations were constantly changing, making it complicated and at times financially unrewarding to legally fish for albacore off the Mexican coast.[8]

By the 1920s, it was possible for large tuna boats to conduct most of their fishing beyond three miles of Mexico's legal territorial waters. The Mexican government felt that American boats were raiding Mexico's marine resources adjacent to its coastal waters. While tuna could be caught outside the three-mile limit, baitfish were more easily caught nearer shore, and American vessels frequently sailed within Mexican territorial waters to acquire them. Also, U.S. fishing boats needed supplies, and they occasionally called at Mexican ports to pick up fuel, water, and food. Mexico levied what American fishermen believed were exorbitant fees, up to $35 per ton, on fish caught in Mexican waters. As there were few Mexican patrol boats, though, the American fishermen often got away without paying the fees. Mexico suffered internal upheavals during the second decade of the twentieth century, enforcement was spotty, and inspectors were frequently bribed or more often just ignored. But other ships were hauled into port and fined. Mexican regulations were a constant irritant to American tuna boats throughout the pre–World War II period.

It was the United States government that first questioned the three-mile limit, for reasons completely unconnected with tuna fishing. Japanese fishermen had been catching salmon beyond the three-mile limit off the coast of the Pacific Northwest and Alaska. Salmon runs dropped off during the 1930s, and American fishermen blamed the Japanese for depletion of these stocks. Salmon were vulnerable when they came up from the continental shelf and headed into rivers to spawn, and catching the fish before they spawned meant fewer salmon in future years. The Japanese began experimenting with mother ships that made it possible to catch, freeze, and store large quantities of salmon. They began operating just beyond the three-mile territorial limit off Bristol Bay, Alaska.

Without U.S. control of the seas beyond the three-mile limit, conservation measures would not be effective. American salmon fishermen pressured Washington for help. A possible solution was for the United States to declare sovereignty over the ocean out to the continental limit. This would place most of the valuable fishing areas in Alaskan waters under American control. Bills were introduced in Congress to accomplish this, but none passed.[9]

The second matter that caused the United States to reconsider the three-mile limit was oil. Surveys proved that the Gulf of Mexico held great reserves of oil—and most was well beyond the three-mile limit. President Roosevelt felt that the United States and Mexico should divide up the Gulf and exploit this valuable resource. He believed that this plan "would be far more sensible than allowing some European nation, for example, to come in there and drill." Roosevelt sent a memorandum to the State Department in 1943 asking for its views.[10] But with American attention and resources focused on World War II, this issue was put on the back burner.

As the war was ending in 1945, Americans began to look toward the future. Recalling the problems with Japan over fishing rights in the Pacific Northwest before the war and Roosevelt's memo, State Department staff recommended that President Truman issue two proclamations, which he did three weeks after Japan formally surrendered in September 1945. The first was the Continental Shelf Proclamation, which declared "the natural resources of the seabed and subsoil of the continental shelf contiguous beyond the three mile limit" to be under U.S. jurisdiction. The second was the "Fisheries Proclamation," which sanctioned the establishment of "conservation zones in those areas of the high seas contiguous to the coasts of the United States wherein fishing activities have been or in the future may be developed and maintained on a substantial scale." This proclamation did not claim sole American jurisdiction regarding fisheries on the continental shelf but noted that the "legitimate" fishing rights of other nations would be regulated by mutual agreement. Any future Japanese fishing in that area would have to deal with new U.S. regulations and restrictions.[11]

Mexican leaders liked the American proclamations, so much so that on October 29, 1945, the president of Mexico signed a single proclamation claiming jurisdiction over Mexico's continental shelf and fisheries therein. The United States gave a qualified acceptance of Mexico's action, providing that Mexico gave "adequate recognition" to American "fishing interests in the area affected by the establishment of such zones." Argentina then followed suit with its own coastal sovereignty declaration.[12]

The Chilean government saw the principle behind these proclamations as a way to solve a problem it had with Russian whalers that were fishing and whaling just beyond Chile's three-mile limit. Issuing a proclamation to cover just the continental shelf, however, would not solve Chile's problem, because the continental shelf on the western coast of South America is very narrow—in some places only a few miles wide. In June 1947 Chile simply declared its control of resources out to 200 nautical miles, "placing within the control of the government especially all fisheries and whaling activities with the object of preventing . . . exploitation . . . to the detriment of the inhabitants of Chile."[13]

Two months later José Luis Bustamante y Rivero, the president of Peru, followed Chile's lead and declared that, for the protection, conservation, and exploitation of natural resources, Peru's boundaries extended 200 miles from its coast. Unlike Chile's coastal waters, where fishing resources were limited, the area off the Peruvian coast was loaded with fish. The Humboldt current emerges from great depths in the Pacific Ocean there, bringing plankton and other matter to the surface. Small fish, such as sardines and anchovies, feed on this, and tuna (and other predators) feed on the small fish. During World War II, the United States had encouraged Peru to develop its fisheries so that more fish could be shipped into the United States to make up for the tuna shortfall during the war. When the war was over, Peruvians wanted to protect their fledgling industry, and the 200-mile declaration seemed the best way to do that.[14]

The United States did not formally protest Chile's and Peru's declarations of 200-mile maritime zones until July 1948, when it claimed that these decisions "differ in large measure from those of the United States Proclamations and appear to be at variance with the generally accepted principles of international law." This response surprised many Latin Americans, who believed that Chile's and Peru's declarations were consistent with the principles proclaimed by President Truman three years before.[15]

U.S. opposition to this turn of events had little to do with American tuna fishing. While tuna clippers had fished off the coast of South America for more than a decade, their activity had been halted during World War II. The U.S. Navy, in an effort to protect the Panama Canal Zone, prohibited American fishing boats from traveling south of 10° north latitude. This put a complete stop to fishing in South American coastal waters and the Galápagos Islands during the war.[16] These restrictions were relaxed in 1944, but at the time, most large tuna clippers, which could easily have made the voyage to South America, had been requisitioned by the U.S. Navy. New boats were soon built, but when Chile and Peru issued their declarations, there were few American clippers fishing off the coast of South America.

The U.S. military's concern was that these declarations would set a precedent that other countries would follow. If all coastal countries extended their sovereignty 200 miles from shore, American naval vessels would be restricted from traveling to and from strategic areas. Likewise, countries that extended their sovereignty might restrict commercial ships from transiting those waters, and world trade could easily be disrupted. Such proclamations might challenge the principle of freedom of the seas and cause economic havoc throughout the world. Freedom of the seas had been a core principle in international law for hundreds of years, and it was crucial that the United States support it.

Rather than back down from their positions, Chile and Peru sought support from other Latin American countries. Costa Rica, El Salvador, and Honduras demonstrated their support by declaring 200-mile limits as well.[17] Ecuador proclaimed a 12-mile limit in 1950, but when the United States protested, Ecuador declared a 200-mile zone, as Peru and

Chile had already done. Representatives of Ecuador, Peru, and Chile met in 1952 in Santiago and declared their commitment to the 200-mile maritime zone around the three countries; they also encouraged other nations to declare their own 200-mile limits. President Eisenhower publicly stated the American position in October 1953: "It will continue to be the policy of the United States to assert the right of its nationals to engage in fishing on the high seas outside the three-mile limit for territorial waters." When the Organization of American States (OAS) met in Caracas in 1954, a resolution recognizing the 200-mile limit for all members was presented by representatives of those nations that already had claimed it. The resolution was opposed by the U.S. delegation, which was able to twist enough arms to defeat it, but it was clear that if it were raised at a future OAS meeting, the United States would likely lose. It was in the economic self-interest of most OAS members to declare a 200-mile limit.[18]

HOSTILITIES COMMENCE

After World War II, new long-range tuna clippers began to be constructed in the United States, and these vessels once again headed south. By the early 1950s, numerous American tuna boats were fishing off the South American coast, well within the 200-mile zone claimed by Peru, Ecuador, and Chile. The three countries warned American tuna-boat captains that they needed to buy licenses and pay fees. The Americans, at the recommendation of the U.S. State Department, refused to do so. In August 1952, Ecuador began seizing American tuna boats fishing off its coast beyond the traditional three-mile limit but within the 200-mile limit proclaimed by Ecuador. In October, it seized two more boats, requiring them to buy licenses and pay fines.[19] As the seizures escalated, the U.S. Congress passed the Fishermen's Protective Act, directing the federal government to pay any fine levied on an American vessel by any nation while fishing in international waters beyond the traditionally recognized three miles. An additional clause authorized the secretary of state "to make claims against the foreign countries for amounts expended under the

Act because of the seizure of a United States vessel."[20] Ecuador and Peru halted their seizure of American tuna boats.

But in early 1955, the Peruvian and Ecuadorian navies again began seizing American boats. After the incident involving the *Arctic Maid* and the wounding of William Peck, the United States requested a meeting in Santiago with representatives of the governments of Chile, Peru, and Ecuador. The United States offered these countries the right to the fish within 12 miles of their coasts, as well as shared fishing responsibility with the United States for the remaining 188 miles. The three South American countries refused, and the negotiations broke down. The American Tunaboat Association (ATA) met privately with Peruvian officials and paid the licensing fees for American tuna boats to fish within the 200-mile exclusion zone. When Chile began seizing U.S. tuna boats in 1957, the ATA once again reached an agreement with the Chilean government. These agreements created a truce that lasted until 1962.[21]

ROUND 2

The agreements between the ATA and the countries of Chile and Peru were based on the assumption that American tuna boats needed to come into port to pick up ice or to catch bait, which was more easily accomplished close to shore. Rather than carry full supplies of bait and ice from their home ports in the United States, it was more efficient to stock up in South American ports and pay for licenses and fees at that time. But two technological changes made it unnecessary for tuna clippers to acquire bait inshore: the invention of sturdy nylon purse seine nets and the power winch—a device that could easily pull in vast schools of yellowfin. In 1958, bait boats made up 80 percent of the tuna fleet, and the remaining 20 percent were purse seiners. As these new inventions began to generate vast profits, bait boats were quickly converted to purse seiners, and new purse seine vessels began to be constructed. By the early 1960s, 80 percent of the tuna boats were purse seiners with much bigger holds. These new vessels could catch yellowfin hundreds of miles off the coast, freeze their catch, and haul it back to the United States without ever entering a foreign port. The eastern tropical Pacific became the main fishing grounds of the new long-range American tuna boats.

The American expansion into the eastern Pacific came at the same time that Peru and Ecuador agreed to pool their resources to build their own tuna industries.[22] In 1962 the Ecuadorian government ordered its patrol boats to seize American fishing boats within Ecuador's 200-mile maritime zone. Twelve vessels were apprehended before May 1963. On May 25, 1963, Peru captured two boats whose captains claimed they had been fishing thirteen miles offshore. Peruvian authorities said that the boats had come within three miles of the coast. Other American tuna boats in the area surrounded the captured vessels to prevent them from being towed into port, and Ecuadorian naval ships fired across the bow of one of the American boats. The two captured boats were hauled into the port of Salinas, and the other tuna boats followed them in to protest the seizures. All boats were impounded. The U.S. State Department demanded that the ships be released. Ecuador rejected the demand but released the tuna boats after their owners paid $26,272 in fees and fines. During the following month two more tuna boats were seized and then released after a fine and fees were paid.[23]

Shortly after these incidents, an Ecuadorian vessel carrying perishable bananas arrived at a California port, where it was picketed by tuna fishermen. Longshoremen refused to cross the picket line, and the bananas rotted. Even with this very serious counterthreat—bananas accounted for 60 percent of Ecuador's export earnings—Ecuador continued to seize American tuna boats until July 11, 1963, when the Ecuadorian government was overthrown by a military coup.[24] The United States quickly recognized the new regime, and Ecuador stopped seizing American fishing boats. The military junta was more favorably disposed toward the United States than the previous government had been, and it engaged in public discussions with the United States regarding tuna fishing. Without making a public announcement, the United States agreed to recognize Ecuador's control up to 12 miles from its coast and to respect its control over specific fishing areas beyond this limit. Ecuador agreed not to seize American boats that were within 200 miles of the coast but outside these restricted areas, and for two years, no American fishing boats were seized by Ecuador.[25]

While this might have been a tactical victory for the United States, it was a strategic blunder. Many South Americans believed that the American Central Intelligence Agency had organized or at least encouraged the military coup in Ecuador. Peru used this belief to convince other South American countries to declare 200-mile limits, and Argentina, Brazil, Uruguay, Panama, and other Latin American countries did so. When the military stepped down in Ecuador, the incoming provisional government again declared that its sovereignty extended to 200 miles. Once again, Peru began seizing American tuna boats.

ROUND 3

The Fishermen's Protective Act of August 1954 proved inadequate for many reasons. American owners of seized boats were reimbursed only for fines levied by foreign governments. They were not compensated for damage done to their boats, lost wages, confiscated cargoes, or many other expenses. The State Department had to examine each case individually, and it often took up to a year for the owners to be reimbursed for fines. In addition, the State Department was unable to collect the monies paid out to boat owners from any of the foreign countries as required by the 1954 act. By 1967, 102 boats had been seized by governments recognizing the 200-mile jurisdiction, and boat seizures were escalating. Congress held hearings, and tuna-boat owners lobbied Congress for changes in the law. Boat owners wanted payment for their actual losses, including fees, fines, and other direct charges, and demanded that an insurance program be established that could compensate boat owners for other costs. They fought for a provision to be added to the legislation directing the secretary of state to withhold an amount equal to the monies paid to boat owners by the U.S. government from the government that seized the vessels.[26]

American views toward fishing off the United States' own coast were evolving. In 1964, the United States had declared control of "sedentary fish" within the continental shelf. (Sedentary fish are those that remain within a specific geographical area, or that return to spawn in specific rivers.) As the continental shelf was more than 200 miles off

Alaska and the coast of New England, this declaration appeared hypo-
critical to many Latin Americans. The United States responded that it
was trying to conserve sedentary fish stocks, and it did not include fish
that migrated from one place to another, such as tuna. At the behest of
America's fishing industry, in 1968 the United States claimed jurisdiction
over all fishing within 12 miles of the U.S. coast. It also recognized other
nations' right to declare similar jurisdiction over similar fishing zones.[27]

Congressman Pelly of Washington was upset by the seizures and
fines, and so proposed an amendment to the Foreign Military Sales Act
that required the United States to suspend sales and services to any
nation that "seizes or takes into custody or fines an American fishing
vessel engaged in fishing more than twelve miles from the coast of that
country." The president was given some discretion if continuation of
the aid was determined to be important to American security. The Pelly
Amendment passed Congress in October 1968.[28]

On February 14, 1969, a Peruvian naval patrol boat shadowed an
American tuna fleet 40 miles off the coast of Peru. When the crew of the
Peruvian boat tried to board the *Mariner*, a tuna seiner, the patrol boat
collided with it, damaging the *Mariner's* superstructure. The Peruvian
boat then headed for another tuna seiner, the *San Juan*, and fired its
machine guns at the ship, which was riddled with bullets. When five
other tuna ships closed in on the Peruvian boat, it ceased firing. When
the *San Juan* put into port in Ecuador, harbor officials asked for the ship's
logbook, which was given to them. The officials declared that the ship
had been fishing in Ecuadorian waters the previous November and
therefore had to pay fines. As the ship had been in port in the United
States at that time, the captain saw the Ecuadorian officials' demands
as an attempted shakedown. Rather than remain in port and pay fines
he claimed that he didn't owe, the captain left the logbook behind and
headed out of port at full speed.[29]

After the incidents with Peru, President Nixon invoked the Pelly
Amendment and halted military sales to Peru. The Peruvian government responded by expelling the American military assistance mission
to Peru. A few months later, however, Nixon concluded that an American
military presence in Peru was more important than Peruvian seizures of

American tuna boats. The United States resumed military aid, and Peru continued seizing tuna boats. By the end of 1970, it had captured thirty-nine vessels.[30] In the United States there were calls for marines to be placed on tuna boats, and for naval escorts to protect the fishing vessels off the coast of South America.

When José María Velasco Ibarra was elected president of Ecuador in 1968, he resumed the tuna war with the United States. In December 1968 U.S. military sales to Ecuador were suspended but were renewed in July 1969. Ecuador seized and fined forty-seven tuna boats in 1969. Talks were held in August and September 1970 but proved fruitless. When Ecuadorian patrol ships again went after U.S. fishing boats in January 1971, the United States suspended military aid and reported that American "economic assistance" to Ecuador was "under review."[31] Ecuador took fifty-three American boats during 1971, and the boat owners were fined $2.5 million, all of which was reimbursed by the United States government.[32] One boat was vandalized, and its crew beaten with rifle butts and then jailed. The tuna-boat owners requested naval escorts to protect their property and personnel.[33] To avoid future problems, the American Tunaboat Association quietly purchased fishing licenses from Ecuador for the tuna fleet. Velasco Ibarra was overthrown by a military junta in February 1972; the tuna war subsided, and American aid was renewed.[34] Again, many Latin Americans blamed the United States for the coup, which had overthrown a democratically elected government.

By the early 1970s, the 200-mile limit was accepted by many nations around the world, and there wasn't much the United States could do about it. The United States finally got on the bandwagon in 1976, when Congress passed the Fisheries Conservation and Management Act (also called the Magnuson Act), which created a 197-mile zone surrounding the United States beyond the existing three-mile international boundary. Only American boats (or those authorized by the United States) could fish within this zone. Control within this area extended only to sedentary fish; the act specifically excluded tuna and other highly migratory fish, which U.S. authorities believed should be managed internationally. (Other countries made no distinction between sedentary and migratory fish.) As a result of the lobbying efforts of the American Tunaboat

Association, the act specifically called for an automatic embargo on fishery products from any nation that seized American boats fishing for tuna more than 12 miles from its coast. This act was intended to revitalize the American fishing industry and still lend legitimacy to American tuna boats fishing within the 200-mile zones of other nations.[35]

The Magnuson Act provided for the recognition of other nations' 200-mile exclusion zones, provided that they did not include migratory fish in their jurisdiction. Few other nations accepted this principle, which would permit American purse seiners to continue fishing within other nations' 200-mile limits. Mexico and other Latin American nations believed otherwise and continued to enforce their sovereignty by seizing American tuna boats fishing within 200 miles of their coasts. When caught by foreign navies, the clippers continued to be hauled into port and charged hefty fines. Many boats also suffered damage, resulting in considerable downtime for the boats and their crews. The United States embargoed tuna imports from nations that seized American fishing boats, but this did not stop the seizures.

ROUND 4

When the United States extended its territorial limits to 200 miles, Canada followed suit, but unlike the United States, Canada claimed control of migratory fish. These declarations created problems for American and Canadian fishermen, who had traditionally fished beyond the three-mile limits of both nations. The two countries signed an interim agreement regarding fishing, which expired in June 1978. U.S. tuna boats continued to fish in waters more than 12 miles from the Canadian coast. In September 1979, Canada seized nineteen American tuna boats that the Canadians claimed were fishing illegally off the coast of British Columbia. They seized the catch and fined the captains $5,000 each. The United States retaliated with a ban on Canadian tuna boats in U.S. ports and also embargoed Canadian fish imports. This conflict was resolved in 1981 when Canada and the United States signed a tuna treaty permitting vessels from either country to fish in each other's waters and to sell their fish in either country.[36]

ROUND 5

The next theater of the tuna war was off the coast of Mexico. While both the United States and Mexico had claimed 200-mile economic zones, Mexico maintained that it had control over all fish—both sedentary and migratory—within the 200-mile limit. In July 1980, after the two countries had tried and failed to reach an agreement, Mexico seized six American tuna boats. In addition, Mexico refused to permit the ships' nets to be retrieved, which put those ships out of commission for quite a while.[37] The United States retaliated by banning Mexican yellowfin tuna imports. This ban lasted for six years. The embargo cost Mexico an estimated $20 million annually in tuna exports to the United States and an additional $15 million in tuna caught by boats of other nations that had previously passed through Mexico to the American market. Historically, the United States was the only buyer of canned and frozen tuna, but by the 1980s, many other countries also imported these products, so this embargo in fact caused little disruption to the Mexican tuna industry. The Mexican tuna industry increased its production from 39,000 metric tons of tuna in 1980 to 100,000 tons in 1985. By that time, Mexico owned the world's second-largest tuna fleet, with about eighty boats.[38]

The United States expanded its imports of frozen tuna, so the loss of fish from Mexico was insignificant. The embargo's burden fell mainly on American operators of small tuna boats, who were unable to fish outside the 200-mile limit. Many small boat owners reregistered their boats in Mexico and continued fishing; others gave up and sold their boats to buyers in other countries. The United States maintained the embargo on Mexico, mainly because of conditions within the California tuna industry. During the six years from 1980 to 1986, the American tuna fishing industry was devastated by cheap foreign imports. Labor costs were simply lower in the South Pacific and Asia; American canneries fled the mainland, first to American Samoa and Puerto Rico and later to Asia. American negotiators feared that if the embargo on Mexican tuna imports was lifted, the United States would be flooded with even more cheap tuna, which might well mean the end of the American tuna industry.[39]

The American embargo on Mexican tuna was finally lifted in 1986, and Mexican tuna exports to the United States tripled in three years from 32,000 tons to 96,000 tons, approximately 15 percent of Mexico's total tuna exports.[40] The embargo was reinstated in August 1990, when a U.S. federal judge again banned tuna imports from Mexico on the grounds that Mexican tuna purse seiners refused to require their tuna boats to follow dolphin-safe techniques as delineated by the U.S. Marine Mammal Protection Act of 1972. This embargo lasted for nine years. It had little effect on the Mexican tuna industry, which was on its way to becoming the largest in the world. Mexico simply shipped its tuna to Japan and Europe, where some of it was canned and then reexported to the United States. On April 20, 1991, the United States extended the embargo to European countries that reexported Mexican yellowfin to the United States. The United States also banned imported yellowfin from other countries, including Canada, Venezuela, and Colombia, because of dolphin safety issues. Mexico and European nations took the United States to a dispute-resolution panel of the General Agreement on Tariffs and Trade (GATT), which ruled against the United States.[41] The Mexican government chose not to have the decision enforced because it wanted the United States to agree to other important international agreements, such as the North American Free Trade Agreement (NAFTA), which was signed in 1994. The United States ended its embargo on Mexican tuna imports, and it phased out tuna tariffs among the three nations. Today, Mexico pays no tariff on tuna imports and is a major supplier of tuna consumed in the United States.

ROUND 6

As controversy raged in the eastern tropical Pacific in the 1980s, many large American purse seiners headed for the western Pacific, where tuna was plentiful, and there were fewer restrictions. There was one problem, however: to protect their marine resources and make a profit selling licenses, many Pacific island nations also declared 200-mile economic exclusion zones around their territories. As these island nations were spread out over vast distances, it was almost impossible for them to enforce their 200-mile zones. However, several acquired aircraft and patrol boats, and they made arrangements with other countries, such as Australia, to help them enforce their laws. When American purse seiners began to violate territorial waters, South Pacific island nations began to seize the American boats. Papua New Guinea seized an American purse seiner in 1982 and then released it after the owners paid a fine. The United States responded by embargoing tuna products from Papua New Guinea. The American Tunaboat Association quietly bought licenses for boats whose owners wanted to fish in those waters. Another seiner was found in waters surrounding the Republic of Kiribati (mainly the former Gilbert and Elice Islands), and Kiribati officials claimed that it was within 12 miles of the islands. Two other American purse seiners were caught off the Solomon Islands, and the island governments complained to the United States. In 1984 an American purse seiner was caught by Solomon Island patrol boats after a 12-mile chase. The owner was fined $72,000, and the boat was confiscated along with its gear and cargo. The United States placed a total ban on fish products from the Solomon Islands and reimbursed the boat owners for their losses. The Solomon Islands banned American fishing vessels from their coastal waters. This ban was lifted when the Solomon Islands sold the boat back to its owners.[42]

The ATA agreed to buy licenses, but the ATA and Kiribati authorities failed to agree on a price. In August 1985 Kiribati sold the annual rights to fish in its waters to the Soviet Union for $1.5 million. The U.S. government panicked at this incursion of Soviet power into what it considered "friendly" waters. In 1987 the United States and Kiribati signed an agreement for economic development, and when the United States gave Kiribati a large foreign aid package, American purse seiners were free to fish in Kiribati waters.[43]

WAR'S END

The United States lost the tuna wars. They caused serious embarrassment for the nation when small countries seized American boats in what the United States claimed were international waters. America could easily have won the wars by sending in naval ships to protect the fishing fleets, but the federal government concluded that other foreign policy objectives were more important than tuna fishing. The effect on the American tuna industry was devastating: the wars made it difficult for American tuna clippers to operate, while the industry was undercut at home by tuna imports from other countries.

When the tuna imports were deluging America, and the tuna wars were heating up, a solution appeared on the horizon. Fishermen had developed a new method of fishing for yellowfin in the eastern tropical Pacific beyond the 200-mile maritime limits claimed by South and Central American nations. This method gave American tuna clippers a competitive advantage so that they could compete with frozen Japanese and other imports. This new method was called porpoise fishing.

POSTSCRIPT

Thomas M. Pelly, congressman from Illinois and author of the Pelly Amendment, retired from Congress in 1972. He died the following year.

William Peck, the injured engineer, was in and out of hospitals and was crippled for life. Washington senator Warren Magnuson, supported by Congressman Pelly, submitted bills in Congress to pay Peck's hospital expenses in 1958.

EIGHT Porpoise Fishing

In the spring of 1966 William F. Perrin, a biology student who was graduating from San Diego State University, was looking for a summer job before he went on to study for an advanced degree at UCLA. One of the places he visited was the U.S. Bureau of Commercial Fisheries at La Jolla, California. He was told that they had no jobs, but he left his name and phone number anyway. A few weeks later he received a call from the bureau's scientist responsible for research on fishing technology. The bureau needed someone to collect data on the performance of purse seines—the large nets used to surround and catch schools of tuna. It was hoped that the study would improve net design so that it could more efficiently catch tuna. Perrin was offered the job of collecting the data on a tuna boat. Although he had never been on a tuna boat, it sounded like an interesting experience, so he readily accepted.[1]

While on the trip, Perrin learned about a surprising phenomenon: schools of dolphins and medium and large yellowfin tuna associate with each other in the eastern tropical Pacific, and tuna fishermen used this relationship as a means of finding tuna. Dolphins are air-breathing mammals, so they remain near the surface of the ocean, where they are clearly visible. Using high-powered binoculars, fishermen scanned the horizon for certain types of birds that are associated with dolphins. Once the birds were spotted, the tuna boats set on the surface-swimming dolphins, and then the fishermen looked for signs of yellowfin in the waters below. They deployed speedboats to herd the dolphins into a small area. Schools of yellowfin below the surface usually remained under the corralled dolphins. Then the fishermen surrounded the dolphins with a large net or seine. The net was then brought on board with a bountiful catch of yellowfin. Along with the yellowfin, however, were often hundreds of dolphins, many of which were caught in the net and had suffocated. For the fishermen, the dolphins simply provided a means of finding yellowfin. As dolphins had no commercial value, the fishermen just discarded the dead bodies. For the fishermen, this was an extremely efficient way of catching yellowfin. For Perrin, the dolphin mortality was shocking.

When his summer job was over, Perrin wrote an article about the tuna/dolphin connection that was accepted for publication in the magazine *Sea Frontiers*. He began working at the Bureau of Commercial Fisheries and in April 1968 again traveled to the eastern tropical Pacific. He collected dolphin specimens and counted the dolphins killed on this voyage. He also took a camera and filmed the operation. When he returned from the trip, he examined logbooks of other purse seine vessels operating in the eastern tropical Pacific and calculated a rough estimate of how many dolphins were killed by tuna boats annually; the number was a staggering 244,000. Perrin worried that the number of dolphins killed might exceed their reproductive capacity, and that dolphin populations might collapse if this mortality rate continued, so he wrote a second article that was accepted for publication in *World Fishing*.[2]

As a result of these articles, Perrin gained visibility among academics and was asked to present a paper at the Conference on Biological

Sonar and Diving Mammals held at the Stanford Research Institute in 1969. His paper, titled "The Problem of Porpoise Mortality in the U.S. Tropical Tuna Fishery," generated attention, but the film that he showed that had been taken onboard a tuna boat caused a sensation. The conference attendees were small in number, but Perrin's paper was circulated to environmental groups who were horrified at the dolphin mortality.[3] Environmentalists jumped on the save-the-dolphin bandwagon. Letters began arriving in the offices of congressmen and senators, who in turn began to ask questions.

GENTLE, AFFECTIONATE CREATURES

Locating large schools of tuna in the open sea presents quite a challenge. Traditionally, fishermen had only their eyes to rely on, so fishing was limited to daylight hours, when tuna could be spotted breaching the water's surface. After World War I, seaplanes were employed for a while to spot schools of tuna. This worked well when the boats stayed close to shore, but as tuna boats began traveling thousands of miles from the U.S. coast, it was less effective. After World War II, both sonar and helicopters were used to locate schools of tuna.

In the tropical waters of the eastern Pacific fishermen noticed that schools of yellowfin congregated under schools of spotted dolphins (*Stenella attenuata*), spinner dolphins (*S. longirostris*), and to a lesser extent, common dolphins (*Delphinus delphis*). The reason for this remains unknown, but this discovery in the 1920s made catching yellowfin much easier. All fishermen had to do was find dolphins and then cast their hooks into the water in hopes that yellowfin tuna were below. This method resulted in few dolphin deaths.

In the 1950s, purse seine operators came up with an even more efficient way of catching yellowfin. Once the dolphins were located, speedboats were launched to herd them into large, bottomless nets sometimes a mile long and 400 feet deep; these nets were buoyed up by a line of cork floats. Yellowfin underneath followed the dolphins into the nets. The nets were then closed by powerful winches. This practice was so successful in catching yellowfin that many bait boats were converted to purse seiners at great expense to their owners. The advent of powerful hydraulic blocks in 1955 and rot-resistant nylon nets the following year made it possible to use even larger nets that could easily capture whole schools of fish. Porpoise fishing was a very efficient way to locate yellowfin. By 1962 it was estimated that 62 percent of the tuna caught in the eastern tropical Pacific were caught by setting on dolphins.[4]

Tuna boats in the eastern Pacific shifted dramatically toward the use of purse seines. By the mid-1970s 75 percent of the 132 tuna boats operating in the eastern Pacific were using purse seines. Added to the fleet were big new "super purse seiners" costing millions of dollars; these vessels could carry as much as 2,000 tons of frozen yellowfin.[5] The tuna fleet as a whole became much more efficient, and the yellowfin catch shot up.

When the nets were pulled close to the boat to haul the yellowfin on board, the dolphins tried to swim through the nets, became entangled, and suffocated. The dolphins wouldn't jump over the cork line, and mothers would not leave their young, so even when part of the net was dropped to permit the dolphins to escape, many remained inside the nets. As the nets were pulled tighter, more dolphins, in a frantic attempt to escape, became entangled in the net and suffocated. There was no market for dolphins in the United States, so the injured, dying, or dead creatures were simply tossed back into the sea, usually ending up as shark food. Sometimes just a few dolphins died, but on other occasions— due to darkness, human error, bad weather, equipment failure, or the panic that set in among the dolphins as the nets closed—the number killed could approach a thousand or more.[6]

Observers pointed out that it was in the fishermen's long-term self-interest to release dolphins alive and uninjured from their nets. It was time-consuming to remove the dead animals from the nets, and dolphins released alive might lead the fishermen to other schools of tuna at some future time. As true as this was, most fishermen just wanted to bring home a good paycheck at the end of their voyage, and their pay was based on the amount of tuna that was caught, not on the number of dolphin that they rescued. Time spent saving dolphins often meant time away from catching yellowfin.

Well before this dolphin mortality was brought to the attention of the public, fishermen developed techniques, such as "backing down," that permitted many dolphins to get away while keeping most tuna in the net. Such techniques were time-consuming, however, and compromised efficiency: even a few escaping dolphins could entice the yellowfin underneath to escape from the closing net. In 1971, just as criticism of the tuna fishing industry began to surface, a purse seiner captain, Harold Medina, developed the Medina panel, consisting of a finer mesh that made it harder for dolphins to become entangled in the net and easier for them to escape when the net was lowered.[7] This technique saved dolphins, but many still died.

Several articles were published about purse seines, yellowfin, and dolphins in the 1960s, but they did not discuss dolphin mortality.[8] The dolphin toll was largely unseen and unknown to anyone other than tuna fishermen until Perrin stepped aboard a tuna boat and began writing articles about his observations and filming the process. Estimates of how many dolphins died annually in the nets ranged from 100,000 in 1959 to 500,000 in the 1960s as more tuna boats were converted to purse seiners.[9]

At the time that reports of dolphin mortality surfaced, Congress was contemplating a ban on the capture of all species of whales. Dolphins were not a congressional concern until letters poured in from environmental groups and political leaders. Dolphin mortality became a topic of a congressional hearing, and William Perrin was one of the speakers. The tuna industry lobbied Congress to include a provision in the legislation exempting fishermen for killing dolphins in procedures incidental to catching tuna. In July 1971 congressional hearings were held on the "International Moratorium of Ten Years on the Killing of All Species of Whales." Dolphins are in the whale family, so when Congress began to consider the proposed Marine Mammal Protection Act (MMPA) restricting fishing for whales, it included dolphins and other sea mammals under the act's protection.

The congressional hearings gave most Americans their first inkling about the connection between tuna and dolphins. Many had seen the 1963 movie "Flipper," about a beloved pet dolphin, and watched the television series based on it. Many Americans had anthropomorphized the dolphins and viewed them as human-like. When they heard about the numbers of dolphins killed by tuna fishing, they were shocked and angry.[10]

Newspapers jumped on the save-the-dolphin issue. The *Los Angeles Times* alerted the general public to the plight of the dolphins in an editorial published on January 30, 1972. The editorial urged that new techniques be developed to diminish the mortality rates of these "gentle, affectionate creatures with so many characteristics of human beings that they are often described as man's first cousin in the animal kingdom."[11] Scott McVay, the chairman of the Environmental Defense Fund's effort to conserve whales, penned an op-ed piece for the *New York Times* titled "The Great Porpoise Massacre." McVay was concerned about the MMPA's exemption for tuna fishermen. Although tuna fishermen had developed methods to limit the number of dolphins they killed, it was unclear how widely used these procedures were, or how effective. Tuna fishermen often refused to allow observers on their boats to determine precisely how many dolphins were killed in this manner, and urged the tuna industry to cooperate with scientists to resolve the matter in "months, not years."[12]

Congress passed the MMPA in October 1972. It prohibited "taking" marine mammals in U.S. waters and by American citizens on the high seas. Courts later defined "taking" as both killing and harassing dolphins. The MMPA required American tuna fishermen to adjust their fishing practices to avoid such deaths. The National Marine Fisheries Service (NMFS), a branch of the Commerce Department, was selected to partially administer the MMPA. It was specifically responsible for establishing dolphin kill quotas, but as the NMFS had little information about the size of existing dolphin stocks, it gave tuna fishermen a two-year waiver from this regulation. This period would allow fishermen time to develop techniques and equipment for avoiding the peril to dolphins while catching yellowfin. During this waiver period, an estimated 440,000 dolphins were killed by tuna boats seining for yellowfin.[13]

The NMFS placed observers aboard U.S. tuna boats to record the number of dolphins killed. In the fall of 1974, it issued a report stating that some dolphin species were endangered due to purse seine tuna fishing. Despite this finding, the agency then gave tuna fishermen another two-year waiver with no limitation on dolphin kills. This decision was challenged in court by the Committee for Humane Legislation and the Environmental Defense Fund. The district court ruled that nets could no longer be used to catch tuna if dolphins were killed in the process. The decision was appealed to the District of Columbia Court of Appeals, which affirmed the lower court's decision. Under court order, the NMFS established a quota of 78,000 dolphins for 1976 and 59,050 for 1977. The tuna industry alleged that both the quota and the MMPA were unconstitutional because they took private property without compensation.[14]

Stanley M. Minasian, a film producer, organized the Marine Mammal Fund in 1973. He had heard that the NMFS had chartered a purse seiner in 1971 to increase the agency's understanding of what happened when purse seines captured dolphins in the process of catching yellowfin. The NMFS's goal was to create a system by which dolphins could escape from the nets. The scientists filmed the procedures. The 800-foot film included sequences of dolphins dying in tuna-boat nets. Minasian asked the NMFS for the film, but he was refused. The NMFS claimed that the film had been shot aboard a tuna purse seiner with permission of the seiner's captain, Joseph Medina, with the understanding that the footage would be used by scientists for research purposes. The agency also claimed that the film showed proprietary technology and procedures that could help foreign vessels learn American techniques. Minasian took the NMFS to court, and when he won, in 1974, the court ordered the NMFS to release the film with the disclaimer that the film was "obtained during government controlled situations in which experiments were conducted and do not necessarily reflect commercial fishing operations."[15] This footage was edited to remove proprietary techniques and served as the basis for a twenty-six-minute television documentary, *Last Day of the Dolphins?* released in 1975. The program, narrated by Dick Cavett, showed dozens of squealing dolphins trying to escape from tuna nets, and dead dolphins left in the nets. These images catalyzed efforts to save dolphins. Minasian continued to produce films on dolphins and tuna, including *Where Have All the Dolphins Gone?* narrated by George C. Scott, and *Dolphins in Danger,* hosted by Bridget Fonda, daughter of Peter

Fonda. These films had a huge impact on other environmental groups and on the general public.

The tuna industry was sluggish in its reaction to the dolphin controversy. Tuna canners, boat owners, and labor groups created the Porpoise Rescue Foundation in 1975 to promote and fund development of porpoise-saving techniques and to train fishermen to reduce dolphin fatalities and injuries. Two years later the tuna industry established the United States Tuna Foundation, which worked on many issues, including the porpoise controversy. The American Tunaboat Association attempted to counter the bad publicity by issuing a film of its own: *Tuna and Porpoise: A Scientific Approach*. Released in 1977, the film had little effect on the continuing controversy. In the same year, a San Diego television station released its own documentary, *The Tragic Tangle: Porpoise and the Fishermen*, illustrating the negative effects of the controversy on the men who manned the boats. It received little national coverage, but around San Diego cars soon sported bumper stickers that read "Tuna fishermen, the latest Endangered Species."[16]

More common were statements supporting dolphins. "In the name of humanity and all that is decent in human nature," proclaimed the Audubon Society, "the time is long overdue when this brutal slaughter must be stopped completely."[17] The Earth Island Institute created the "Save the Dolphins" project, which collected information about dolphin mortality and published it in a newsletter beginning in 1976; the organization Friends of Animals launched a campaign with the slogan "Would You Kill Flipper for a Tuna Sandwich?" The tuna industry's apparent insensitivity to the dolphin kills contributed to public indignation. Members of Friends of Animals picketed the piers used by tuna boats. More bumper stickers were printed and letter-writing campaigns were launched, all opposing the taking of dolphins by tuna fishermen.[18]

The NMFS identified the spinner dolphin as "numerically depleted," which meant that fishermen who caught even one were subject to a substantial fine and a term in jail. The American Tunaboat Association opposed virtually all regulations regarding dolphin kills; August Felando, the organization's manager, believed it impossible for yellowfin to be caught without also taking spinner dolphins. Purse seine owners began to register their boats in other countries to avoid the new regulations. By January 1977, 30 of the 130 purse seine boats in California had registered or applied for registration in other countries, and several were sold abroad. Other boats just stayed in San Diego harbor, their crews refusing to fish.[19] They hoped that economic pressure, especially the loss of jobs for thousands of people in the San Diego area, would convince the NMFS to change the regulation.

Purse seiners finally went back out to sea a few months later, when the NMFS relaxed its rulings on spinner dolphins. Tuna fishermen had some new technology, and they established procedures to safeguard dolphins. Floodlights helped at night, and rubber rafts were also used to help dolphins escape the nets. These techniques helped reduce dolphin mortality but did not end it.

The newly amended MMPA called for observers to be placed on U.S.-registered tuna boats. Their job was to tally the number of dolphins killed on each voyage. The Reagan administration, which took office in January 1981, was not a strong supporter of the legislation. NMFS observers were cut by half, and NMFS funds for research on dolphin-saving gear were slashed. Regulations were also relaxed. The American Tunaboat Association sued to have observers removed from member boats and won an injunction ordering just that. In the end, the injunction was overturned, but for three years federal observers were not permitted on tuna boats. When the courts ruled against the ATA, the few observers who ended up on the boats faced harassment from the crews. Observers claimed that if they underreported their dolphin figures they would be treated better by captain and crew.[20]

Estimated dolphin mortality on American tuna boats decreased during the following years, averaging 16,072 per year for the next decade.[21] However, these official statistics included only those dolphins killed in the nets, and not those that died after being removed from the nets and thrown back into the sea. Many such animals were exhausted and disoriented, with injuries such as broken beaks or broken flippers. Many more died shortly after release, either from their injuries or due to their inability to defend themselves from shark attacks, which were quite common. In addition, these figures were only for American tuna boats.

As the American fleet declined in the eastern tropical Pacific, vessels from other nations began operating without similar restrictions of dolphins. Overall, dolphin kills increased to an estimated 100,000 in 1986.[22]

This loss was too high for many environmental organizations. The Friends of Animals launched a campaign to boycott tuna.[23] The boycott picked up steam in January 1988, when a coalition of environmental groups launched a campaign to boycott tuna that was not "dolphin-safe," which meant that tuna boats could not use purse seines in the presence of dolphins. The Earth Island Institute's International Marine Mammal Project paid for magazine ads announcing "The Dolphin Massacre off Our Coasts and What You Can Do to Stop It." The Earth Island Institute urged a boycott not just of tuna canned by major American companies, but also of nontuna products of the H. J. Heinz Company, the canner of StarKist tuna. Ecology-minded children and Hollywood movie stars joined the boycott.[24] A "Just Say No to Tuna" comic book was published by Jason Salisbury, and magazines published articles similarly titled.[25] Kenneth Brower's article "The Destruction of Dolphins," which appeared in the July 1989 issue of the *Atlantic Monthly*, presented the issue to an even wider audience.[26]

Brower's piece told the story of Sam LaBudde, a biologist and fisherman who hid his environmentalist affiliations for five months while working on a Panamanian-registered tuna boat out of Ensenada, Mexico. He took a camera on board and filmed the operations of the purse seine. Once dolphins were spotted, speedboats were launched, and explosive charges called "seal bombs" were used to keep the dolphins in the net until it could be closed and pursed. At the time it was illegal in the United States to set on some types of dolphins, but the captain ignored the regulations. LaBudde then filmed the dolphins trying to escape. In one instance, the captain did not use the "backing down" method, and all the dolphins died except one newborn, which was released by a crew member. Unable to nurse or fend for itself, the baby dolphin likely died shortly thereafter. After the incident, the boat's captain filleted a dead dolphin and served it to the crew. Sam LaBudde's films were shown on news programs on the CBS and ABC networks, and he later testified in a congressional hearing at which his film was shown.[27] The footage of squealing dolphins dying in nets increased visibility and generated greater public support for the tuna boycott.

DOLPHIN-SAFE?

Despite the boycott, between 1988 and 1990, sales of StarKist tuna increased from $115 million to $145 million.[28] Nevertheless, the controversy had generated a great deal of bad publicity for Heinz, which owned the brand, although its tuna business was a relatively small and nonessential part of the multinational's operation. Heinz's president believed that the company could seize "the environmental high ground by offering the only tuna guaranteed not caught off dolphins."[29] On April 12, 1990, Heinz voluntarily agreed to use only tuna that was not caught on dolphins. The canners of Chicken of the Sea tuna followed Heinz's lead. When Bumble Bee brand tuna did not immediately follow suit, environmental groups waged a campaign against them. Advertisements in magazines advised consumers: "To save Dolphins from being caught in tuna nets, you can buy StarKist or Chicken of the Sea Tuna."[30] Bumble Bee management finally caved in. Staff at the Earth Island Institute, however, discovered that Bumble Bee was still using tuna that was not dolphin-safe, and the institute paid for ads attacking the company for breaking its pledge. Meetings were held with environmental groups to "resolve the confusion."[31] As a result of the intense public and political pressure, the U.S. tuna fleet stopped using the "setting on dolphins" method of catching tuna.[32]

Companies that canned tuna using these methods could display a "dolphin-safe" symbol on their tuna labels. These voluntary agreements to pack only dolphin-safe tuna were enshrined in the Dolphin Consumer Protection Information Act passed by Congress in 1990. It established a label that indicated that the tuna was dolphin-safe. Its intent was to discourage Americans from consuming tuna caught with purse seiners in the eastern tropical Pacific as well as tuna harvested with drift nets in the northern Pacific, which also had serious bycatch problems. Loopholes in the law led to passage of the International Dolphin Conservation Act in 1992.

While these laws reduced the number of dolphin deaths caused by tuna fishing, dolphin fatalities continued, and the tuna industry continued to be blamed for them. When the National Research Council looked into this matter in 1992, it concluded that "promising new techniques for finding and catching yellowfin tuna without killing porpoises" in the eastern tropical Pacific "are elusive, may be costly to develop, and may require considerable investment in new vessels and equipment."[33]

The MMPA also banned imported tuna from countries in which dolphin deaths from tuna fishing exceeded deaths from U.S. tuna fishing by more than 25 percent. While the NMFS, the governmental entity responsible for carrying out this provision, believed that its job was to maintain optimal sustainable populations of dolphins, environmental groups believed that dolphin kills should be reduced to "insignificant levels approaching zero." The NMFS failed to adopt rules to enforce this provision, so Congress amended the MMPA in 1988 to require foreign fleets wishing to export to the United States to comply with American regulations regarding the catching of yellowfin.

When the federal government failed to comply with this amendment promptly, the Earth Island Institute took the United States government to court, demanding that the import provisions of the MMPA be enforced. The district court found for the plaintiffs and prohibited importation of yellowfin until the provisions of the 1988 amendment were carried out. When the government appealed the decision, the appellate court upheld the ruling, and yellowfin imports from Mexico, Venezuela, Panama, Ecuador, and the South Pacific island nation of Vanuatu were banned.

Mexican government leaders believed that this was an attempt by the United States to protect its tuna industry at the expense of Mexican tuna fishing. They tried to end the boycott quietly behind the scenes, but when the United States refused to budge, Mexico challenged the ban as a violation of the free trade provisions in GATT, the predecessor to the World Trade Organization. The GATT dispute resolution panel charged with investigating the matter found that American restrictions on importing Mexican tuna indeed violated agreements. The broader implication of this provision was that no nation could impose its views of environmental protection on other nations. Environmentalists took great exception to this and called for a revision of GATT agreements. Before the ruling took effect, the United States negotiated agreements with the affected nations. The Panama Declaration was signed by several Central and South American countries, France, and the United States in 1995. In it, the United States agreed to end the boycotts of tuna from those countries, and it accepted purse seining of yellowfin tuna, provided that no more than 5,000 dolphins were killed annually. In addition, the United States agreed to provide Mexican fishermen with the technology to reduce the number of dolphin fatalities, and Mexico, not wanting to provoke environmental groups to oppose other international agreements, accepted the restrictions.[34] The best estimate of total dolphin mortality in 1996 in the eastern Pacific was about 2,600, which, according to Martin A. Hall, head of the Tuna-Dolphin Program, Inter-American Tropical Tuna Commission, was "not significant from the population point of view."[35]

After agreements were made with other nations that supplied tuna to the United States, the Dolphin Protection Consumer Act was amended in 1997 to give the secretary of commerce the ability to consider whether a modified encirclement method could qualify for a dolphin-safe label. On December 31, 2002, Donald L. Evans, secretary of commerce, concluded that this fishing method created "no significant adverse effect" on dolphin populations. He relaxed the prohibition on the encirclement method, allowing fishermen to use the technique and still qualify for the dolphin-safe label on their cans.[36]

By this time, few American purse seiners fished in the eastern tropical Pacific, so this ruling meant that the dolphin-safe symbol could be placed on yellowfin caught by Mexican and other Latin American countries even though dolphins were killed in the process of catching it. According to an account published in the New York Times in 2003, two scientists claimed that scientific reports were ignored by the secretary of commerce and that political pressure had been brought to bear on the NMFS to discontinue funding of data collection on dolphins killed by tuna fishermen. The best scientific data indicated that dolphin populations had not regenerated even after a decade of reduction of dolphin kills.[37]

Led by the Earth Island Institute, nine environmental groups took the matter to court. The Southwest Fisheries Science Center (SWFSC) in La Jolla issued a report warning that dolphin populations were not recovering despite all the efforts to avoid killing them. Environmental groups asserted that the secretary of commerce had ignored science, while Secretary Evans claimed that the report was not "conclusive."[38] In August 2004, the court ruled that the administration had "failed to do the scientific research required to relax tuna-labeling laws" and had engaged in "a pattern of delay and inattention" to build support for the secretary's position.[39] The Department of Commerce appealed the decision, but in April 2007 the attempt to weaken the dolphin-safe symbol was rejected.

The Mexican tuna fleet invested heavily in the technology to minimize dolphin losses, claiming that it met international standards, but it did not meet the U.S. requirements for a voluntary label saying that the tuna was caught in a dolphin-safe manner. Mexico complained to the World Trade Organization (WTO) in 2008 that the American law discriminated against Mexican tuna imports, and therefore was a violation of WTO regulations. A three-member dispute settlement panel considered the matter, and in September 2011, two panelists (with one panelist dissenting) gave a weak victory for the Mexican position, finding that the U.S. law did not discriminate against Mexican producers, but that the voluntary dolphin-safe label was more restrictive than necessary. The decision was appealed and remains unresolved.[40] Forty years after the tuna/dolphin controversy erupted, the issues have not been resolved. Although shifts since the early 1990s in methods used by purse seiners in the eastern tropical Pacific to catch yellowfin have greatly reduced dolphin mortality, the spotted dolphin population has not recovered, and other dolphin populations remained stressed. Some groups, such as the Humane Society, report that purse seining continues to kill 4,000 to 5,000 dolphins annually, and they want strict criteria for the "dolphin-safe" label. Others favor a less "strict dolphin-safe standard." They believe that purse seining is not harming dolphin populations as a whole and that progress has been made in reducing dolphin fatalities. Strict guidelines, argue some, damage U.S. trade relations with Mexico and other countries. As long as purse seiners continue to fish for dolphins, the controversy will continue.[41]

POSTSCRIPT

William F. Perrin completed his doctorate at the University of California, Los Angeles, and received his Ph.D. in 1972. His dissertation was on the spotted and spinner dolphins of the eastern tropical Pacific and Hawaii, a subject about which he knew little before he made his fateful trip aboard a purse seine boat in 1966. He continues to work for the Southwest Fisheries Science Center (SWFSC) in La Jolla, California. He has completed a book on dolphins and tuna.

In 1997 the SWFSC in consultation with the U.S. Marine Mammal Commission and the Inter-American Tropical Tuna Commission conducted a survey of dolphin mortality in the eastern tropical Pacific. The report concluded that spotted dolphins are at 20 percent and eastern spinner dolphins at 35 percent of their previous levels. Neither population is recovering at a rate consistent with the levels of depletion and the reported kills.[42]

August Felando, the manager of the American Tunaboat Association from 1960 to 1991, lives in San Diego. In 2011 he coauthored *The Tuna/Porpoise Controversy* with Harold Medina, the creator of the panel to help dolphins escape from nets.

NINE Parts Per Million

Dr. Bruce McDuffie, an analytical chemistry professor at the State University of New York at Binghamton, had been examining a variety of freshwater fish, hoping to learn something about the amount of mercury in them when a graduate student remarked: "The only fish I eat is tuna. Why don't you analyze some?" McDuffie thought it unlikely that tuna would have much mercury. Seawater does contain naturally occurring mercury, but only at a level of about 0.5 parts per billion (ppb), and the oceans are so vast that any mercury entering the water from pollution or industrial waste would soon be dissipated. But McDuffie's wife also wanted to know about mercury in tuna, and the test was simple enough, so he went to the Grand Union supermarket and came back with several cans of the fish, which he began testing in December 1970. Tests revealed that tuna had mercury at levels exceeding the standards of the U.S. Food and Drug Administration (FDA). McDuffie's findings came as a complete surprise to scientists, the tuna canning industry, and American consumers and would spark a controversy that has continued for more than forty years.

TOXICITY

Mercury is an element found naturally in the environment. It is a heavy metal, but unlike most other metals, it is liquid at room temperature. Inorganic mercury is not easily absorbed by the human body, and small amounts can be ingested without known adverse effects.

Mercury is also released into the environment as a result of human activity—from industrial waste and power plants that burn fossil fuels, especially coal. When coal is burned, the mercury in it is released into the air as a gas. The airborne mercury is redeposited on the earth through precipitation and drains into rivers and lakes, where it becomes a component in mud. Bacteria methylate (or convert) the mercury, creating methylmercury, an organic compound, which is easily absorbed by aquatic plants. Fish that feed on these plants ingest the methylmercury. Unlike inorganic mercury, which tends not to accumulate in fish, methylmercury is absorbed, and bioaccumulation or bioconcentration occurs. Predator fish, such as tuna, that consume other fish with methylmercury, have much higher levels of mercury in their bodies than does the water in which they swim. When humans eat contaminated fish, methylmercury is easily absorbed into the body, where it accumulates.

Methylmercury had been identified as a serious health hazard throughout the world. In 1953, in the area around Minamata Bay, in Japan, cats began to develop neurological problems and exhibit strange behavior—including jumping into the bay and drowning. Then people living near the bay became ill, and many died. It took years to determine that the main cause of illness and death in the area was mercury in the waste discharged from industrial plants sited near the bay. Eventually, 2,265 people were certified as having contracted illnesses, of whom 1,784 died from ingesting methylmercury.[1] Following this disaster in Japan, methylmercury poisonings were uncovered in such diverse locations as the Faeroe Islands, the Amazon River basin, and Sweden.

Studies have demonstrated that if organic methylmercury is ingested in large enough quantities, it can damage the nervous and renal systems and cause brain damage. Investigations demonstrated that methylmercury is easily absorbed and accumulated by the human body. Methylmercury's half-life in the human body (the time it takes to decrease by 50 percent) is in excess of fifty days. Mild methylmercury poisoning in adults can cause profuse sweating, elevated heart rate, blurred vision, and impaired hearing and speech. Higher levels of exposure may result in serious neurological damage, blindness, deafness, kidney damage, brain damage, heart attack, anorexia, and, ultimately, coma and death. In utero exposure to high doses of methylmercury is known to cause damage to the fetus's central nervous system (brain and spinal cord) and may result in delayed physical development, impaired cognitive development, autism, and physical coordination problems.[2] Severe damage caused by methylmercury is irreversible.

In the late 1960s, Canadian researchers wondered if there might be problems with mercury contamination in freshwater rivers and other bodies of water in which industries had discharged waste. Sure enough, researchers found extremely high levels of mercury in fish in Lake St. Clair, Cedar Lake, the Saskatchewan River, the Red River, and, subsequently, in other rivers and lakes. The Canadians had set a "zero tolerance" level for mercury in food, but now they placed the permissible limit at 0.5 parts per million (ppm) as an interim action guideline. The Canadians estimated that the lowest levels of adverse effects of methylmercury poisoning were reached at 5 ppm, and then they simply divided this figure by 10 to be on the safe side. Lakes and rivers with fish above this level were identified, and commercial fishing was banned from these bodies of water, warnings about mercury contamination were posted at the water's edge, and where there was severe toxicity, all fishing was banned.

At the time, no mercury at all was permitted in food in the United States, but the FDA went along with the Canadian recommendation, setting the level at 0.5 ppm in 1969. The United States did not test for mercury in rivers and lakes until the Canadians reported their findings in February 1970. When American authorities began looking for methylmercury contamination, they too found it in many lakes and rivers throughout the United States.

In May 1970 Michigan senator Philip Hart held congressional hearings on mercury contamination. While the hearings were under way, state after state reported mercury contamination in lakes and rivers. Eventually, thirty-three states filed such reports, and some sites were declared disaster areas. Freshwater commercial fishing was restricted or banned in places in some states, causing severe economic problems for the local fishing industry.[3]

METHYLMERCURY AND TUNA

Although water from mercury-polluted rivers and bays circulates into the ocean, and airborne mercury from industrial facilities and power plants adds to that naturally present in the sea, it was believed that mercury from industrial waste would dissipate as it went farther out to sea. As tuna is an oceanic fish and spends little time in polluted coastal waters, it was believed to be unlikely that tuna would have high levels of methylmercury. But it was theoretically possible. Bacteria in coastal areas absorb mercury and convert it into methylmercury, which is then absorbed by marine plants. The fish that feed on those plants become contaminated, and as these fish are eaten by larger fish, methylmercury accumulates in the predator species. Tuna and other fish at the upper end of the aquatic food chain might end up with high levels of methylmercury.[4]

Bruce McDuffie's tests found mercury at levels of 0.75 ppm, which exceeded the FDA's limit (0.5 ppm). On December 3, 1970, he forwarded his results to the FDA, which immediately began its own investigation into canned tuna. On December 15, 1970, the FDA reported that 23 percent of the canned tuna it had tested exceeded the agency's limit for methylmercury, with some canned tuna containing as much as 1.23 ppm. By extrapolation, this meant that an estimated 207 million of the 900 million cans of tuna packed that year likely had levels of mercury above the limit set by the FDA. The FDA advised tuna companies to recall 921,000 cans containing the highest levels of mercury. Even as the FDA recalled tuna, the agency reassured the public that the canned fish—even the recalled product—was safe to eat; it just shouldn't be eaten too often. In May 1971, after further testing, the FDA downgraded the total estimate of methylmercury-contaminated tuna, stating that just 3.6 percent had been above the limit and that a mere 1 to 2 percent contained "excessive" amounts. The reason was that the FDA had concluded that harmful levels of mercury were found in only two tuna species—bigeye and yellowfin. Eventually, tuna canners withdrew a total of 12.5 million cans, and canners lost an estimated $84 million.[5]

The Tuna Research Foundation, formed in the 1950s by StarKist, Bumble Bee, Chicken of the Sea, and other canners to serve as a voice for the industry on legislative and regulatory issues, reported that the mercury scare caused sales to drop off nearly 40 percent in some areas.[6] Tuna canners claimed that a person would have to eat two cans of contaminated tuna every day for a full year before suffering any ill effects.[7] But the recall was carried out. Since then, no evidence has surfaced that any adult in the United States has ever died or even become ill due to methylmercury poisoning caused by eating canned tuna. Others have worried that the advisories issued by government agencies about the methylmercury in some fish may have discouraged consumers from eating any seafood. They argued that the small potential risk of methylmercury needed to be weighed against the benefits associated with fish consumption.[8]

Public and industry concern over methylmercury in tuna continued well after the initial scare. While methylmercury is also present in beef, pork, and grains, it is estimated that 95 percent of methylmercury in the human diet comes from fish and seafood; and 37 percent of the fish and seafood consumed in America is tuna.[9]

The tuna industry disagreed with the limit set by the FDA. One company, Anderson Seafoods, in Florida, challenged the 0.5 ppm limit. In 1978 a district court in Florida concluded that the FDA had not systematically considered the evidence before setting its 0.5 ppm limit. Unable to justify that number, the FDA reset the limit at 1.0 ppm.[10]

When the methylmercury scare began, tuna was tested as fishing boats brought their catch into the cannery. If any fish were found to contain levels higher than 0.5 ppm, the whole load was impounded. To avoid losing their entire catch, fishermen, believing that large fish contained more mercury than smaller ones, just tossed out specimens weighing more than 50 pounds.[11] When the FDA raised the limit to 1.0 ppm, virtually all tuna tested at "safe" levels. The FDA believed that the problem had been fixed. Testing of fresh fish at canneries was discontinued, and the FDA stopped testing for methylmercury in canned tuna.

DON'T EAT THESE FISH

Other research indicated that methylmercury from fish might well pose a risk for pregnant women and young children. In 1997 the Environmental Protection Agency (EPA) issued a report to Congress summarizing the current state of knowledge of methylmercury's effects on human health.[12] In 1999 Kathryn R. Mahaffey, the EPA's top mercury expert, expressed concern about methylmercury exposure levels, particularly in sensitive populations such as pregnant women.[13] These findings persuaded the FDA to reexamine its conclusions about methylmercury. In July 2000, while the FDA review was in progress, the Committee on the Toxicological Effects of Methylmercury of the National Academy of Science (NAS) issued an extensive report recommending that pregnant women, women who might become pregnant, and young children eat less fish and seafood high in methylmercury. On its list of species to be avoided or eaten sparingly was white tuna. It seemed likely that the FDA would use these guidelines to formulate new recommendations of its own,[14] and in January 2001 the agency did just that, stating that pregnant women should not eat certain fish—swordfish, shark, king mackerel, and tilefish—because these species contained enough methylmercury to potentially harm a fetus. Much to the dismay of some observers, the FDA did not include a warning about white tuna.[15]

This omission was inconsistent with the NAS report and contrary to considerable evidence that had surfaced during the preceding three decades. Robert Goyer, who had chaired the NAS committee that issued the report, criticized the FDA's advisory, saying that the agency should simply say to pregnant women, "Don't eat these fish." A month after issuing the new advisory, the FDA claimed that tuna had not been mentioned "because consumers did not eat enough to cause a significant risk." This contradicted all previous research, including that conducted by the FDA itself; it was widely known that tuna was (and is) the single most important fish in the American diet.[16] Later, the FDA claimed that if the advisory had cautioned against *some* tuna, pregnant women might have misunderstood the advice, and the general public might have stopped eating fish entirely. In support of this claim, the FDA explained that it had convened focus groups while studying the matter, and that was what had emerged from those groups. The FDA's position was that eating some fish (and risking possible exposure to mercury) was better for pregnant women than not eating any fish.[17]

The FDA's response sounded fishy to two nonprofit advocacy groups, the Environmental Working Group (EWG) and Ralph Nader's U.S. Public Interest Research Group. They disagreed with the FDA's omission of tuna from the health advisory and urged the FDA to warn pregnant women about eating too much tuna.[18] When the FDA declined, the EWG filed a Freedom of Information Act request for all transcripts and reports used by the FDA in determining that tuna should not be included in the warning. The transcripts showed that tuna had been on the initial list of fish high in methylmercury. Following three meetings attended by FDA officials and industry leaders from the U.S. Tuna Foundation, Bumble Bee, StarKist, Chicken of the Sea, and the National Food Processors Association, tuna was removed from the warning list. The food company representatives had argued that the research on methylmercury and tuna was inconclusive, and that if tuna were mentioned in the FDA advisory, tuna consumption would drop by 19 to 24 percent. Tuna canners also feared that they "would face the distinct possibility of numerous class action lawsuits" if the warning were issued.[19]

According to the transcripts, Clark Carrington, an FDA official, stated that canned light tuna was classified as low in methylmercury "to keep market share at a reasonable level." Many observers believed that market share, not science, had guided the FDA's decisions; the agency denied the charge.[20] In addition, evidence from the focus groups was exactly the opposite of what FDA had claimed. Focus group members easily understood the potential warning about some types of tuna for pregnant women. As soon as the transcripts were released, the FDA announced that it had decided to review its advisory recommendation regarding fish consumption by pregnant women.

As this reexamination got under way, one member of the advisory panel charged that the FDA was going to "'disregard science' and not warn consumers about the real health risks of eating tuna." This adviser then resigned from the committee.[21] In February 2004, the EPA reported that about 630,000 of the 4 million children born each year are at risk for lowered intelligence and learning problems caused by exposure to high levels of mercury in the womb.[22] Kathryn R. Mahaffey reported that "fetuses concentrate more mercury in their blood than do pregnant women." Mahaffey believed this was because once fetuses had accumulated methylmercury, they were less able to purge it.[23]

After due reconsideration, the FDA and the EPA jointly issued a health advisory in March 2004 warning about tuna consumption by pregnant women, women who could become pregnant, nursing mothers, and young children. This time, the FDA reported: "Albacore ('white') tuna has more mercury than canned light tuna. So, when choosing your two meals of fish and shellfish, you may eat up to 6 ounces (one average meal) of albacore tuna per week." No warning was given about canned light tuna, which frequently contained species of tuna known to have high levels of mercury. At the same time, the FDA proclaimed that "fish and shellfish are an important part of a healthy diet."[24] Despite this confusing disclaimer, tuna sales dropped 10 percent in the United States after the warning was issued, causing an estimated revenue loss of nearly $150 million.[25]

To help reverse this trend, the U.S. Tuna Foundation applauded the decision for emphasizing that "consumption advice was not necessary for the general population."[26] It then announced in advertisements that federal guidelines reassured "pregnant and nursing women and young children" that canned tuna "is absolutely safe to eat." Ads concluded:

"No government study has ever found unsafe levels of mercury in women or young children who eat canned tuna."[27]

Some researchers believed that the FDA's warning should have been stronger, and public interest groups have continued to wage campaigns to inform Americans about methylmercury in fish. Specific concern has focused on the potential effects of methylmercury on fetuses. In December 2005, reporters from the *Chicago Tribune* sent cans of tuna to two labs, and many cans were found to have high levels of methylmercury. They reported that three decades after methylmercury had first been uncovered that high levels of mercury were still found in canned tuna.[28]

In July 2006, Consumer's Union (CU) performed its own tests on canned tuna and found that some cans were much higher in methylmercury than the FDA reported. CU recommended that pregnant women not eat tuna of any kind. CU again conducted tests on canned and pouched tuna in 2010 and found all the samples contained measurable levels of mercury, ranging from 0.018 to 0.774 ppm. Samples of white tuna had 0.217 to 0.774 ppm of mercury and averaged 0.427 ppm. The investigators concluded that if women of childbearing age or children consumed just 2.5 ounces of the tested samples, they would exceed the daily mercury amounts that federal agencies advised them to avoid.[29]

Studies conducted in 2005 and 2008 indicated that children of women who consumed fish with low mercury levels while pregnant scored highest on tests of intelligence and motor skills when compared with women who had eaten fish with the highest mercury levels. These studies raised the possibility that "no level of methylmercury exposure is without appreciable risk to the developing brain."[30] Mercury researchers met in 2006 and issued a "declaration" affirming that there was a general global consensus among scientists that "methylmercury affects nervous system development and there is sufficient evidence to warrant the prudent selection of fish in the diet, specifically for pregnant women and children."[31]

In late 2008, just before President Bush left office, the FDA was ready to abandon its nearly five-year-old seafood advisory. The FDA claimed that research "argued that nutrients in fish, including omega-3 fatty acids, selenium and other minerals could boost a child's IQ by three points. The greatest benefits . . . would come from eating more than 12 ounces of fish a week, which is the current limit advised for pregnant women, women of childbearing age, nursing mothers and young children." Kathryn Mahaffey, who had just left the EPA, proclaimed that the FDA had used an "oversimplified approach" that might well result in more Americans ingesting methylmercury.[32]

It was not just canned tuna that contained methylmercury. In 2010, researchers examined the methylmercury content of sushi served in restaurants and supermarkets. They found that sushi sold in grocery stores had less methylmercury than did sushi served in restaurants. Supermarket sushi is usually made from inexpensive yellowfin, which is lower in mercury than the costlier bluefin used in high-quality sushi bar offerings that usually are sold in high-end restaurants. Another sample in Los Angeles found that 20 percent of sushi (not all of which was tuna) that was tested exceeded federal guidelines, and several other samples were just under the limit. Recent research has also shown that mercury levels are higher in different fish tissues—so sushi made from *akimi* (the dark red muscle) contains more mercury than sushi made from *toro* (the fatty parts), even if they're both taken from the very same bluefin. The researchers urged restaurants to tell their customers from which tuna species their sushi was made, and from what part of the fish: "Species names and clearer labeling would allow consumers to exercise greater control over the level of mercury they imbibe."[33]

Some scientists, such as Tom Brenna at Cornell University and Michael Crawford of the Institute of Brain Chemistry and Human Nutrition at London Metropolitan University, have concluded that the methylmercury in fish and seafood is not a serious problem, even for pregnant women and young children. They have reported that the benefits of omega-3 fatty acids and other nutrients in seafood far outweigh any potential harm from the methylmercury. They have specifically recommended consuming light tuna, which tends to be lower in methylmercury than albacore or white tuna. Brenna and Crawford have asked the FDA to change its recommendations regarding methylmercury.

Many other scientists and environmental organizations disagree.

They maintain that fish and seafood low in methylmercury is good to eat; other fish, such as tuna, is not, especially for pregnant women and young children. In April 2010, a study undertaken by the environmental scientist Edward Groth III concluded: "Tuna (canned light, canned albacore and fresh/frozen varieties) accounts for 37.4 percent of total mercury inputs."[34]

One reason for tuna's rapid rise to culinary stardom was the widely held view that it was a healthful, nutritious food. It is indeed an excellent low-fat source of protein, contains B vitamins and omega-3 fatty acids, and has half the fat and cholesterol of an equal portion of chicken. Tuna has long been promoted as a diet food and was an important component of the Weight Watchers program. But when word got out that canned tuna contained methylmercury, tuna's image as a wholesome food was severely tarnished.

The controversy over mercury in tuna has flared up again and again, and the FDA, the EPA, independent researchers, and environmental groups have all regularly issued warnings about tuna consumption. The tuna industry and other researchers have maintained that tuna is safe to eat and that the small amount of mercury in tuna is far outweighed by the fish's nutrients. The controversy continues unabated today.

POSTSCRIPT

Bruce McDuffie, the professor at the State University of New York at Binghamton who first raised concerns about methylmercury in 1970, retired in 1988 and began competing in international triathlons and other endurance events.[35]

Kathryn Mahaffey left the EPA in 2008 and became a lecturer at the George Washington University School of Public Health.[36]

The U.S. Tuna Foundation was dissolved in 2007. The Tuna Council in the National Fisheries Institute was created to carry on the foundation's work.

It was once thought that levels of methylmercury were closely related to the age and size of the fish—that larger and older tuna would have accumulated more methylmercury. Recent studies have demonstrated that tuna of the same age and weight can still have differing amounts of methylmercury. One study concluded that the amount of methylmercury was related to the depth at which the individual species feed. The deeper the water, the higher the methylmercury. This finding suggested that the methylmercury in fish, squid, and shrimp comes from natural processes and may not be due to pollution caused by humans.[37]

Epilogue

The American tuna fleet was the largest in the world at the end of the Second World War. This began to change in the early 1950s, when foreign imports flooded into the United States. Fishermen and cannery workers in other countries were willing to accept a fraction of the wages that American workers expected. Even with tariffs, it was still lucrative for foreign companies to import frozen and canned tuna into the United States, and the American tuna industry suffered the consequences.

Historically, tuna fishing was a family affair. Boats were owned by families and passed down from father to son. By the early 1960s, however, the only tuna boats that remained profitable were the large "super seiners." Their price—often between $5 million and $6 million apiece—was too steep for most families, and the largest boats were underwritten by canneries. Control of the tuna fleet went from family businesses to huge corporations. Smaller boats were no longer able to make the tuna business pay.[1] Those willing to upgrade went into debt to acquire the latest boats with the best technology.

The 200-mile economic exclusion zones established by Latin American nations in the eastern tropical Pacific were problematic for tuna fishermen, but the tuna fishing in this area was extremely profitable, especially when the federal government began picking up the tab for fines and fees. It made financial sense to fish for tuna in the eastern tropical Pacific and pay the licenses and fees (or just try to evade the patrol boats). By 1970, the American tuna fleet of 124 purse seiners caught almost 85 percent of the yellowfin in the eastern tropical Pacific.

Then came the crisis related to dolphin mortality. The United States passed laws and created regulations intended to reduce the number of dolphin fatalities. These restrictions increased operating costs of American-flagged vessels and made it more difficult for them to catch tuna. Worse, the image of squealing dolphins in tuna fishing nets caused a massive public relations disaster for the industry. Many tuna boats were reregistered in countries that had less stringent regulations than the United States. Often, these boats operated with the same captain as before; the foreign ownership was just a dodge to avoid U.S. laws and regulations. Tuna boats based in San Diego often picked up crews in Mexico or Panama, where the labor costs were much lower than in California or Puerto Rico.[2]

Meanwhile, other nations expanded their tuna fleets and industries. For a time, new tuna seiners continued to be built in the United States using the latest technology, but these were mainly sold to foreign buyers. Traditionally, the tuna companies maintained their own fleets or contracted with independent fishing boats. Beginning in 1975, canners increasingly relied on the international market for their tuna supply. They divested themselves of their corporate fleets and limited their contracts with domestic independent tuna boat owners. By 1980 only 30 percent of the tuna sold in the United States was supplied by American tuna boats and fishermen.[3] The U.S.-flagged purse seine boats in the eastern tropical Pacific dropped to thirty-six in 1985, and then eleven in 1991. By 1997, 189 purse seiners were operating in the eastern tropical Pacific, but only seven carried an American flag. Mexico had become the major tuna-fishing nation in the eastern tropical Pacific.[4]

Few tuna boats are based in mainland American ports. To avoid the dolphin controversy and issues related to 200-mile economic zones, most American purse seiners headed for the western Pacific. As this was too far away for the boats to return regularly to ports on the American mainland, owners shifted their bases of operations to other countries in the western Pacific. Captains occasionally fly home to the United States to visit families and friends.

THE CLOSE OF BUSINESS

It wasn't just the American tuna fishermen and boat owners who faced extinction. In the early 1960s, twelve tuna canneries remained in operation on the U.S. mainland. When significant commercial catches of tuna were made in the Atlantic in 1960, tuna canners began leaving California and setting up plants in Puerto Rico, where unemployment was higher, and labor was much cheaper. Puerto Rico offered tax incentives for companies relocating to the island, and its location was also advantageous. It was cheaper to ship product to East Coast cities from Puerto Rico than it was from California. And for boats fishing off the west coast of South America, the Panama Canal made Puerto Rico more readily accessible than California ports. Puerto Rico was also closer to the new tuna fishing area discovered off the west coast of Africa. By 1972, 56 percent of tuna canning was done outside California, and Puerto Rico's tuna production was two-thirds that of California.[5]

Tuna canneries on the mainland began to close. The Maryland cannery—the last tuna packer on the East Coast—closed in 1977. Between 1979 and 1989, five more facilities closed, with 40 percent of the industry's workers losing their jobs. The cannery in Astoria, Oregon—the last one in the Pacific Northwest—closed in 1979. StarKist closed its last plant on Terminal Island in 1984. San Diego lost its title of "Tuna Capital of the World" in 1984, when its last large cannery closed. The last tuna cannery in Hawaii ceased operations the following year.

Six more plants have closed since 1990. The Chicken of the Sea facility in San Pedro—the last full-scale tuna cannery on the American mainland—shut down in 2001. In all, 20,000 cannery workers lost their jobs during the thirty-year period from 1979 to 2009.[6] As the main source of tuna moved to the western Pacific, Puerto Rican canneries began to close as well. During the ten-year period from 1982 to 1992, an estimated 10,000 jobs in the industry were lost in Puerto Rico.[7] Today, only one tuna processing plant remains in operation there. Thousands more jobs on the mainland and in Puerto Rico indirectly connected with the canneries were also lost.

As the western and central Pacific developed into the center of world tuna fishing, canneries in American Samoa expanded, and all three major U.S. tuna companies opened plants in Pago Pago, the capital. American Samoa, like Puerto Rico before it, offered cheap labor and the advantage of proximity. It was closer to the new Pacific fishing grounds.

The main reason for the disappearance of American tuna canneries is wages. U.S. cannery workers make about $11.50 per hour. The average hourly rate in Thailand is 88 cents; in Ecuador, it's 69 cents.[8] American canneries have tried to get around this in a variety of ways. One is through technology; U.S. facilities are highly automated. Another is to have the labor-intensive work of cleaning the fish done outside the mainland, and then have frozen tuna loins or disks shipped to American canneries.

In January 2007, the incoming Democratic Congress passed a bill that increased the minimum wage to $7.25 per hour. This was not at all unusual, except for one small provision that gradually raised wages in American territories to the new level. American Samoa, a territory of 65,000 inhabitants, had a minimum wage of $3.25; the amendment would increase this by 50 cents per year until it reached $7.25.[9]

By the beginning of the twentieth-first century, some canned tuna sold in the United States was cleaned and packed in American Samoa, an unincorporated territory south of the equator. It was the last American-controlled locality to boast canneries owned by two of the world's largest tuna companies, Chicken of the Sea and StarKist. Both located in the port city (and capital), Pago Pago, they exported an estimated $445 million in canned tuna to the U.S. mainland.[10]

Even before the minimum wage increase in 2007, the Samoan tuna industry was in trouble. Its main competition paid its workers much less than Samoan workers received. With the wage increase mandated in 2007, employees of the Pago Pago canneries would eventually be earning ten times as much as Thai tuna packers. Once it became known that the minimum wage would be applied to Samoa, the Chicken of the Sea plant closed.[11] This left only the StarKist cannery in Pago Pago. In 2006 it had a staff of 3,000. Because of the wage increase, StarKist let go all but 1,200 of its employees in 2010.[12] In 2010, the U.S. Food and Drug Administration inspected the plant and told StarKist: "Your canned tuna and pouched packed tuna are adulterated, in that they have been prepared, packed or held under unsanitary conditions whereby they may have been rendered injurious to health."[13] If this plant closes, no full-scale tuna cannery will remain in operation in the United States or its territories.

CORPORATE SHUFFLE

Historically, tuna packing companies were launched by hardworking and creative entrepreneurs. In some cases leadership was continued by the founder's family. Consolidation of the tuna industry began in the 1920s and 1930s, and by the late 1940s most tuna production was in the hands of just a few companies. As second- and third-generation family canners began to retire, larger corporations acquired their companies as subsidiaries. Three major tuna brands, controlling about 80 percent of the tuna sold in America, emerged in the 1950s: Chicken of the Sea, Bumble Bee, and StarKist.

The Van Camp Sea Food Company remained in family hands through the third generation of Van Camps. They made the company, with its Chicken of the Sea and White Star brands, the world's largest tuna packer. Van Camp adopted the mermaid logo in 1952 and launched an innovative advertising campaign in 1955 by sponsoring the "Chicken of the Sea Pirate Ship" at the newly opened Disneyland in Anaheim, California. Gilbert C. Van Camp III sold the company to Ralston Purina in 1963. A few years later, the brand undertook a major promotional effort around the jingle "Ask any mermaid you happen to see, 'What's the best tuna?' Chicken of the Sea."

As the crisis with dolphins gave rise to tuna boycotts, Ralston Purina sold the Van Camp Seafood division in 1988 to Mantrust, one of Indonesia's largest food companies. In 1997, the company was purchased by Tri-Union Seafoods, the second largest tuna canner in the world. It was renamed Chicken of the Sea International, based in San Diego. In 2000, Thai Union Frozen Seafood Products of Bangkok acquired the company. Today, Chicken of the Sea operates a tuna processing plant in Georgia. The company launched several new advertising campaigns during the past decade, including a major one around "Tommy Tuna" that was intended to reach young adults. Chicken of the Sea is America's third most popular brand today.

In 1950, Bumble Bee was acquired by Castle & Cook, a prominent Hawaii-based food company. Ten years later, the company launched Bumble Bee Seafoods as a wholly owned subsidiary. In 1977 Bumble Bee acquired a tuna cannery in Puerto Rico and a fishing operation in Ecuador. Beginning in the 1980s, Bumble Bee went through a series of ownership changes, including its purchase by Pillsbury, which sold it to Unicord, based in Bangkok, Thailand. In 1997 it was sold to International Home Foods, Inc. In 2000, Bumble Bee was acquired by the American multinational ConAgra, but three years later it was sold to Connors Bros., a Canadian firm. In 2008 Centre Partners, an American private equity firm, acquired Bumble Bee Foods. Three years later, Centre Partners sold it for an estimated $980 million to Lion Capital LLP, a British private equity firm. Bumble Bee remains headquartered in San Diego, and it operates processing plants in Mayagüez, Puerto Rico, and Santa Fe Springs, California. Despite the corporate shake-ups over the past sixty years, Bumble Bee has remained one of America's most popular tuna brands, second only to StarKist.

StarKist launched a major advertising blitz in 1961. The Chicago advertising agency of Leo Burnett created a campaign for the brand that starred the ambitious "Charlie the Tuna," who was sure he'd be chosen by StarKist but never was. The doleful voice-over line "Sorry, Charlie" became a national catchphrase. The promotional campaign greatly increased sales, which encouraged the Pittsburgh-based food company H. J. Heinz to buy StarKist in 1962.

In 1992 StarKist introduced Charlie's Lunch Kit, a do-it-yourself tuna salad package that contained tuna fish and packets of mayonnaise and relish. StarKist sells about 1 billion cans of tuna annually and is America's largest-selling brand. StarKist also started packing pouch tuna in Thailand and Malaysia, some of which was imported into the United States. Despite this success, Heinz sold StarKist to Del Monte in 2002. When the price of fuel oil increased in 2007, this ran up costs of catching skipjack in the western Pacific. What with all the other problems the industry was having, Del Monte decided that StarKist just wasn't worth it and put the subsidiary up for auction. The winner was Dongwon Industries of Seoul, South Korea, which bought StarKist for $359 million in December 2008.[14] StarKist remains America's most popular brand of tuna, in part due to Charlie the Tuna, who continues, fifty years after his first appearance, to remain a popular advertising figure.

Advertising worked. Throughout the last half of the twentieth century, smaller tuna canners have gone out of business, and the three largest canners, StarKist, Bumble Bee and Chicken of the Sea, gained market share. Three large companies controlled 71 percent of the U.S. canned tuna market in 1989. Today, they control more than 82 percent. However, the amount of tuna Americans consume annually has dropped from 3.4 pounds a year in 2003 to 2.5 pounds six years later. To counteract this decline, the three companies began a joint advertising campaign under the umbrella of the Tuna Council to encourage Americans to buy tuna.

ENVIRONMENTALLY CHALLENGED BLUEFIN

The demand for sushi, especially in Japan, which consumes 80 percent of the bluefin caught worldwide, has greatly affected the bluefin populations of both the Atlantic and the Pacific. International groups have established quotas for the number of bluefin that can be caught in each of these oceans in any year, but extensive evidence indicates that these quotas have been exceeded on a regular basis.[15]

Atlantic bluefin are known to spawn in only two places: the eastern Mediterranean and the Caribbean. Many environmentalists are deeply concerned about the overfishing of this species, particularly in the Mediterranean.[16] The World Wildlife Fund has predicted that unless the Mediterranean fishery is closed, the bluefin that spawn there will be "functionally extinct" by 2012.[17] Greenpeace has campaigned against fishing for bluefin and also against restaurants that serve it. After four years of pressure from environmental groups, the Nobu restaurant chain, created by Nobuyuki Matsuhisa and Robert De Niro, agreed not to serve bluefin. In spite of this promise, when Greenpeace members took sushi from three Nobu restaurants in London and had a DNA analysis of the fish done, the results showed that Nobu was in fact still serving endangered northern Atlantic bluefin. Greenpeace activists in New York demonstrated at the Nobu restaurant in Tribeca.[18] The activists who had reservations tried to replace Nobu's menu with a fake one of their own that featured endangered species. Demonstrators tried to substitute their menu for Nobu's and plastered the fake menus on restroom doors. The organizer of the demonstration, Casson Trenor, author of *Sustainable Sushi* (2009), called the demonstration a success. Nobu restaurants responded by placing a note at the bottom of their menu stating that bluefin was "environmentally challenged," and suggested that concerned diners ask their server for alternatives.[19]

It just wasn't Western environmental groups that were concerned with the plight of bluefin. The International Commission for the Conservation of Atlantic Tunas (ICCAT), an intergovernmental organization that sets quotas for East Atlantic and Mediterranean bluefin tuna, was also concerned. The current Atlantic bluefin tuna population is less than 15 percent of the original population.[20] Japanese scientists led by Toshio Katsukawa, an associate professor at Mie University, demonstrated that overexploitation of large-sized fish led to a rise in the catch of small juvenile fish less than three years old. If young bluefin are caught before they spawn, there will be far fewer bluefin in future generations.[21]

Despite many such studies, the Convention on International Trade in Endangered Species of Wild Fauna and Flora (CITES) turned down a proposal to ban international commercial trade in Atlantic bluefin tuna in March 2010. This ban had been proposed by the United States and the

European Union, but the Japanese delegation opposed the ban, and it was not passed.

Today, bluefin that spawn in the Caribbean are at just 20 percent of their 1960s levels—and this was before BP's Deepwater Horizon oil spill in the Gulf of Mexico. The full effects of the oil spill on this bluefin population will not be known for three or four years, when this cohort of bluefin reaches adulthood.

Where intergovernmental organizations have had a difficult time coming to consensus, conservation groups have begun to take the lead in protecting the bluefin. According to the U.S. conservation organization Center for Biological Diversity (CBD) 22,000 people as of May 2011 have pledged to boycott eating bluefin tuna or visiting any restaurant that serves the imperiled species.

Boycotts to the contrary, in May 2011 the National Oceanic and Atmospheric Administration (NOAA) reported that the Atlantic bluefin tuna was not in imminent danger of extinction and that it did not warrant species protection under the Endangered Species Act. NOAA planned to reexamine the species' status in 2013 when the effects of the Deepwater Horizon oil spill are better understood. This was not enough for the CBD, which notified the National Marine Fisheries Service that it planned to sue the agency for failing to protect Atlantic bluefin tuna.

FARMED AND CAPTURE-BASED TUNA

Despite the real concerns for the future of tuna, all may not be lost. The good news is that mature female tuna spawn between 1 million and 30 million eggs over a few months. In the wild, it is estimated that only three of these eggs will reach maturity. Several operations are under way around the world to hatch tuna eggs, support their early development, and then turn them loose into the ocean.

The Japanese have been experimenting with tuna farms since the 1970s. By the 1980s, some of the kinks had been worked out, and innovators had found ways of getting bluefin to spawn in captivity. Today there are many tuna "farms"—usually 100 feet in diameter—in operation. In Japan, where most of the experimental work was done, bluefin farms provided their first commercial fish in 2004. An estimated 400,000 bluefin were raised this way, mainly in Japan. They were marketed as "farm-raised" and priced about 30 percent less than wild bluefin.[22] These farmed fish are now served in a few American restaurants.

Yet another system that's still evolving is "capture-based" tuna. Such operations are currently under way in Malta, Spain, Greece, Croatia, Australia, and Mexico. In the Baja California farm, juvenile bluefin are captured in the open sea around Ensenada and then fattened in pens for three to four months. Their main diet is sardines collected in the area. When sardines are unavailable (due to a variety of oceanic conditions), the tuna are sometimes fed frozen sardines shipped in from Los Angeles. The fish harvested in Baja are mainly sent to Japan, although small amounts are consumed in Mexico and the Los Angeles area. To date, few people claim that they can see, taste, or smell the difference between farmed and wild tuna, and there does not seem to be any nutritional differences either.[23]

This type of aquaculture has been criticized by environmentalists. The ratio of feed to fish is about ten to one—10 pounds of sardines go into feeding the captured fish for every pound of tuna produced. Also, because immature adults are captured, they are prevented from spawning, and there is fear that operations like this will continue to deplete the numbers of wild tuna.

Despite the criticism, similar enterprises are under construction around the Pacific and Mediterranean. In 2009, Hawaii Oceanic Technology was approved to create an "environmentally friendly open ocean farm" off the coast of Hawaii; it will artificially hatch bigeye tuna and raise them until they weigh about 100 pounds. Once operational, the farm is projected to generate 6,000 tons of bigeye tuna per year.[24]

THE END OF AMERICAN TUNA?

Americans began canning tuna in the early twentieth century, and it quickly became an important industry. The industry has gone through many changes during the last century. Today, all three of the largest tuna companies are foreign owned, and no full-scale tuna canning facilities operate inside the United States.

Historically, American tuna was caught within a few hundred miles of the west coast of the United States. Today, less than 1 percent of our tuna comes from American waters. Some tuna that Americans eat is from the Indian Ocean, about 15 percent is from the eastern tropical Pacific, and most of the rest is from the western Pacific. Today, most tuna that Americans consume is caught by fishermen from other countries. There are relatively few American tuna boats in the eastern tropical Pacific, and a total of only about seventy U.S. boats left, most of which work in the western Pacific. Many of their crew members are foreign nationals. Today, Mexico has the largest tuna fleet in the world.

Today, the United States consumes 29 percent of the canned tuna produced worldwide, and virtually all of the tuna is imported. While tuna remains the most frequently consumed fish in America, its per capita consumption has declined, and it was dethroned in 2001 as the nation's most consumed seafood by shrimp, most of which is farmed in Southeast Asia.

Historical Tuna Recipes

During the research for this book, I ran across many historical recipes published in nineteenth- and early twentieth-century cookbooks, corporate promotional pamphlets, and magazines. Only a few copies of the many cookbooks, pamphlets, and booklets have survived. I have included twenty-seven recipes here as illustrative examples of the early ways that tuna was recommended for use in the United States.

Baked Tuna Spanish

To one pound of White Star Brand Tuna add two medium size potatoes and one onion minced fine. Season to suit the taste and place in baking pan. Cover with Spanish sauce of onions, chili and tomatoes, and bake in hot oven half an hour.

Source: White Star Canning Co., *White Star Brand Tuna Fish. "Chicken of the Sea"* (Los Angeles: White Star Canning Co., [ca. 1914]).

Tuna Canapes

1 cup tuna fish	1 tablespoon lemon juice
1 tablespoon tomato ketchup	½ tablespoon olive oil
½ teaspoon salt	¼ teaspoon paprika

Chop fish, add seasonings, and spread on small rounds of lightly toasted bread. Garnish with sliced pimolas.

Source: Marietta McPherson Greenough, *Better Meals for Less Money* (New York: H. Holt and Co., 1917), 18.

Tuna En Casserole

To 1 shredded tin of Blue Sea Tuna Fish add 2 whole eggs, ½ cup of cream, 4 tablespoons catsup, ½ cup of pepper relish with cracker crumbs and salt and pepper to taste. Place in casserole, cover with cracker crumbs, add 3 tablespoons of melted butter over top. Bake in moderate oven.

Source: Southern California Fish Co., *14 Tasty Recipes for Serving Blue Sea Extra Fancy Brand Tuna* (Terminal Island, Calif.: Southern California Fish Co., [ca. 1930s]).

Tuna Chowder—California

Chop medium sized onion, medium sized piece of bacon, a small piece of salt pork, and in a tablespoonful of butter fry the whole until the bacon and pork are brown and crisp. Have ready three cups of cooked diced potatoes. Season with salt and pepper. Mix all with a can of BLUE SEA BRAND of canned TUNA fish. Bring to the boiling point one quart of rich milk and pour in. Add oyster crackers and serve hot. The oil in the can makes this dish richer than where butter is used. This is better chowder than clam.

Source: Southern California Fish Company label, ca. 1912.

Tuna Croquettes

Melt two and one-half tablespoons butter, add one half tablespoon finely chopped onion and cook till onion is yellow, add one-third cup flour, cook to smooth, add one cup stewed tomatoes and cook stirring constantly till boiling, add one can AVALON BRAND TUNA, and one cup finely chopped boiled potato. Season to taste with salt and pepper, form into balls, dip in egg, roll in crumbs and fry in hot deep grease.

Source: *Boston Cooking-School Magazine* 18 (October 1913): 239.

Deviled Tuna Baked in Shells

One can of White Star Brand Tuna, cut into small pieces, half cup of bread crumbs, two hard boiled eggs chopped fine, juice of one lemon and Worcester sauce to taste. Mix all with a cream sauce, one cup of milk, piece of butter, one tablespoon of flour, salt, pepper, then fill shells with mixture. Cook till it thickens, then fill shells with mixture, sprinkle over the top with cracker crumbs and grated cheese and bake. Very fine.

Source: White Star Canning Co., *White Star Brand Tuna Fish "Chicken of the Sea"* (Los Angeles: White Star Canning Co., [ca. 1914]).

Tunny Fish or Horse Mackerel, Fried with Arrowroot Mayonnaise Sauce

Lift the fillets from a young tunny fish or from a horse mackerel, suppress the skin and from the meats cut some lengthwise slices or aiguillettes, lay these on a dish to season with salt, mignonette, slices of onions, sprigs of parsley, thyme, bay leaf, oil and vinegar. Leave to marinate for two hours, then drain and wipe dry, dip them in eggs, then in bread-crumbs, fry to a good color; drain and dress on a folded napkin placing a bunch of fried parsley on top. Serve separately arrowroot mayonnaise sauce.

Source: Charles Ranhofer, *The Epicurean* (New York: R. Ranhofer, 1893), 468.

"Tunny" Fritters

Stir up a batter of a pint of milk, four eggs, a pinch of salt, one large teaspoonful baking powder and flour enough to make batter thicker than batter cakes. Stir in the PIERCE'S Brand TUNNY minced fine and fry like any fritters.

Source: C. E. Pierce Co., "Pierce's Brand California Tunny" (San Francisco: C. E. Pierce Co., 1913).

Tuna Loaf

Empty contents of one can AVALON BRAND TUNA. Beat two eggs and add one cup bread crumbs, one teaspoonful lemon juice, chopped parsley, green peppers; salt and pepper to taste. Mould and bake moderately one-half hour. Garnish with parsley and sliced stuffed olives. Serve hot or cold. If eaten hot serve with fish sauce.

Source: *Boston Cooking-School Magazine* 18 (November 1913): 325.

Preparation of a Tuna Omelet

Take, for six people, two well-cleaned carp roes which you will blanch by plunging them for five minutes into water already boiling and lightly salted.

Have to hand a piece of fresh tuna the size of a hen's egg, to which you will add a small shallot finely minced.

Chop together the roes and the tuna so that they are well blended, toss the mixture into a casserole with an adequate lump of very good butter, and heat just until the butter is melted. This last is what gives the omelet its special savor.

Take a second lump of butter, blend it with parsley and chives, and put it in a fish-shaped platter destined to hold the omelet; sprinkle it with the juice of a lemon, and put it over a gentle heat.

Then beat twelve eggs (the freshest are the best), and add the hot mixture of roe and tuna and mix together thoroughly.

Make the omelet in the usual way, and take care that it is long in shape, thick enough, and soft. Slide it skillfully onto the platter which you have prepared for it, and serve it, to be eaten at once.

This dish should be reserved for especially good luncheons, and for those reunions of enthusiasts who appreciate what is served to them and eat it thoughtfully and slowly. Let it be floated downward on a fine old wine, and miracles will happen.

Theoretical Notes on the Preparation of This Dish

(1) The roes and tuna must be thoroughly heated in the butter, but not allowed to bubble in it, so that they do not become hard; this would keep them from blending thoroughly with the eggs.

(2) The platter must be deep, so that the sauce will collect in it and be easy to serve with a spoon.

(3) The platter must also be lightly warmed: if it were cold, the porcelain would absorb the heat of the omelet and would not leave enough in it to melt the herb butter on which the mixture rests.

Source: Jean-Anthelme Brillat-Savarin, *The Physiology of Taste or Meditations on Transcendental Gastronomy*, trans. M. K. F. Fisher (Washington, D.C.: Counterpoint, 1986), 268–69.

Blue Sea Pie

Boil together 2 diced carrots, 2 small chopped onions and 3 diced potatoes. Add small can of peas. White sauce made of 2 tablespoons butter, 3 tablespoons of flour and 3/4 cup of milk, season and add 1 tin of Blue Sea Tuna Fish shredded. Line baking dish with pastry and fill with alternate layers of tuna and vegetables. Cover with upper crust and bake until brown.

Source: Southern California Fish Co., *14 Tasty Recipes for Serving Blue Sea Extra Fancy Brand Tuna* (Terminal Island, Calif.: Southern California Fish Co., [ca. 1930s]).

Blue Sea Rarebit

Brown toasted bread dipped in milk and placed in pan with melted butter. Add ½-inch layer of Blue Sea Tuna Fish, shredded; a tablespoon of cream and sprinkle with grated cheese. Melt in hot oven and serve hot.

Source: Southern California Fish Co., *14 Tasty Recipes for Serving Blue Sea Extra Fancy Brand Tuna* (Terminal Island, Calif.: Southern California Fish Co., [ca. 1930s]).

Thon Mariné Salad

Tunny fish can be obtained in cans, the best quality being the French brands. Break up the fish with the fingers, and place on a platter with leaves of lettuce. The fish should be in pieces about one inch and a half thick. Sprinkle with salt, pepper, chopped parsley, chervil, and a little finely sliced chives, and a sauce of one-third vinegar and two-thirds olive oil.

Source: Victor Hirtzler, *The Hotel St. Francis Cook Book* (Chicago: The Hotel Monthly Press, 1919), 27.

Botargo Sandwiches

Botargo (which is the dried eggs of the Tonno) makes a delicious sandwich. That put up in either Genoa or Tunis being considered by epicures the best. Season with lemon juice and make according to directions, using unbuttered bread slices.

Source: [Mrs. Alexander Orr Bradley,] *Beverages and Sandwiches for Your Husband's Friends by One Who Knows* (New York: Brentano's, 1893), 37.

Tuna Sandwiches

Shred the contents of one can of Pierce's brand of Tuna fish, add finely chopped celery, green pepper, olives and nuts; mix with mayonnaise, placing crisp lettuce leaves between thin slices of bread and spreading the mixture upon them.

Source: The Council of Jewish Women, *The Neighborhood Cook Book* (Portland, Ore.: Press of Bushong & Co., 1914), 285.

Blue Sea Souffle

Use 2 tablespoons butter, 2 tablespoons flour, 1 cup of milk, 1 tin of Blue Sea Tuna Fish, ½ teaspoon salt, 3 eggs separated and ½ cup of soft bread crumbs. Melt butter, add flour, mix and cook until frothy, add milk and stir until thickened. Add shredded Blue Sea Tuna Fish, bread crumbs, beaten egg yolks and seasonings. Place in baking dish in pan of hot water and bake in moderate oven for 30 minutes.

Source: Southern California Fish Co., *14 Tasty Recipes for Serving Blue Sea Extra Fancy Brand Tuna* (Terminal Island, Calif.: Southern California Fish Co., [ca. 1930s]).

Tuna Fish Soup

2 tablespoons grated carrots	2 cups hot milk
¼ teaspoon paprika	¼ cup sifted crumbs
1 tablespoon grated onions	1 cup tuna fish
2 cups boiling water	1 teaspoon salt
¼ teaspoon Worcestershire	¼ tablespoon butter

Cook vegetables, water, and milk in double boiler for twenty minutes; add crumbs, seasonings, tuna fish separated into flakes, and butter; cook five minutes.

Source: Marietta McPherson Greenough, *Better Meals for Less Money* (New York: H. Holt and Co., 1917).

Tuna a la Newberg

One can White Star Brand Tuna, one tablespoon butter, one tablespoon flour, yolks of two eggs, one cup of cream. Melt the butter, add the flour and cook till it thickens. Beat the yolks of the eggs till they are light, mix in the cream and pour it over the flaked Tuna, stir until heated well, but do not allow to boil.

Source: White Star Canning Co., *White Star Brand Tuna Fish "Chicken of the Sea"* (Los Angeles: White Star Canning Co., [ca. 1914]).

Tomatoes Stuffed with "Tunny"

Slice the tops from the required number of tomatoes and scoop out the centers. Mix with contents of can PIERCE'S Brand **Tunny:** One cup cracker crumbs, one teaspoonful salt, and paprika to taste. Replace all into the tomato shell and bake twenty minutes in quick oven. Serve with slices of lemon.

Source: C. E. Pierce Co., "Pierce's Brand California Tunny" (San Francisco: C. E. Pierce Co., 1913).

Pierce's "Tunny" Fish au Gratin

One can TUNNY, one-half cup cracker crumbs, one-half pint of cream sauce. Season well with salt, pepper, paprika, celery salt. First layer of fish in baking dish, then layer of cheese, then layer of cracker crumbs. Sprinkle with chopped parsley. Pour over part of cream sauce on each layer. Bake in quick oven until it boils up in the middle and cracker crumbs are brown.

Source: C. E. Pierce Co., "Pierce's Brand California Tunny" (San Francisco: C. E. Pierce Co., 1913).

Pierce's "Tunny" Cocktail

Two tablespoons Cocktail sauce, two tablespoonfuls Pierce's **Tunny,** few drops lemon juice, pepper, salt and a little dash of paprika. A most delicious appetizer.

Source: C. E. Pierce Co., "Pierce's Brand California Tunny" (San Francisco: C. E. Pierce Co., 1913).

Tuna Fish Balls

Mix one can White Star Brand Tuna with equal parts of mashed potatoes and eggs well beaten. Season and make into small cakes. Roll in flour and fry in hot butter or olive oil.

Source: White Star Canning Co., *White Star Brand Tuna Fish "Chicken of the Sea"* (Los Angeles: White Star Canning Co., [ca. 1914]).

Creamed Tuna Fish
(Sufficient to Serve Six)

3 Tb. butter	⅛ tsp. paprika
3 Tb. flour	1½ c. hot milk
½ tsp. salt	1½ c. tuna fish
⅛ tsp. pepper	1 egg

Melt the butter in a saucepan and add the flour, salt, pepper, and paprika. Stir well, pour in the milk, and when this has thickened, add the tuna fish. Allow this to heat thoroughly in the sauce. Just before serving, add the slightly beaten egg and cook until this has thickened. Pour over toast and serve.

Source: *Woman's Institute Library of Cookery: Soup, Meat, Poultry, and Game Fish and Shell Fish* (Scranton, Pa.: Woman's Institute of Domestic Arts and Sciences, Inc., 1918), 34.

Blue Sea Tuna Ring

1 can Blue Sea Tuna Fish drained and shredded. Add ½ cup of chopped pimientos, 2 cups mashed potatoes, the liquid from 1 can of asparagus, the tuna liquid and seasoning. Stir, heat and add chopped asparagus

tops. Mold in buttered ring mold and brown 20 minutes in oven. Serve with green peas center.

Source: Southern California Fish Co., *14 Tasty Recipes for Serving Blue Sea Extra Fancy Brand Tuna* (Terminal Island, Calif.: Southern California Fish Co., [ca. 1930s]).

Tuna Stuffed Eggs

Cut off top and remove yolks of half a dozen boiled eggs and stand on crisp lettuce. Fill the inside with stuffing made from 1 small tin Blue Sea Fish, 2 tablespoons minced ripe olives, tablespoon chopped celery, mix with mayonnaise and chopped egg yolks.

Source: Southern California Fish Co., *14 Tasty Recipes for Serving Blue Sea Extra Fancy Brand Tuna* (Terminal Island, Calif.: Southern California Fish Co., [ca. 1930s]).

Beech-Nut Tuna Fish and Spaghetti

Prepare creamed tuna fish by the usual recipe. Allow three cupfuls of white sauce to a half pound can of tuna fish. Add two cupfuls of coarsely chopped Beech-Nut Spaghetti, half a tablespoonful lemon juice, one tablespoonful minced parsley and serve hot.

Source: Ida Bailey Allen, *The Beech-Nut Book of Menus & Recipes* (Canajoharie, N.Y.: Beech-Nut Packing Co., 1924), 21.

Veal with Tunny (Vitello tomato)

Take two pounds of meat without bones, remove the fat and tendons, then lard it with two anchovies. These must be washed and boned and cut lengthwise, after opening them, making in all eight pieces. Tie the piece of meat not very tight and boil it for an hour and a half in enough water to cover it completely. Previously put into the water one quarter of an onion larded with clover, one leaf of laurel, celery, carrot and parsley. Salt the water generously and don't put the veal in until it is boiling. When the veal is cooked, untie, dry it and keep it for two or three days in the following sauce in quantity sufficient to cover it.

Grind ¼ pound tunny fish preserved in olive oil and two anchovies, crush them well with the blade of a knife and rub through a sieve adding good olive oil in abundance little by little, and squeeze in one whole lemon, so that the sauce should remain liquid. Finally mix in some capers soaked in vinegar.

Serve the veal cold, in thin slices, with the sauce.

The stock of the veal can be rubbed through a sieve and used for risotto.

Source: Maria Gentile, *The Italian Cook Book* (New York: Italian Cook Book Co., 1919), 69.

Notes

PROLOGUE

1. Roberta S. Greenwood, R. O. Browne, and John E. Fitch, *A Coastal Chumash Village: Excavation of Shisholop, Ventura County, California* ([Los Angeles, Southern California Academy of Sciences], 1969), 57; Mark A. Roeder, *Archaeological Study of Ca-Ven-110, Ventura, California: Fish Remains* (Pacific Palisades: Greenwood and Associates, 1987), 3, 4, 5, 6.

2. W. Michael Mathes, "Early California Propaganda: The Works of Fray Antonio de la Ascencion," *California Historical Quarterly* 50 (June 1971): 197.

3. William Ingraham Kip, *Historical Scenes from the Old Jesuit Missions* (New York: Anson D. F. Randolph, [1875]), 60.

4. Kay Sanger, "A Fish Story: Realism or Symbolic Communication? Arroyo de las Piedras Pintas, Baja California," in Paul Faulstich, ed., *Rock Art as Visual Ecology* (Tucson, Ariz.: American Rock Art Research Association, IRAC Proceedings, 1997), 82.

5. Greenwood, Browne, and Fitch, *Coastal Chumash Village*, 57; Roeder, *Archaeological Study of Ca-Ven-110*, 3, 4, 5, 6.

6. Frederick William Beechey, *Narrative of a Voyage to the Pacific and Beering's [sic] Strait* (Philadelphia: Carey & Lea, 1832), 341.

7. *Bulletin of the Pan-Pacific Union,* n.s., 55 (May 1924): 10.

8. John Josselyn, *New-England Rarities Discovered* (London: G. Widdowes, 1672; repr., Boston: Massachusetts Historical Society, 1972), 23.

9. Timothy Dwight, *Travels in New-England and New-York* (New York: T. Dwight, 1821), 3:46.

10. Boston *News,* September 4, 1818; *Commercial Advertiser,* September 7, 1818.

11. David Humphreys Storer and William Bourn Oliver Peabody, *Reports on the Fishes, Reptiles and Birds of Massachusetts / Published Agreeably to an Order of the Legislature, by the Commissioners on the Zoological and Botanical Survey of the State* (Boston: Dutton and Wentworth, State Printers, 1839), 47; *Gazette of the U.S.,* May 24, 1798; Thomas F. Devoe, *The Market Assistant* (New York: Hurd and Houghton, 1867), 268.

12. *Salem Gazette,* as quoted in Thomas F. Devoe, *The Market Assistant* (New York: Hurd and Houghton, 1867), 270.

13. "Tunny Fishing," *New York Times,* October 25, 1874, p. 3.

14. *Appleton's Journal* 13 (May 29, 1875): 701.

15. Devoe, *Market Assistant,* 268.

16. P.H. Felker, *The Grocer's Manual: A Guide Book for the Information and Use of Grocers,* 2nd ed. (New York: The American Grocer Publishing Association, 1878), 269.

17. Artemas Ward, *The Grocers' Hand-Book and Directory for 1883* (Philadelphia: The Philadelphia Grocer Publishing Co., 1882), 268.

18. G. Ripley and C.A. Dana, eds., *The New American Cyclopædia* (New York: D. Appleton, and Co., 1862), 15:640.

19. Todd S. Goodholme, ed., *Goodholme's Domestic Cyclopedia of Practical Information,* new rev. ed. (New York: Charles Scribner's Sons, 1889), 541.

20. *Fishing Gazette,* as quoted in W.A. Wilcox, "New England Fisheries in April 1885," in *Bulletin of the United States Fish Commission* (Washington, D.C.: Government Printing Office, 1885), 5:168.

21. G. Brown Goode, *American Fishes: A Popular Treatise upon the Game and Food and Food Fishes,* 2nd ed., rev. and enl. Theodore Gill (Boston: L.C. Page & Company, 1903), 216.

22. G. Brown Goode, *The Fisheries and Fishery Industries of the United States,* Section I, U.S. Commission of Fish and Fisheries (Washington, D.C.: Government Printing Office, 1884), 321.

23. *Fishing Gazette,* as quoted in Wilcox, "New England Fisheries," 168.

24. F.L Harding, "The Oceanic Game Fishes of the United States, Comparative Notes by an Angler on Their Size, Distribution, Food, Appearance and Manner of Capture—Third Paper," *Field and Stream* 8 (July 1906): 437.

25. Stillhunter, "In Catalina's Shadow," *Western Field: The Sportsman's Magazine of the West* 8 (February 1906): 7.

26. David Starr Jordan and Barton Warren Evermann, *American Food and Game Fishes: A Popular Account of All the Species Found in America North of the Equator, with Keys for Ready Identification, Life Histories, and Methods of Capture* (Garden City, N.Y.: Doubleday, Page & Co., 1908), 282.

27. *American Food Journal* 12 (December 1917): 667.

28. *Carte de Restaurant Français des Frères Delmonico* (New York: T. & C. Wood, 1838), 1.

29. Alessandro Filippini. *The Table: How to Buy Food, How to Cook it, and How to Serve It* (New York: Charles L. Webster & Company, 1889), 190.

30. Charles Ranhofer, *The Epicurean* (New York: R. Ranhofer, 1893), 367, 468.

31. Pierre Blot, *Hand-Book of Practical Cookery* (New York: D. Appleton and Co., 1867), 143, 147, 370.

32. Felix Déliée, *The Franco-American Cookery Book* (New York: G. P. Putnam's Sons, 1884), 232–33, 239.

33. *Commercial Relations of the United States with Foreign Countries* (Washington, D.C.: Department of State, United States, Bureau of Foreign and Domestic Commerce, 1866), 143.

34. United States Centennial Commission, *Reports and Awards* (Philadelphia: J. B. Lippincott, 1877), 4:646.

35. *Chicago Daily Tribune*, October 10, 1876. This reference was located by Janet Clarkson.

36. *Sprague, Warner & Co., Importers and Jobbers of Fine Groceries and Table Luxuries* (Chicago: Sprague, Warner, & Co., 1885), 20–21.

37. "Price List of S. S. Pierce & Co., 1886–7" (Boston: S. S. Pierce & Co., 1886), n.p.

38. *Catalogue of Fine Groceries* (New York: Park & Tilford, Summer & Spring 1906); *Modern Housekeeping and Food News* (New York: Siegel Cooper Co., January 1907), 40.

39. "The Rival Fish Dealers," *New York Times*, October 11, 1897, p. 3.

40. Henrietta Sowle, *I Go A-Marketing* (Boston: Little, Brown and Company, 1900), 70.

41. "A Mediterranean Fish Far Astray," *San Francisco Examiner*, August 18, 1895, as reprinted in *New York Times*, August 25, 1895, p. 12.

1. ANGLING FOR A BIG FISH

1. Charles F. Holder, "The Return of the Leaping Tuna," *The Outing Magazine* 55 (February 1910): 538.

2. Colleen J. Sheehy, "American Angling: The Rise of Urbanism and the

Romance of the Rod and Reel," in Kathryn Grover, *Hard at Play: Leisure in America, 1840–1940* (Amherst: University of Massachusetts Press; Rochester, N.Y.: Strong Museum, 1992), 78.

3. Sheehy, "American Angling," 78–82; Charles E Goodspeed, *Angling in America: Its Early History and Literature* (Boston: Houghton Mifflin, 1939).

4. Sheehy, "American Angling," 84.

5. Pierre Fortin, "Continuation of the List of Fish of the Gulf and River St. Lawrence," in *Annual Report for 1863* (Quebec, 1864), 60–72.

6. *Proceedings of the Boston Society of Natural History* (Boston: Dutton and Wentworth, 1844): vol. 1 (1841–1844), p. 81.

7. Philip Tocque, *Wandering Thoughts, or Solitary Hours* (London: Thomas Richardson and Son, 1844), 330.

8. Charles F. Holder, *The Big Game Fishes of the United States* (New York: Macmillan Company, 1903), 54.

9. J. Richard Dunn, "Charles H. Gilbert, Pioneer Ichthyologist and Fishery Biologist," *Marine Fisheries Review* 58 (Winter-Spring 1996): 1–2.

10. David S. Jordan, and Charles H. Gilbert, "Notes on the Fishes of the Pacific Coast of the United States," *The Proceedings of the United States National Museum* 4 (1881): 45.

11. David S. Jordan, "The Fisheries of the Pacific Coast," in G. Brown Goode, ed., *The Fisheries and Fishing Industries of the United States;* and J.W. Collins, "Report on the Fisheries of the Pacific Coast of the United States," as cited in Arthur F. McEvoy, *The Fisherman's Problem: Ecology and Law in the California Fisheries, 1850–1980* (New York: Cambridge University Press, 1990), 65.

12. McEvoy, *Fisherman's Problem,* 89.

13. G. Brown Goode, *American Fishes: A Popular Treatise upon the Game and Food and Food Fishes of North America* (Boston: Estes and Lauriant, 1887), 212–13, 220.

14. Holder, *Big Game Fishes,* 56; Charles F. Holder and David Starr Jordan, *Fish Stories Alleged and Experienced* (New York: Henry Holt and Company, 1909), 205; Holder, "Return of the Leaping Tuna," 537.

15. George Reiger, *Profiles in Saltwater Angling: A History of the Sport; Its People and Places, Tackle and Techniques* (Englewood Cliffs, N.J.: Prentice-Hall, 1973), 78.

16. Charles F. Holder, "Attempts to Protect the Sea Fisheries of Southern California," *California Fish and Game* 1 (October 1914): 9.

17. Holder, "Return of the Leaping Tuna," 538.

18. Arthur N. Macrate, *The History of the Tuna Club* (Avalon, Calif.: n.p., [1948]), 27.

19. Charles F. Holder, *Cosmopolitan,* as quoted in Horace Annesley Vachell, "Sea Fishing in Californian Waters," *Overland Monthly* 30 (December 1897): 484.

20. *Pasadena Daily News,* June 2, 1898, as quoted in Reiger, *Profiles in Saltwater Angling,* 76.

21. Vachell, "Sea Fishing in Californian Waters," 484.

22. Charles F. Holder, *The Log of a Sea Angler* (Boston: Houghton, Mifflin, and Co., 1906), 212.

23. Holder, *Log of a Sea Angler*, 206.

24. *Los Angeles Daily News*, as quoted in Reiger, *Profiles in Saltwater Angling*, 77.

25. Reiger, *Profiles in Saltwater Angling*, 77–78.

26. Charles F. Holder, *The Channel Islands of California: A Book for the Angler, Sportsman, and Tourist* (Chicago: A.C. McClurg & Co., 1910), 78–79.

27. "Santa Catalina Island," *Los Angeles Times*, August 20, 1899, p. A7.

28. Holder, *Log of a Sea Angler*, 206.

29. Holder, *Log of a Sea Angler*, 206–7.

30. Dwight G. French, "Fishing at Santa Catalina Island—Its Development and Methods," *California Fish and Game* 2 (1916): 14–19.

31. Macrate, *History of the Tuna Club*, 93; *San Francisco Examiner*, August 25, 1911, as cited in Michael L. Farrior, *The History of the Tuna Club, 1898–1998* (Avalon, Santa Catalina Island, Calif.: Tuna Club Foundation, 2004).

32. Macrate, *History of the Tuna Club*, 49.

33. Holder, *Channel Islands of California*, 77.

34. Zane Grey, *Tales of Fishes* (New York: Harper & Brothers, 1919), 221–25.

35. Earl Chapin May, *The Canning Clan: A Pageant of Pioneering Americans* (New York: Macmillan Company, 1937), 196.

36. Zane Grey, *Tales of Swordfish and Tuna* (New York: Grosset & Dunlap, 1927), pl. II, p. 96.

37. Ernest Hemingway, "Tuna Fishing in Spain," *Toronto Star Weekly*, February 18, 1922; Thomas H. Lineaweaver, "Test Time for Tuna," *Sports Illustrated*, September 10, 1956, http://sportsillustrated.cnn.com/vault/article/magazine/MAG1131724/index.htm.

38. Ernest Hemingway, *Old Man and the Sea* (New York: Scribner's Sons, 1952), 43, 64, 66, 82.

39. Hemingway, *Old Man and the Sea*.

40. See the menu of the annual banquet, sponsored by the Tuna Club, at the Metropole Hotel, Santa Catalina Island, California, June 15, 1901, http://digitalgallery.nypl.org/nypldigital/id?471754.

41. May, *Canning Clan*, 191.

42. Holder, *Channel Islands of California*, 68.

43. Charles Holder, *Salt Water Game Fishing* (New York: Outing Publishing Co., 1914), 106.

44. Holder, *Log of a Sea Angler*, 206.

45. Holder, "Attempts to Protect the Sea Fisheries," 12.

46. "Question Is Answered: Dearth of Tuna Comprehensible When the Activity of Japanese Fishermen Is Considered," *Los Angeles Times*, September 26, 1913, sec. 2, p. 8.

47. "Oppose Fish Bill," *Los Angeles Times*, May 15, 1915, sec. 2, p. 8.

48. *Pacific Fisherman* 17 (September 1919): 56; *Pacific Fisherman* 18 (July 1920): 66.

49. Grey, *Tales of Fishes*, 252.

50. Holder, *Big Game Fishes*, 78; F. L. Harding, "The Oceanic Game Fishes of the United States, Comparative Notes by an Angler on Their Size, Distribution, Food, Appearance and Manner of Capture—Third Paper," *Field and Stream* 8 (July 1906): 435.

51. "Ship Four Tons of Fish: Big Catch of Barracuda and White Sea Bass Sent from Catalina Island to Mainland," *Los Angeles Times*, March 9, 1910, sec. 2, p. 10.

52. Tom Meade and Paul C. Nicholson, *The Atlantic Tuna Club: Then and Now* ([South Kingstown, R.I.]: The Club, 1992).

53. George R. Carter, *Preliminary Catalogue of Hawaiiana in the Library of George R. Carter* (Boston: The Heintzemann Press, 1915), 79; H. Gooding Field, "Hawaiian Fish and Fishing," *American Angler* 1 (Winter 1916): 241–45.

54. Sealord Products, *Fin 'N' Shell Cookery, with Favorite Recipes of Members and Friends of the Bay Shore Tuna Club, Inc.* (Bay Shore, N.Y.: Bay Shore Tuna Club, 1971).

55. Charles Bradford, "The New Tuna Club," *The American Angler* 2 (February 1918): 510.

2. LOOKS LIKE CHICKEN

1. The phrase "Chicken of the Sea" had been used since the nineteenth century; however, it did not refer to tuna, but to other fish, specifically sheepshead and whiting. Nineteenth- and early twentieth-century observers compared tuna to veal. Nobody knows who first compared canned albacore to chicken, but the most commonly cited story is the one related above, Albert P. Halfhill and Sig Seeman's conversation, which happened in 1908. In his own writings, Halfhill made no such claim. When Seeman wrote about the early days of the tuna industry and his relationship with Albert Halfhill, he also made no mention of the chicken-tuna connection. The incident wasn't first recorded until 1932, eight years after Halfhill's death and two years after Seeman's. Halfhill's sons and others embellished this tale for the next thirty years. It was a good story, and it has been repeated so often that it is enshrined in books and articles. See Jonathan Pereira, *A Treatise on Food and Diet: with Observations on the Dietetical Regimen* (New York: Fowler & Wells, 1843), 133; "Our Modern Mercury," *Once a Week* 11 (February 2, 1861): 151; *Cassell's Dictionary of Cookery* (London: Cassell Petter & Galpin, [ca. 1870]), 999; "Tunny Fishing," *New York Times*, October 25, 1874, p. 3; *Appleton's Journal* 13 (May 29, 1875): 701; J. L. W. Thudichum, *The Spirit of Cookery:*

A Popular Treatise on the History, Science, Practice and Ethical and Medical Import of Culinary Art (London and New York: Frederick Warne and Co., 1895), 539; "The Pioneer of the Tuna Industry," in *Pacific Fisherman Year Book* (Seattle: Pacific Fisherman, 1923), 79; "Trials of Tuna Pioneers as Told by the Late Sig Seeman," *Pacific Fisherman* 29 (February 1931): 20; Earl Chapin May, *The Canning Clan: A Pageant of Pioneering Americans* (New York: Macmillan Company, 1937), 191, 194; *The Federal Reporter* 56 (1932): 798; John Springer and Seymour Francis, "Los Angeles-Long Beach: Development by the Fishing Industry, among Others, the Great Ports Are Atomic-Age Wonders," *Pan-American Fisherman* 3 (December 1948): 32; C. P. Halfhill, *Birth of a Mighty Industry* (Long Beach, Calif.: Halfhill Company, South Pacific Canning, 1951); *Pacific Fisherman* 60 (January 1962): 25.

2. "Trials of Tuna Pioneers," 20.

3. W. Lyman Underwood, "Incidents in the Canning Industry of New England," in Arthur I. Judge, ed., *A History of the Canning Industry: Souvenir of the Seventh Annual Convention of the National Canners' Association and Allied Associations* (Baltimore: The Canning Trade, 1914), 12–14; Mary B. Sim, *Commercial Canning in New Jersey: History and Early Development* (Trenton: New Jersey Agricultural Society, 1951), 16.

4. May, *Canning Clan*, 107–10; Mary de Sales McLellan, "William Hume, 1830–1902," *Oregon Historical Quarterly* 35 (September 1934).

5. Donald Hume Fry, *The Ring Net, Half Ring Net, or Purse Lampara in the Fisheries of California* ([Sacramento: California State Print. Off., 1931]), 7; Thomas Wolff, *In Pursuit of Tuna: The Expansion of a Fishing Industry and Its International Ramifications—The End of an Era* (Tempe: Center for Latin American Studies, Arizona State University, 1980), 1.

6. "Pioneer of the Tuna Industry," 79; James Terry White, *The National Cyclopaedia of American Biography* (Ann Arbor, Mich.: University Microfilms, 1967), 33:375; May, *Canning Clan*, 190.

7. Charles F. Holder, *The Log of a Sea Angler* (Boston: Houghton, Mifflin, and Co., 1906), 198; F. L Harding, "Comparative Notes by an Angler on Their Size, Distribution, Food, Appearance and Manner of Capture—Third Paper," *Field and Stream* 8 (July 1906): 435; James Miller Guinn, *History of California and an Extended History of Los Angeles* (Los Angeles: Los Angeles Record Company, 1915), 2:141; *Pacific Fisherman* 15 (June 1917): 26; Hugh M. Smith, "Notes on a Reconnaissance of the Fisheries of the Pacific Coast of the United States in 1894," *Bulletin of the United States Fish Commission for 1894*, vol. 14 (Washington, D.C.: Government Printing Office, 1895), 230; Charles H. Smith, *The History of Fuller's Ohio Brigade, 1861–1865: Its Great March* (Cleveland: A. J. Watt, 1909), 376.

8. "The California Sardines," *New York Times*, November 12, 1899, p. 26; Tage Skogsberg, "Preliminary Investigation of the Purse Seine Industry of Southern California," *Fish Bulletin* 9 (Sacramento: California Division of Fish and Game,

1925), 9; W. L. Scofield, "Purse Seines and Other Roundhaul Nets in California," *Bulletin,* no. 81 (Sacramento: California Department of Fish and Game, 1951), 26–27; Wolff, *In Pursuit of Tuna,* 1.

9. A. Bert Bynon, *San Pedro: Its History* (Los Angeles: Boyle Heights Press, 1899), 18; "The California Sardines," 26; Springer and Francis, "Los Angeles-Long Beach," 31.

10. Springer and Francis, "Los Angeles-Long Beach," 31.

11. Springer and Francis, "Los Angeles-Long Beach," 31.

12. "Pioneer of the Tuna Industry," 79; Harris Newmark, *Sixty Years in Southern California (1853–1913)* (New York: Knickerbocker Press, 1916), 619; May, *Canning Clan,* 192.

13. A. W. Bitting, *Appertizing; or, the Art of Canning* (San Francisco: Trade Pressroom, 1937), 842.

14. E. C. Johnston, "Long-Finned Tuna: Albatross 1916" (unpublished manuscript, 1916), 16; "Trials of Tuna Pioneers," 20.

15. *Long Beach Evening Tribune,* October 27, 1904, as cited in Ann M. Peterson, "Recollections of Andrea Gomez: Terminal Island Fish Cannery Employee and Union Organizer, 1924–1965" (master's thesis, California State University, Long Beach, 2005), 9.

16. *Report of the Commissioner for the Year Ending June 30, 1897,* United States Fish Commission, pt. 23 (Washington, D.C.: Government Printing Office, 1898), clx; Guinn, *History of California,* 3:797–98; May, *Canning Clan,* 192; quote from Halfhill, *Birth of a Mighty Industry;* "New Sea Food Given World," *Los Angeles Times,* July 26, 1914, sec. 2, p. 3; Springer and Francis, "Los Angeles-Long Beach," 31.

17. Deborah Belgum, "Another Try for Tuna Industry: A San Pedro Cannery Reopens, Bringing Signs of Life Back to the Waterfront," *Los Angeles Times,* July 9, 1996, p. 1.

18. "Pioneer of the Tuna Industry," 79; Guinn, *History of California,* 2:140; "New Sea Food Given World," 3.

19. "The Housekeeper's Directory," *Good Housekeeping* 45 (December 1907): 755.

20. Vermont State Board of Health, *Bulletin* 4 (March 1, 1910): unpaginated appendix.

21. "Pioneer of the Tuna Industry," 79; "Trials of Tuna Pioneers," 20; *The Federal Reporter* 56 (1932): 798; *Trade-Mark Reporter* 23, 2nd ser. (1933): 373; May, *Canning Clan,* 191.

22. Guinn, *History of California,* 2:140; Transcript on Appeal, Southern California Fish Company vs. White Star Canning Corporation, in the Superior Court of the State of California in and for the County of Los Angeles, filed May 14, 1919, pp. 42, 64, 68.

23. N. B. Scofield, "The Tuna Canning Industry of Southern California,"

Twenty-Third Biennial Report of the Board of Fish and Game Commission of the State of California for the Years 1912–1914 (Sacramento: State Printing Office, 1914), 116; Wolff, *In Pursuit of Tuna*, 1; John Cornish Swift, "The Tuna Fishery of Southern California" (master's thesis, University of California, Berkeley, 1956), 52, 61.

24. A.C. Hoff, comp. and ed., *Salads and Salad Dressings by the World Famous Chefs, United States, Canada, Europe* (Los Angeles: International Publishing Co., 1913), 19.

25. *Post-Standard* (Syracuse), January 6, 1913, p. 9; *Pacific Fisherman* 11 (January 1913): 86; *Brooklyn Daily Eagle*, February 2, 1913, p. 3.

26. "Are You Enjoying Tuna Fish?" *The Mercury* (Hobart, Tasmania), April 28, 1916, p. 4.

27. *Pacific Fisherman* 15 (July 1915): 29.

28. *White Star Brand Tuna Fish "Chicken of the Sea"* (Los Angeles: White Star Canning Co., [ca. 1914]).

29. *Indianapolis Star*, December 5, 1912; Frances Barber Harris, *Florida Salads* (Jacksonville, Fla.: n.p., 1914), 18; Edwin L. Hedderly, "Report of the Los Angeles District Office," *Twenty-Fourth Biennial Report of the Board of Fish and Game Commission of the State of California for the Years 1914–1916* (Sacramento: State Printing Office, 1916), 146.

30. C.E. Pierce Co., "Pierce's Brand California Tunny" (San Francisco: C.E. Pierce Co., 1913), n.p.; "Tuna Fish: Sea Chicken," *Trenton Evening Times*, June 10, 1915, p. 11; *American Angler* 1 (Summer 1916): 61; Guy T. Keene, "Catching and Canning Sea Chicken," *The Rotarian* 11 (December 1917): 529; Mae Savell Croy, *Putnam's Household Handbook* (New York: G.P. Putnam's Sons, 1916), 101.

31. In October 1914 Warren C. King sent a letter to other tuna packers informing them that they could not use "the word 'chicken' in any form or in any wording." They ignored his edict. Over the following two decades, lawsuits were generated over who had the legal right to the tuna-chicken connection. These were resolved in the 1930s with the decision that the word "chicken" was a generic term and could not be patented or trademarked. From then on, packers were free to compare their tuna to chicken. See Transcript on Appeal, Southern California Fish Company vs. White Star Canning Corporation, in the Superior Court of the State of California in and for the County of Los Angeles, filed December 15, 1916; *The Federal Reporter* 56 (1932): 798; or *Trade-Mark Reporter*, 23, 2nd ser. (1933): 373.

32. *Los Angeles Times*, June 1, 1913, sec. 3, p. 17.

33. "Make Fortunes Canning Fish," *Los Angeles Times*, July 13, 1913, p. 11; Guinn, *History of California*, 2:139–41; Transcript on Appeal, Southern California Fish Company vs. White Star Canning Corporation, in the Superior Court of the State of California in and for the County of Los Angeles, filed May 14, 1919, pp. 6, 64, 68; "First Tuna Packer Dies," *Los Angeles Times*, May 8, 1924, p. 1; *Pacific Fisherman* 11 (August 1913): 32; Scofield, "Tuna Canning Industry," 116.

34. *Pacific Fisherman* 12 (September 1914): 29.

35. *Pacific Fisherman* 11 (September 1913): 66; C. E. Pierce Co., "Pierce's Brand California Tunny."

36. "Make Fortunes Canning Fish," 11; Scofield, "Tuna Canning Industry," 116.

37. Transcript on Appeal, Southern California Fish Company vs. White Star Canning Corporation, in the Superior Court of the State of California in and for the County of Los Angeles, filed May 14, 1919, p. 68.

38. Springer and Francis, "Los Angeles-Long Beach," 31.

39. *Pacific Fisherman* 11 (April 1913): 21; *Pacific Fisherman* 11 (September 1913): 66; *Pacific Fisherman* 11 (October 1913): 24.

40. Guinn, *History of California*, 2:140, 3:797.

41. *Pacific Fisherman* 15 (February 1915): 25; White, *National Cyclopaedia of American Biography*, 33:375.

42. Guinn, *History of California*, 2:139–41; *Pacific Fisherman* 14 (March 1916): 25; Transcript on Appeal, Southern California Fish Company vs. White Star Canning Corporation, in the Superior Court of the State of California in and for the County of Los Angeles, filed May 14, 1919, p. 64, 68; "First Tuna Packer Dies," 1.

43. Guinn, *History of California*, 2:140; Transcript on Appeal, Southern California Fish Company vs. White Star Canning Corporation, in the Superior Court of the State of California in and for the County of Los Angeles, filed May 14, 1919, p. 64, 68.

44. *Pacific Fisherman* 11 (April 1913): 21; *Pacific Fisherman* 11 (August 1913): 32.

45. *Pacific Fisherman* 11 (January 1913): 86.

46. *Pacific Fisherman* 13 (December 1915): 24; "Tuna Packers Investigate New Methods," *Pacific Fisherman* 14 (March 1916): 25; "Still Believe Purse Seines Will Catch Tuna," *Pacific Fisherman* 14 (April 1916): 21; "Pioneer of the Tuna Industry," 79.

47. "New Cannery Promised: San Pedro Concern Which Makes Specialty of Tuna, Will Double Its Capacity—News Briefs," *Los Angeles Times*, March 17, 1914, sec. 2, p. 8; Anthony Hallett and Diane Hallett, *Entrepreneur Magazine Encyclopedia of Entrepreneurs* (New York: Wiley, 1997), 464; May, *Canning Clan*, 292; "Gilbert Van Camp Dies; Developed Tuna Industry," *Los Angeles Times*, September 10, 1978, p. SD_A12.

48. "Tuna Industry Leaps Forward," *Los Angeles Times*, April 29, 1914, sec. 2, p. 7; "The Story of Tuna Is the Story of Van Camp," *Tuna Fisherman* 1 (April 1949): inside cover.

49. Springer and Francis, "Los Angeles-Long Beach," 33.

50. *Pacific Fisherman* 12 (February 1914).

51. Scofield, "Tuna Canning Industry," 114.

52. N. B. Scofield, "Report of Department of Commercial Fisheries," *Twenty-*

Fourth Biennial Report of the Board of Fish and Game Commission of the State of California for the Years 1914–1916 (Sacramento: State Printing Office, 1916): 84.

53. "The Tuna Industry," *Los Angeles Times,* September 26, 1914, sec. 2, p. 4.

54. *Long Beach Daily Telegram,* June 30, 1914, as cited in Peterson, "Recollections of Andrea Gomez," 10.

55. *Pacific Fisherman* 15 (October 1915): 24.

56. "A War Time Need," *Pacific Fisherman* 18 (April 1918): 55.

57. N.B. Scofield, "Commercial Fishery Notes," *California Fish and Game* 3 (January 20, 1917): 34–35.

58. *Long Beach Press,* July 16, 1915, as quoted in Peterson, "Recollections of Andrea Gomez," 10.

59. Scofield, "Report of Department of Commercial Fisheries," 84.

60. "Tuna Passes Salmon; Worth More to State," *Los Angeles Times,* April 13, 1916, sec. 3, p. 3; *Pacific Fisherman* 14 (June 1916): 31; "Tuna Canning Industry," 86, 89; John Bentley Robinson, "In the News Net," *The American Angler* (December 1917): 446; *Pacific Fisherman* 50 (August 1952): 22; Lenna F. Cooper, *How to Cut Food Costs* (Battle Creek, Mich.: Good Health Pub. Co., 1917), 36.

61. "Tuna Jumps to Double Price," *Los Angeles Times,* October 23, 1916, p. 17.

62. "Eat More Fish," *Pacific Fisherman* 17 (September 1917): 17.

63. *Federal Reserve Bulletin* 4 (January 1, 1918): 50.

64. *The Norwegian American Chamber of Commerce Bulletin* 3 (February-March 1920): 17; May, *Canning Clan,* 192.

65. Springer and Francis, "Los Angeles-Long Beach," 33.

66. *American Food Journal* 12 (May 1917): 265; E.C. Starks, "Common Names of Fishes," *California Fish and Game* 4 (October 1918): 188; Bitting, *Appertizing,* 843.

67. *Pacific Fisherman* 12 (March 1914): 20; Kanichi Kawasaki, "The Japanese Community of East San Pedro, Terminal Island, California" (master's thesis, University of Southern California, 1931), 44, 46.

68. *Fourteenth Biennial Report of the State Board of Fish Commissioners for the Years 1895–96* (Sacramento: State Printing Office, 1896), 15–16; Swift, "Tuna Fishery of Southern California," 53; Frederick Bohme, "The Portuguese of California," *California Historical Society Quarterly* 35 (September 1956): 239–40.

69. *Walker's Manual of California Securities and Directory of Directors,* 12th Annual Number (San Francisco: H.D. Walker, 1920), 188.

70. Arthur F. McEvoy, *The Fisherman's Problem: Ecology and Law in the California Fisheries, 1850–1980* (New York: Cambridge University Press, 1990), 133.

71. *Pacific Fisherman* 20 (August 1922): 32; "News of the Trade," *American Food Journal* 17 (July 1922): 33.

72. Hallett and Hallett, *Encyclopedia of Entrepreneurs,* 464.

73. *Pacific Fisherman* 19 (June 1921): 50.

74. *Pacific Fisherman* 21 (July 1923): 32.

75. Swift, "Tuna Fishery of Southern California," 62.

76. *Tuna Fisherman* 1 (February 1948): 17–18; William C. Richardson, "The Fishermen of San Diego" (master's thesis, San Diego State University, 1981), 112.

77. August J. Felando, "California's Tuna Clipper Fleet: 1918–1963; Part 1," *Mains'l Haul* 32:4 (1996): 6; *The Tuna Fishing and Packing Industry of California* (Los Angeles: William R. Staats Co., 1949), 1.

78. Geraldine Conner, "Expansion of Tuna Fishing Areas," in "The Commercial Fish Catch of California for the Year 1929," *Fish Bulletin* 30 (Sacramento: Bureau of Commercial Fisheries, 1931), 23–31.

79. Richard Pourade, *The History of San Diego* (San Diego: Union-Tribune Pub. Co., 1967), 6:99.

80. Conner, "Expansion of Tuna Fishing Areas," 23–31; American Fishermen's Research Foundation, http://wfoa-tuna.org/health/historyalbacoreindustry.pdf.

81. *National Geographic* 95 (May 1949): 560; John Springer, "Editorial," *Pan-American Fisherman* 5 (July 1951): 6; Richard Ellis, *Tuna: A Love Story* (New York: Alfred A. Knopf, 2008), 217.

82. *Pacific Fisherman* 15 (August 1915): 19.

83. *Statistical Digest,* Issue 59 (Washington, D.C.: U.S. Fish and Wildlife Service, Bureau of Commercial Fisheries, 1967), 387.

84. Oliver Vickery, *Harbor Heritage: Tales of the Harbor Area of Los Angeles, California* (Mountain View, Calif.: Morgan Press/Farag, 1978), 90.

85. *Pacific Fisherman* 15 (July 1915): 29; Newmark, *Sixty Years in Southern California,* 628; *Pacific Fisherman* 15 (April 1917): 14; *Pacific Fisherman* 21 (October 1923): 46; James Collins, *The Story of Canned Foods* (New York: E.P. Dutton and Company, 1924), 132; *The Federal Reporter* 56 (1932): 798; May, *Canning Clan,* 194; A.W. Anderson, W.H. Stolting, et al., *Survey of the Domestic Tuna Industry,* U.S. Fish and Wildlife Services, Special Scientific Report: Fisheries, no. 104 (Washington, D.C.: Department of the Interior, 1952), 12.

86. Kenneth Crist, "Tuna! All Hands on Deck!" *Los Angeles Times,* October 28, 1934, p. J10.

87. *Pacific Fisherman* 22 (April 1924): 33; "Gilbert Van Camp Dies," p. SD_A12.

3. ENEMY ALIENS

1. Kanichi Kawasaki, "The Japanese Community of East San Pedro, Terminal Island, California" (master's thesis, University of Southern California, 1931), 31–37.

2. *Twenty-First Biennial Report of the Board of Fish and Game Commissioners of the State of California for the Years 1909–10* (Sacramento: Superintendent State Printing, 1910), 41.

3. Kawasaki, "Japanese Community of East San Pedro," 37–41.

4. Earl Chapin May, *The Canning Clan: A Pageant of Pioneering Americans* (New York: Macmillan Company, 1937), 192; Kawasaki, "Japanese Community of East San Pedro," 39, 41.

5. Kawasaki, "Japanese Community of East San Pedro," 43.

6. Roger Daniels, *Prejudice of Prejudice: The Anti-Japanese Movement in California and the Struggle for Japanese Exclusion* (Berkeley: University of California Press, 1977), 54–55, 98.

7. Census and immigration data, as presented in Daniels, *Prejudice of Prejudice*, 1; John Modell, *The Economics and Politics of Racial Accommodation: The Japanese of Los Angeles, 1900–1942* (Urbana: University of Illinois Press, 1977), 17.

8. Helen R. Crane, "A Japanese Fishing Village," *Los Angeles Times,* November 24, 1929, p. F13; John Cornish Swift, "The Tuna Fishery of Southern California" (master's thesis, University of California, Berkeley, 1956), 62–67.

9. Kawasaki, "Japanese Community of East San Pedro," 43; David Metzler and Allyson Nakamoto, "The Lost Village of Terminal Island" (Culver City, Calif.: Our Stories, 2007), DVD (this DVD interviews Terminal Islanders).

10. Kawasaki, "Japanese Community of East San Pedro," 46; Charles Langdon White and Edwin Jay Foscue, *Regional Geography of Anglo-America*, 2nd ed. (New York: Prentice-Hall, 1954), 384.

11. *Pacific Fisherman* 15 (June 1917): 26.

12. *Pacific Fisherman* 14 (March 1916): 25.

13. Kanshi Stanley Yamashita, "Terminal Island: Ethnography of an Ethnic Community; Its Dissolution and Reorganization to a Non-spatial Community" (PhD diss., University of California, Irvine, 1985), 83.

14. Daniels, *Prejudice of Prejudice*, 87–88.

15. Samuel Lawrence, "Fishing Village Brings Atmosphere of Old Japan to Los Angeles Harbor," *Los Angeles Times,* April 25, 1926, p. B10; Crane, "Japanese Fishing Village," F13; Kawasaki, "Japanese Community of East San Pedro," 48; "One Hour Away," *Los Angeles Times,* April 28, 1935, pp. 11, 18, B10; Lilian Takahashi Hoffecker, "A Village Disappeared," *American Heritage* 52 (November/December 2001), www.americanheritage.com/articles/magazine/ah/2001/8/2001_8_64.shtml.

16. Crane, "Japanese Fishing Village," F13; Kawasaki, "Japanese Community of East San Pedro," 50.

17. James Miller Guinn, *History of California and an Extended History of Los Angeles* (Los Angeles: Historic Record Company, 1915), 3:798.

18. *Twenty-Third Biennial Report of the Board of Fish and Game Commission of the State of California for the Years 1912–1914* (Sacramento: State Printing Office, 1914), 118.

19. Kenneth Crist, "Tuna! All Hands on Deck!" *Los Angeles Times*, October 28, 1934, p. J10.

20. *Report of the United States Commissioner of Fisheries for the Fiscal Year Ending June 30, 1914*, document 807 (Washington, D.C.: Bureau of Fisheries, 1915), 36; Russell Palmer, "California Tuna Canning," in *Pacific Fisherman Year Book* (Seattle: Pacific Fisherman, 1915), 76.

21. *Report of the United States Commissioner of Fisheries for the Fiscal Year Ending June 30, 1914*, 36.

22. William C. Richardson, "Fishermen of San Diego: The Italians," *Journal of San Diego History* 27 (Fall 1981), https://www.sandiegohistory.org/journal/81fall/fishermen.htm.

23. William C. Richardson, "Fishermen of San Diego" (master's thesis, San Diego State University, 1981), 47.

24. *Pacific Fisherman*, as quoted in *Fish and Game Commission* 1 (October 1914): 72.

25. N. B. Scofield, "Commercial Fishery Notes," *California Fish and Game* 3 (January 20, 1917): 34–35.

26. *Pacific Fisherman* 15 (November 1915): 24; *Pacific Fisherman* 19 (May 1921): 46; Gunki Kai, "Economic Status of the Japanese in California" (master's thesis, Stanford University, 1922), 57.

27. John Modell, "The Japanese of Los Angeles: A Study in Growth and Accommodation, 1900–1946" (PhD diss., Columbia University, 1969), 101.

28. Kawasaki, "Japanese Community of East San Pedro," 44; Modell, *Economics and Politics of Racial Accommodation*, 119.

29. *Pacific Fisherman* 13 (December 1915): 24; "Floating Cannery for Packing Tuna," *Los Angeles Times*, February 1, 1916, sec. 2, p. 10; Kawasaki, "Japanese Community of East San Pedro," 42–44, 47, 130; *Pacific Fisherman* 14 (April 1916): 21.

30. "Japanese Fishermen's Association Opens Office," *Pacific Fisherman* 14 (April 1916): 21; Kawasaki, "Japanese Community of East San Pedro," 44.

31. "Japs Break Up Harbor Strike," *Los Angeles Times*, April 30, 1914, sec. 2, p. 8.

32. "White Fishermen to Break Jap Monopoly," *Pacific Fisherman* 15 (March 1915): 28; "Jap Fishermen Come to Terms," *Los Angeles Times*, May 7, 1915, sec. 2, p. 8; Swift, "Tuna Fishery of Southern California," 64–65.

33. *Pacific Fisherman* 14 (December 1916): 25.

34. "Tuna Jumps to Double Price," *Los Angeles Times*, October 23, 1916, p. 17.

35. *Pacific Fisherman* 18 (May 1918): 47 and 49; "Cannery Wages Cut; Fifty Workers Quit," *Los Angeles Times*, June 13, 1918, p. 16; "Crandall Says Japs Must Fish," *Los Angeles Times*, July 5, 1918, sec. 1, p. 11; "Japanese Fishermen Refuse Price Offer," *Los Angeles Times*, July 15, 1918, p. 13; "Fishermen's Strike Ends;

Bonus Allowed," *Los Angeles Times*, July 16, 1918, sec. 2, p. 5; *Pacific Fisherman* 18 (July 1918): 51; *Pacific Fisherman* 18 (1918): 42; William Clinton Mullendore, *History of the United States Food Administration, 1917–1919* (Stanford, Calif.: Stanford University Press, 1941), 276; Modell, *Economics and Politics of Racial Accommodation*, 125.

36. Swift, "Tuna Fishery of Southern California," 69.

37. *Pacific Fisherman* 17 (June 1919): 46; *Pacific Fisherman* 17 (July 1919): 67.

38. Edwin Fitton Bamford, *Social Aspects of the Fishing Industry at Los Angeles Harbor*, Studies in Sociology, Sociological Monograph, no. 18, vol. 5 (January, 1921) (Los Angeles: The Southern California Sociological Society, University of Southern California, [1921]).

39. Modell, "Japanese of Los Angeles," 184.

40. *Pacific Fisherman* 19 (June 1921): 52.

41. Donald H. Estes, "Asama Gunkan: The Reappraisal of a War Scare," *Journal of San Diego History* 24 (Summer 1978), www.sandiegohistory.org/journal/78summer/asama.htm; Daniels, *Prejudice of Prejudice*, 70–71.

42. Daniels, *Prejudice of Prejudice*, 27.

43. Daniels, *Prejudice of Prejudice*, 44.

44. Modell, *Economics and Politics of Racial Accommodation*, 5; Yamashita, "Terminal Island," 75–76.

45. Daniels, *Prejudice of Prejudice*, 63.

46. Sidney Lewis Gulick, *Anti-Japanese War-Scare Stories* (New York: Fleming H. Revell Company, 1917), 20.

47. Modell, *Economics and Politics of Racial Accommodation*, 52.

48. Modell, *Economics and Politics of Racial Accommodation*, 53.

49. "Will Wipe Out Fish Industry," *Los Angeles Times*, June 12, 1919, sec. 2, pp. 1, 3.

50. *Pacific Fisherman* 18 (August 1920): 34.

51. *Pacific Fisherman* 21 (February 1923): 46.

52. *Pacific Fisherman* 16 (January 1918): 49; *Pacific Fisherman* 17 (October 1919): 58; *Administration of Immigration Laws: Hearings Before the Committee on Immigration and Naturalization, House of Representatives, Sixty-Sixth Congress, Second Session, March 30 and 31 and April 6, 1920* (Washington, D.C.: Government Printing Office, 1920), 362; *Pacific Fisherman* 18 (September 1920): 55; *Pacific Fisherman* 21 (January 1923): 40; *Tuna Imports: Hearings Before the Committee on Finance, United States Senate, Eighty-Second Congress* (Washington, D.C.: Government Printing Office, 1952), 23.

53. *Pacific Fisherman* 19 (May 1921): 46; *Pacific Fisherman* 22 (February 1924): 46; *Pacific Fisherman* 22 (April 1924): 34.

54. *Press Reference Library: Notables of the Southwest* (Los Angeles: Los Angeles Examiner, 1912), 458.

55. David Starr Jordan, "The Perennial Bogey of War," *The World's Work* 25 (November 1912): 195; Don Estes, "Kondo Masaharu and the Best of All Fishermen," *Journal of San Diego History* 23 (Summer 1977): 2; José Adán Cháirez A., *Historia de la pesca del atún en México* (Ensenada, B.C., Mexico: Editorial Chairez, 1996), 1:190–94.

56. Jordan, "Perennial Bogey of War," 195; Estes, "Kondo Masaharu," 18; Eugene Keith Chamberlin, "The Japanese Scare at Magdalena Bay," *Pacific Historical Review* 24 (November 1955): 348.

57. Estes, "Asama Gunkan"; Chamberlin, "Japanese Scare at Magdalena Bay," 348.

58. *Pacific Fisherman* 12 (September 1914): 29; *Twenty-Third Biennial Report of the Board of Fish and Game Commission*, 116; Jeffery M. Dorwart, *The Office of Naval Intelligence: The Birth of America's First Intelligence Agency, 1865–1918* (Annapolis, Md.: Naval Institute Press, 1979), 179.

59. Gulick, *Anti-Japanese War-Scare Stories*, 31–33; Frank F. Chuman, *The Bamboo People: The Law and Japanese-Americans* (Del Mar, Calif.: Publisher's Inc., 1976), 75; Estes, "Asama Gunkan."

60. *New York Times*, December 14, 1918, p. 1.

61. Gulick, *Anti-Japanese War-Scare Stories*, 28–30.

62. *Pacific Fisherman* 22 (June 1924): 36.

63. Van Antwerp to Cable Censor, San Francisco, November 27, 1918, file 20955–636, as quoted in Dorwart, *Office of Naval Intelligence*, 139.

64. Chuman, *Bamboo People*, 228–29.

65. Don Estes, "'Offensive Stupidity,' and the Struggle of Abe Tokunosuke," *Journal of San Diego History* 28 (Fall 1982), http://www.sandiegohistory.org/journal/82fall/offensive.htm; Modell, "Japanese of Los Angeles," 342.

66. Eiji Tanabe, "The History of Japanese Commercial Fishing," *Pacific Citizen*, March 27, 1948, p. 6.

67. Modell, "Japanese of Los Angeles," 344–45.

68. Tanabe, "History of Japanese Commercial Fishing," 6.

69. Modell, *Economics and Politics of Racial Accommodation*, 175.

70. Estes, "Struggle of Abe Tokunosuke"; August J. Felando, "California's Tuna Clipper Fleet: 1918–1963; Part 2," *Mains'l Haul* 33:1 (1997): 19.

71. John L. Spivak, *Honorable Spy* (New York: Modern Age Books, 1939).

72. "Dies Reports Sabotage Plot; Terminal Isle Center of Japanese Ring Headed by Navy Officers, F.B.I. Told," *Los Angeles Times*, August 1, 1941, p. 1.

73. Chuman, *Bamboo People*, 227; Modell, "Japanese of Los Angeles," abstract.

74. Modell, "Japanese of Los Angeles," 340.

75. Yamashita, "Terminal Island," 139.

76. "Eviction of Jap Aliens Sought," *Los Angeles Times*, January 28, 1942, p. 1; Hoffecker, "Village Disappeared," 64–71; Ann M. Peterson, "Recollections of

Andrea Gomez: Terminal Island Fish Cannery Employee and Union Organizer, 1924–1965" (master's thesis, California State University, Long Beach, 2005), 27; Yamashita, "Terminal Island," 38–39.

77. *Tuna Imports: Hearings Before the Committee on Finance, United States Senate, Eighty-Second Congress,*410.

78. Estes, "Kondo Masaharu," 17.

79. *Fish and Game Code* (Sacramento: California Department of Fish and Game, 1943), 170.

80. Hoffecker, "Village Disappeared."

81. *Pacific Fisherman* 20 (May 1922): 43.

82. Cháirez A., *Historia de la pesca del atún*, 1:189.

83. Bill Hosokawa, *Nisei: The Quiet Americans* (New York: W. Morrow, 1969), 144.

84. Justice Frank Murphy, as quoted in Chuman, *Bamboo People*, 232.

85. Yamashita, "Terminal Island," 139, 144.

86. Estes, "Kondo Masaharu."

4. THIS DELICIOUS FISH

1. Mrs. G. H. Acklin, "Bee-Keeping in Southern California," *Gleanings in Bee Culture* 39 (April 1, 1911): 198.

2. *Boston Cooking-School Magazine* 18 (December 1913): 401. Unfortunately, a copy of the Avalon Brand Tuna booklet has not been located, but the recipes published in Avalon Tuna advertisements were likely ones taken from the booklet.

3. For more information about advertising cookbooklets, see Andrew F. Smith, "Advertising and Promotional Cookbooks," *The Cookbook Collectors' Exchange* (September/October 1999): 5–9.

4. *Argo Red Salmon Cook Book: How to Eat Canned Salmon* (San Francisco: Alaska Packers Association, 1906).

5. A copy of the Avalon Brand "Tuna Receipe Booklet" has not been located. It is mentioned in Avalon Tuna advertisements that appeared in several issues of the *Boston Cooking-School Magazine: Boston Cooking-School Magazine* 18 (November 1913): 325; *Boston Cooking-School Magazine* 18 (December 1913): 401.

6. C. E. Pierce Co., "Pierce's Brand California Tunny" (San Francisco: C. E. Pierce Co., 1913), n.p.

7. *White Star Brand Tuna Fish "Chicken of the Sea"* (Los Angeles: White Star Canning Co., [ca. 1914]).

8. *Panama Brand Tuna Recipes* (Long Beach, Calif.: Los Angeles Tuna Canning Co., [ca. 1914]).

9. Blue Sea Brand Tuna label, ca. 1912.

10. Blue Sea Brand Tuna label, ca. 1912.

11. *Blue Sea Tuna* (Los Angeles: Southern California Fish Co., n.d.).

12. "Hot-House Tomatoes, with Tunny," *Boston Cooking-School Magazine* 17 (February 1913): 558.

13. *Boston Cooking-School Magazine* 18 (August-September 1913): 122.

14. *Boston Cooking-School Magazine* 18 (August-September 1913): 122–23; *Boston Cooking-School Magazine* 18 (October 1913): 210–11; *Boston Cooking-School Magazine* 18 (February 1914): 547–48.

15. *American Cooking* 20 (December 1915): 390.

16. *Brooklyn Daily Eagle*, February 2, 1913, p. 3.

17. *New York Tribune*, August 20, 1914, p. 5.

18. *New York Tribune*, September 10, 1914, p. 5.

19. *New York Tribune*, October 31, 1914, p. 7.

20. *New York Tribune*, March 19, 1914, p. 7.

21. "Serving Tuna Fish," *Aberdeen Daily News*, February 10, 1915, p. 7.

22. "Tuna Now Popular Fish Food," *Christian Science Monitor*, February 19, 1913, p. 11.

23. A.C. Hoff, comp. and ed., *Salads and Salad Dressings by the World Famous Chefs, United States, Canada, Europe* (Los Angeles: International Publishing Co., 1913), 18–19.

24. A.C. Hoff, comp and ed., *Relishes and Appetizers of the World Famous Chefs, United States, Canada, Europe* (Los Angeles: International Book Publishing Co., 1914), 21.

25. Victor Hirtzler, *The Hotel St. Francis Cook Book* (Chicago: The Hotel Monthly Press, 1919), 27, 332.

26. *Recipes for Preparing Steeles Premium California Tuna: Packed in Perfectly Blended Oils* (San Diego: Premier Packing Co., n.d.), n.p.

27. Council of Jewish Women, *The Neighborhood Cook Book*, 2nd ed. (Portland, Ore.: Press of Bushong & Co., 1914), 285.

28. Amelia Doddridge, *Liberty Recipes* (Cincinnati: Stewart & Kidd Co., 1918), 67.

29. "The Housekeeper's Directory," *Good Housekeeping* 45 (December 1907): 755.

30. Olive Green [Myrtle Reed], *One Thousand Salads* (New York and London: G.P. Putnam's Sons, 1909), 87.

31. *The Palisades Cook Book* (Tenafly, N.J.: Ladies' Aid Society, Tenafly Presbyterian Church, 1910), 73.

32. Associated College Women Workers, *The Cook County Cook Book* (Chicago: Press of McElroy Publishing Co., 1912), 489.

33. Hoff, *Salads and Salad Dressings*, 18.

34. C.E. Pierce Co., "Pierce's Brand California Tunny."

35. *Panama Brand Tuna Recipes.*

36. Blue Sea Brand Tuna label, ca. 1912.

37. Frances Barber Harris, *Florida Salads* (Jacksonville, Fla.: n.p., 1914), 18; *Boston Cooking-School Magazine* 18 (February 1914): 548; Ladies' Aid Society, *Up-to-Date Cook Book 1914* (Newark, N.J.: South Park Presbyterian Church, 1914), 77.

38. "Tuna Industry Leaps Forward," *Los Angeles Times,* April 29, 1914, sec. 2, p. 7.

39. Elizabeth Condit and Jessie A. Long, *How to Cook and Why* (New York: Harper and Brothers, 1914), 181.

40. Daughters of the American Revolution, *Favorite Dishes Contributed by the Daughters of the American Revolution* (Clinton, Iowa: Daughters of the American Revolution, Clinton Chapter, 1916), 98.

41. Elizabeth David, *French Provincial Cooking,* rev. ed. (Harmondsworth, Eng.: Penguin, 1970), 171.

42. [Mrs. Alexander Orr Bradley], *Beverages and Sandwiches for Your Husband's Friends by One Who Knows* (New York: Brentano's, 1893), 37–38.

43. *The Rotarian* 6 (June 1915): 18; Transcript on Appeal, Southern California Fish Company vs. White Star Canning Corporation, in the Superior Court of the State of California in and for the County of Los Angeles, filed May 14, 1919, pp. 76–77.

44. Mae Savell Croy, *Putnam's Household Handbook* (New York: G. P. Putnam's Sons, 1916), 101.

45. "The Soda Fountain," *North Western Druggist* 28 (November 1920): 68.

46. *Los Angeles Times,* October 6, 1968, p. WS12; *Family Circle* (June 1975): 115. These references were located by Barry Popik.

47. Reah Jeannette Lynch, *"Win the War" Cook Book* (St. Louis: St. Louis Woman's Committee, Council of National Defense, Missouri Division, 1918), 60.

48. *PTA Cook Book,* 2nd ed. (Petersburg, Alaska: Petersburg Parent Teachers' Association, 1947), 101.

49. *Woman's Day Collector's Cookbook* (New York: Simon and Schuster, 1973), 197–98.

50. *News-Advocate* (Price, Utah), April 9, 1931, p. 7; *Chronicle-Telegram* (Elyria, Ohio), September 18, 1937, p. 9. Other early tuna noodle casserole recipes appeared in *Christian Science Monitor,* January 22, 1937, p. 12; *Chronicle-Telegram* (Elyria, Ohio), July 11, 1939, p. 13. These references were located by Barry Popik.

51. Lyla G. Maxwell, "It Is the Taste That Tells," *Christian Science Monitor,* July 19, 1933, p. 10; "Favorite Recipes in Our Family," *Christian Science Monitor,* January 22, 1937, p. 12; *Daily News* (Frederick, Md.), July 29, 1938, p. 2; *Easy Ways to Good Meals: 99 Delicious Dishes Made with Campbell's Soups* (Camden, N.J.: Campbell Soup Company, 1941), 16.

52. *PTA Cook Book,* 101.

53. Nell Beaubien Nichols, *Good Home Cooking across the U.S.A.: A Source Book of American Foods* (Ames: Iowa State College Press, 1952), 394.

54. Lily Haxworth Wallace, *The Woman's World Cook Book* (Chicago: Reilly & Lee Co., 1931), 285.

55. "Tuna Surprise Croquettes," *Life* 38 (March 21, 1955): 100.

56. *Pacific Fisherman* 62 (February 1964): 5–6; *Life* 56 (February 14, 1964): 46.

57. *White Star Brand Tuna Fish "Chicken of the Sea."*

58. C. E. Pierce Co., "Pierce's Brand California Tunny."

59. *Panama Brand Tuna Recipes.*

60. *Recipes for Preparing Steeles Premium California Tuna.*

61. *Recipes for Preparing Steeles Premium California Tuna.*

62. Jessup Whitehead, *The Steward's Handbook and Guide* (Chicago: [J. Anderson & Co.], 1893), 280.

63. Sunyowe Pang, "Chinese in America," *New York Times Magazine Supplement*, January 5, 1902, p. SM15.

64. *Boston Cooking-School Magazine* 18 (February 1914): 548.

65. *Boston Cooking-School Magazine* 18 (November 1913): 325.

66. *Hoppy's Bar-20 Ranch Recipes Featuring . . . Chicken of the Sea . . . Hoppy's Favorite Brand!* (Los Angeles: V.C.S.F. Co., Inc., 1951).

67. *The Coral Tuna Cookbook* (Honolulu: Hawaiian Tuna Packers, Ltd., 1956).

68. Sheila Metcalf, *The Tuna Cookbook* (Garden City, N.Y.: Doubleday & Company, 1972).

69. Andy Black, *A Can of Tuna: The Complete Guide to Cooking with Tuna* (Santa Rosa, Calif.: Prism Press, 1995).

70. Joie Warner and Drew Warner, *Joie Warner's Take a Tin of Tuna: 65 Inspired Recipes for Every Meal of the Day* (San Francisco: Chronicle Books, 2004).

71. U.S. Department of Labor, "The Tuna Processing Industry," http://www.dol.gov/whd/as/sec3.htm.

72. http://www.vegieworld.com/cart/product_pages.asp?id = 376.

73. *Pacific Fisherman* 15 (December 1917): 29.

5. CAUCASIANS WHO HAVE TASTED AND LIKED THIS SPECIALITY

1. Jane Nickerson, "Japan Big Contributor to the American Table," *New York Times*, October 25, 1956, Family/Style, p. 38.

2. June Owen, "News of Food: Raw Fish Is Appetizer or Main Dish in Various Parts of the World," *New York Times*, August 18, 1954, p. 19; Jane Nickerson, "Japanese Culinary Art for the New Year," *New York Times Magazine*, December 26, 1954, p. 30.

3. Craig Claiborne, "Restaurant on Review; Kabuki Is Japanese and One of the Best," *New York Times*, April 4, 1961, Food, Fashions, Family, Furnishing, p. 40.

4. Craig Claiborne, "Food News from Tokyo," *New York Times*, June 9, 1962, Real Estate, p. 12.

5. Craig Claiborne, "Restaurants on Review; Variety of Japanese Dishes Offered, But Raw Fish Is Specialty on Menu," *New York Times*, November 11, 1963, Real Estate, p. 37.

6. Craig Claiborne, "Food News," *New York Times*, October 17, 1964, Food, Fashions, Family, Furnishings, p. 32.

7. Craig Claiborne, "New Yorkers Take to Tempura and Chopsticks with Gusto," *New York Times*, March 10, 1966, Real Estate, p. 22.

8. Craig Claiborne, "1960s: Haute Cuisine in America," *New York Times*, January 1, 1970, Food, Fashions, Family, Furnishings, p. 27.

9. Josephine E. Tilden, "Algae Collecting in the Hawaiian Islands," in Thomas G. Thrum, ed., *Hawaiian Annual for 1905* (Honolulu: Black & Auld, 1904), 133.

10. Erna Fergusson, *Our Hawaii* (New York: A.A. Knopf, 1942), 32; Owen, "Raw Fish Is Appetizer or Main Dish," 19.

11. Katherine Bazore, *Hawaiian and Pacific Foods: A Cook Book of Culinary Customs and Recipes Adapted for the American Hostess* (New York: M. Barrows and Co., 1940).

12. Aya Kagawa, *Japanese Cook Book*, rev. ed. (Tokyo: Japan Travel Bureau, Inc., 1967), 164.

13. A.W. Anderson, W.H. Stolting, et al., *Survey of the Domestic Tuna Industry*, U.S. Fish and Wildlife Services, Special Scientific Report: Fisheries, no. 104 (Washington, D.C.: Department of the Interior, 1952), 20.

14. *American Magazine* 121 (1936): 130; Owen, "Raw Fish Is Appetizer or Main Dish," 19.

15. David Starr Jordan, *Fishes* (New York: Henry Holt and Co., 1907), 478.

16. "A Fishing Yarn from Japan," *New York Times Magazine*, January 24, 1909, p. 10.

17. Clarence Edwords, *Bohemian San Francisco: Its Restaurants and Their Most Famous Recipes; The Elegant Art of Dining* (San Francisco: Paul Elder and Company, 1914), 59.

18. Koyoshi Uono, "The Factors Affecting Geographical Aggregation and Dispersion of the Japanese Residences in the City of Los Angeles" (master's thesis, University of Southern California, 1927), 54.

19. B.M. Little, "What You Can Eat In Los Angeles," *Los Angeles Times*, September 23, 1934, sec. 1, p. 5.

20. *The Federal Reporter* 36 (1930): 424–25; Atsuko Kanai, "How Sushi Came to California and How Edamamé Came to Be Served There with Sushi," in Wil-

liam Shurtleff and Akiko Aoyagi, eds., *History of Edamamé, Green Vegetable Soybeans, and Vegetable-Type Soybeans* (Lafayette, Calif.: Soyinfo Center, 2009), 631–33.

21. Sasha Issenberg, *The Sushi Economy: Globalization and the Making of a Modern Delicacy* (New York: Gotham Books, 2007), 84.

22. Helen R. Crane, "A Japanese Fishing Village," *Los Angeles Times*, August 24, 1929, p. F13.

23. Kaneko Tezuka, *Japanese Food* ([Tokyo]: Board of Tourist Industry, Japanese Government Railways, 1936), 27.

24. Pearl V. Metzelthin, *World Wide Cook Book: Menus and Recipes of 75 Nations* (New York: J. Messner, 1939), 335.

25. Justus George Frederick, *Long Island Seafood Cook Book* (New York: The Business Bourse, 1939), 279.

26. Issenberg, *Sushi Economy*, 84; Trevor Corson, *The Story of Sushi: An Unlikely Saga of Raw Fish and Rice* (New York: Harper Perennial, 2008), 45.

27. Issenberg, *Sushi Economy*, 85.

28. Kanai, "How Sushi Came to California," 631–33.

29. Issenberg, *Sushi Economy*, 88; David Kamp, *The United States of Arugula: How We Became a Gourmet Nation* (New York: Broadway Books, 2006), 315.

30. Issenberg, *Sushi Economy*, 88.

31. Those crediting Ichiro Mashita with inventing the California Roll are John F. Mariani, *The Encyclopedia of American Food & Drink* (New York: Lebhar-Friedmann Books, 1999), 53; Kanai, "How Sushi Came to California," 631–33; Kamp, *United States of Arugula*, 315; Issenberg, *Sushi Economy*, 90.

32. The earliest located references to the California Roll are "Food Fad," *Ocala Star-Banner*, November 25, 1979, p. 14; "More and More Going for Sushi," *Palm Beach Post*, November 30, 1979, p. 36; *Westways* 71 (November 1979): 76; *Los Angeles Times*, November 25, 1979, Calendar, p. 117; Christine Winter, "News for You; War between the States," *Chicago Tribune*, November 23, 1981, p. F2.

33. Kamp, *United States of Arugula*, 315.

34. Mimi Sheraton, "East Side Steak and Side Dishes of Japan," *New York Times*, March 30, 1981, www.nytimes.com/1981/03/20/arts/restaurants-by-mimi-sheraton-east-side-steak-and-side-dishes-of-japan.html. For other early references to the California Roll, see Florence Fabricant, "Dining Out; Japanese Food with Inventiveness," *New York Times*, March 7, 1982, http://query.nytimes.com/search/sitesearch?date_select = full&query = Japanese+Food+with+Inventiveness%2C&type = nyt&x = 12&y = 8; Florence Fabricant, "Adapting American Foods to Japanese Cuisine," *New York Times*, October 6, 1982, p. C8; Jared Lubarsky, "Studying Art of Sushiology," *Los Angeles Times*, November 24, 1985, p. AB93.

35. Craig Claiborne, "Portland Is Just Full of Restaurant Surprises," *New York Times*, September 7, 1965, Food, Fashions, Family, Furnishings, p. 43; Gregory Curtis, "San Francisco, An Off-Beat Guide," *Texas Monthly* 2 (February 1974): 100.

36. John J. Doherty, "John Belushi," in Ray Browne and Pat Browne, eds., *The Guide to United States Popular Culture* (Bowling Green, Ohio: Bowling Green State University Popular Press, 2001), 78; Rich McHugh, J. P. Anderson, Chris Barsanti, and Mark Ellwood, *Chicago* (New York: Rough Guides, Distributed by the Penguin Group, 2003), 154; Corson, *Story of Sushi*, 46.

37. Jeanne Voltz, "Sushi: A Great New Snack from Japan," *Los Angeles Times*, February 7, 1971, p. 36; Lois Dwan, "Roundabout: Sushi Bar Featured at Masukawa," *Los Angeles Times*, March 28, 1973, p. H11.

38. Corson, *Story of Sushi*, 46–48.

39. "More and More Going for Sushi," 36.

40. Matao Uwate, *Sushi* (Los Angeles: M. Uwate, 1975), 3, 6.

41. Mimi Sheraton, "Restaurants; Stuffed Cabbage and Sushi on East Side," *New York Times*, June 9, 1978, p. C14.

42. Florence Fabricant, "It's Japanese and It's Excellent," *New York Times*, October 14, 1979, p. LI15.

43. Mimi Sheraton, "Restaurants; Sushi Delights and East Side Italian," *New York Times*, December 26, 1980, p. C26.

44. Mimi Sheraton, "Sushi and Sashimi, the Best in the City," *New York Times*, April 15, 1983, p. C1.

45. Kanai, "How Sushi Came to California," 632.

46. "513-Pound Tuna Auctioned for $177,000," *Boston Globe*, January 6, 2010, http://www.boston.com/news/world/asia/articles/2010/01/06/513_pound_tuna_auctioned_for_177000.

47. Dave Lowry, *The Connoisseur's Guide to Sushi: Everything You Need to Know about Sushi* (Boston: Harvard Common Press, 2005), 195–202.

48. Day Zschock, *The Little Black Book of Sushi: The Essential Guide to the World of Sushi* (White Plains, N.Y.: Peter Pauper Press, 2005), 26–27; Lowry, *Connoisseur's Guide to Sushi*, 202–7; Corson, *Story of Sushi*, 247–48.

49. Nobu Matsuhisa with Florence Fabricant, "The Chef; Sashimi That Isn't: A Star Is Born," *New York Times*, September 12, 2001, www.nytimes.com/2001/09/12/dining/the-chef-sashimi-that-isn-t-a-star-is-born.html; Kamp, *United States of Arugula*, 317.

50. For an early tuna steak recipe, see Inez Nellie Canfield McFee, *Food and Health: A Book for the Lay Reader Who Believes That Health Is What We Make it* (New York: Thomas Y. Crowell Co., 1924), 148.

51. "Best and Worst," *Cincinnati Magazine* 20 (October 1986): 77.

52. Gael Green, "Trio con Brio," *New York Magazine* 21 (July 19, 1988): 41.

53. Patricia Sharpe and Helen Thompson, "Around the State," *Texas Monthly* 16 (July 1988): 22.

54. Linda Bird Francke with Scott Sullivan and Seth Goldschlager, "Food: The New Wave," *Newsweek* 134 (August 11, 1975): 51.

55. Katie Robbins, "The Man Who Invented Tuna Tartare," *The Atlantic*, June 8, 2010, http://www.theatlantic.com/food/archive/2010/06/the-man-who -invented-tuna-tartare/57799.

56. *Texas Monthly* 18 (June 1990): 42

57. Bryan Miller, "Diner's Journal; Brunches to Samba By," *New York Times*, December 16, 1983, http://www.nytimes.com/1983/12/16/arts/diner-s-journal -brunches-to-samba-by.html.

58. Gael Green, "The Real Thing," *New York Magazine* 27 (November 27, 1989): 60.

59. Sam Choy and Lynn Cook [Joannie Dobbs, ed.], *Sam Choy's Poke: Hawaii's Soul Food* (Honolulu: Mutual Publishing, 1999); Patrick Evans-Hylton, "Sonoma's Tuna Poke Delivers Big Flavor," *The Virginia Pilot*, June 14, 2010, http://hampton roads.com/2010/06/sonoma%E2%80%99s-tuna-poke-delivers-big-flavor.

60. "More and More Going for Sushi," 36; interview with restaurant consultant Clark Wolf, May 23, 2010.

61. Ruth Reichl, "Restaurants; A Surprise for the Reluctant Gourmet," *New York Times*, October 7, 1998, http://www.nytimes.com/1998/10/07/dining/ restaurants-a-surprise-for-the-reluctant-gourmet.html.

6. FOREIGN TUNA

1. August J. Felando, "California's Tuna Clipper Fleet: 1918–1963; Part 2," *Mains'l Haul* 33:1 (1997): 21–23.

2. Richard Crawford, "The Way We Were: Fishermen Became WWII's 'Pork Chop Express,'" *San Diego Union-Tribune*, May 27, 2010, http://www.sign onsandiego.com/news/2010/may/27/sd-fishermen-became-wwiis-pork-chop -express.

3. These requisitioned tuna boats were designated in the Yard Patrol (YP) class and became known as "Yippee boats." Their original fishing crews were asked to enlist in the navy to man the boats. In February 1942 a mass meeting was held at the Naval Reserve Armory in San Diego, and 600 commercial fishermen volunteered to serve aboard their former boats. Naval personnel were assigned to the boats to train the crews and handle the armaments. Some YP boats engaged in coastal patrols, hunting for Japanese submarines; others transported food, supplies, and troops, often in war zones. The Yippee boats participated in every major naval campaign from Guadalcanal to the occupation of Japan. When President Roosevelt urged that soldiers fighting on Guadalcanal be given a turkey dinner on Thanksgiving, it was Yippee boats that delivered holiday meals to soldiers fighting in the jungle. Twenty-one of these boats and many of their crew were lost during the war, some killed by enemy fire and others lost

at sea due to weather or mechanical failures. For more information, see Lawrence Oliver, *Never Backward: The Autobiography of Lawrence Oliver, a Portuguese-American* (San Diego: Neyensch Printers, 1972), 102–3; Leonard Bernstein, "Tuna Crews That Fished to Fame, Cited Glory Days Recalled, Demise Is Lamented at Statue's Unveiling," *Los Angeles Times*, October 27, 1986, San Diego edition, p. 1; Fern Chandonnet, *Alaska at War, 1941–1945: The Forgotten War Remembered* (Anchorage: Alaska at War Committee, 1995), 215.

4. *Tuna Imports: Hearing Before a Subcommittee of the Committee on Ways and Means, House of Representatives Eighty-Second Congress, First Session* (Washington, D.C.: Government Printing Office, 1951), 22, 24.

5. *Tuna Imports: Hearing Before a Subcommittee of the Committee on Ways and Means, House of Representatives* (statement of Lewis S. Ballif), 9; A. W. Anderson, W. H. Stolting, et al., *Survey of the Domestic Tuna Industry*, U.S. Fish and Wildlife Services, Special Scientific Report: Fisheries, no. 104 (Washington, D.C.: Department of the Interior, 1952), 23–25.

6. Thomas Wolff, *In Pursuit of Tuna: The Expansion of a Fishing Industry and Its International Ramifications—The End of an Era* (Tempe: Center for Latin American Studies, Arizona State University, 1980), 8.

7. William C. Richardson, "Fishermen of San Diego: The Italians," *Journal of San Diego History* 27 (Fall 1981), https://www.sandiegohistory.org/journal/81fall/fishermen.htm.

8. August J. Felando, "California's Tuna Clipper Fleet: 1918–1963; Part 3," *Mains'l Haul* 33:3 (1997): 28.

9. *Pacific Fisherman* 22 (March 1924): 37; Earl Chapin May, *The Canning Clan: A Pageant of Pioneering Americans* (New York: Macmillan Company, 1937), 196; Thomas A. Petit, "The Impact of Imports and Tariffs on the American Tuna Industry," *American Journal of Economics and Sociology* 19 (April 1960): 280; Richardson, "Fishermen of San Diego: The Italians."

10. Geraldine Conner, "Expansion of Tuna Fishing Areas," in "The Commercial Fish Catch of California for the Year 1929," *Fish Bulletin* 30 (Sacramento: Bureau of Commercial Fisheries, 1931), 23.

11. Richardson, "Fishermen of San Diego: The Italians."

12. Richardson, "Fishermen of San Diego: The Italians."

13. "Growth of Tuna Fleet Results in Division of San Diego Groups," *29th Annual Statistical Number* (Astoria, Ore.: Pacific Fisherman, 1931), 161; "Tuna Institute Formed," *Pacific Fisherman* 29 (August 1931): 34. The American Fishermen's Tunaboat Association (AFTA) was previously part of the American Fishermen's Protective Association, which broke into two groups in 1930. The AFTA was the forerunner of the American Tunaboat Association, which was formed about 1943.

14. "Tuna Institute Is Organized" *Pacific Fisherman* 30 (May 1932): 27.

15. May, *Canning Clan*, 195–96; *Problems of the Fishing Industry: Hearings Before the Subcommittee on Fisheries and Wildlife Conservation of the Committee on Merchant Marine and Fisheries, House of Representatives, Eighty-First Congress, First Session, February 15–16, 1949* (Washington, D.C.: Government Printing Office, 1949), 126; Thomas A. Petit, "The Impact of Imports and Tariffs on the American Tuna Industry," *American Journal of Economics and Sociology* 19 (April 1960): 281; Sayuri Shimizu, *Creating People of Plenty: The United States and Japan's Economic Alternatives, 1950–1960* (Kent, Ohio: Kent State University Press, 2001), 103.

16. *The Champion* 3 (1937): 28; T. A. Bisson, "American Trade and Japanese Aggression," *Annals of the American Academy of Political and Social Science* 211 (September 1940): 127.

17. "Too Much Tuna," *Wall Street Journal*, September 11, 1951, as quoted in *Tuna Imports: Hearing Before a Subcommittee of the Committee on Ways and Means, House of Representatives*, 3; Clair Wilcox, "Trade Policy for the Fifties," *American Economic Review: Papers and Proceedings of the Sixty-Fifth Annual Meeting of the American Economic Association* 43 (May 1953): 66.

18. *United States Tariff Policy* (Washington, D.C.: Government Printing Office, 1954), as quoted in Jane Underhill Abrams, "A Case Study of Some of the Political Ramifications of the American Tuna Problem" (master's thesis, San Diego State College, 1957), 56.

19. Shimizu, *Creating People of Plenty*, 103–4.

20. Wilcox, "Trade Policy for the Fifties," 70.

21. Shimizu, *Creating People of Plenty*, 104.

22. Shimizu, *Creating People of Plenty*, 104.

23. "Tuna Fish," in *Report on Investigation Conducted Pursuant to a Resolution by the Committee on Finance of the United State Senate Dated August 20, 1957* (Washington D.C.: Government Printing Office, 1958); Thomas A. Petit, "The Impact of Imports and Tariffs on the American Tuna Industry," *American Journal of Economics and Sociology* 19 (April 1960): 281.

24. *Tuna Imports: Hearing Before a Subcommittee of the Committee on Ways and Means, House of Representatives*, 17; *Tuna Imports: Hearings Before the Committee on Finance, United States Senate, Eighty-Second Congress* (Washington, D.C.: Government Printing Office, 1952), 27.

25. *Tuna Imports: Hearings Before the Committee on Finance, United States Senate, Eighty-Second Congress*, 163–64.

26. A Bill to Amend the Tariff Act of 1930 to Impose Certain Duties upon the Importation of Tuna Fish, H.R. 5429, 82nd Cong., 1st Session.

27. *Tuna Imports: Hearings Before the Committee on Finance, United States Senate, Eighty-Second Congress*, 28–37, 43, 408, 411–16.

28. Anderson, Stolting, et al., *Survey of the Domestic Tuna Industry*.

29. Abrams, "Political Ramifications of the American Tuna Problem," 47–54.

30. Abrams, "Political Ramifications of the American Tuna Problem," 39–43.

31. Shimizu, *Creating People of Plenty*, 107.

32. "Tariff Deal Fails to Face Problem of Tuna-in-Brine," *Pacific Fisherman* 53 (July 1955): 1, 13, 15; "How California Canners Look at Tuna Tariff," and "Japanese Reaction to Tariff Concessions," *Pacific Fisherman* 53 (August 1955): 11; "Harold Cary Discusses Effect of Tuna Imports," *Pacific Fisherman* 53 (November 1955): 33; "Pacific Fishery Troubles Told to Senate Committee," *Pacific Fisherman* 53 (November 1955): 25–26; Abrams, "Political Ramifications of the American Tuna Problem," 47–54.

33. Michael Cornell Dypski, "The Caribbean Basin Initiative: An Examination of Structural Dependency, Good Neighbor Relations, and American Investment," *Journal of Transnational Law and Policy* 12 (Fall 2002): 95–136.

34. Keith Bradsher, "U.S. Trade Bill Could Hurt Philippine Tuna Industry, Officials Will Tell Powell in Manila," *New York Times*, August 1, 2002, http://www.nytimes.com/2002/08/01/world/us-trade-bill-could-hurt-philippine-tuna-industry-officials-will-tell-powell.html.

35. "Testimony of Christopher D. Lischewski, President/CEO Bumble Bee Foods before the U.S. International Trade Commission, March 2, 2010, United States Trans-Pacific Partnership Trade Agreement," p. 2, http://www.usitc.gov/press_room/documents/testimony/131_034_005.pdf.

36. "Tuna Fish," in *Report on Investigation . . . Dated August 20, 1957*; Petit, "Impact of Imports and Tariffs," 287.

37. "Testimony of Christopher D. Lischewski."

38. U.S. Department of Labor, *Economic Report: The Minimum Wage in American Samoa, 2007*, http://www.dol.gov/whd/AS/EconomicReport-2007.pdf.

7. TUNA WARS

1. *To Protect Rights of United States Vessels on High Seas: Hearing Before the Subcommittee on Fisheries and Wildlife Conservation of the Committee on Merchant Marine and Fisheries, House of Representatives, Eighty-Fifth Congress, First Session, on H.R. 5526* (Washington, D.C.: Government Printing Office, 1957), 44–46; W.J. Fenrick, "Legal Limits on the Use of Force by Canadian Warships Engaged in Law Enforcement," *Canadian Yearbook of International Law* 18 (1980): 140.

2. "Ecuador Captures Two U.S. Vessels," *New York Times*, March 29, 1955, p. 14; *To Protect Rights of United States Vessels on High Seas: Hearing Before the Subcommittee on Fisheries and Wildlife Conservation of the Committee on Merchant Marine and Fisheries, House of Representatives, Eighty-fifth Congress, First Session*, 44–46; Fenrick, "Legal Limits on the Use of Force," 140.

3. *To Protect Rights of United States Vessels on High Seas: Hearing Before the*

Subcommittee on Fisheries and Wildlife Conservation of the Committee on Merchant Marine and Fisheries, House of Representatives, Eighty-fifth Congress, First Session, 2, 44–46; Fenrick, "Legal Limits on the Use of Force," 140.

4. *To Protect Rights of United States Vessels on High Seas: Hearing Before the Subcommittee on Fisheries and Wildlife Conservation of the Committee on Merchant Marine and Fisheries, House of Representatives, Eighty-fifth Congress, First Session*, 22.

5. "Your Move Mr. Dulles," *Pacific Fishermen* 53 (May 1955): 13.

6. For an extended discussion of the three-mile limit, see Robert Jay Wilder, "The Three-Mile Territorial Sea: Its Origins and Implications for Contemporary Offshore Federalism," *Virginia Journal of International Law* 32 (1991–1992): 681–746.

7. John Cornish Swift, "The Tuna Fishery of Southern California" (master's thesis, University of California, Berkeley, 1956), 64.

8. *Pacific Fisherman* 15 (March 1917): 21; *Pacific Fisherman* 19 (January 1921): 51; Swift, "Tuna Fishery of Southern California," 70.

9. Charles B. Selak Jr., "Recent Developments in High Seas Fisheries Jurisdiction under the Presidential Proclamation of 1945," *American Journal of International Law* 44 (October 1950): 672; Thomas Wolff, *In Pursuit of Tuna: The Expansion of a Fishing Industry and Its International Ramifications—The End of an Era* (Tempe: Center for Latin American Studies, Arizona State University, 1980), 47–48; Wilder, "Three-Mile Territorial Sea," 721–26.

10. Memorandum from President Roosevelt to Secretary of State Hull, June 9, 1943, Department of State file no. 811.145/I1–2844, as quoted in David C. Loring, "The United States-Peruvian 'Fisheries' Dispute," *Stanford Law Review* 23 (February 1971): 397; Selak, " High Seas Fisheries Jurisdiction," 671.

11. Selak, "High Seas Fisheries Jurisdiction," 670–71; Loring, "United States-Peruvian 'Fisheries' Dispute," 397; Wolff, *In Pursuit of Tuna*, 47; Wilder, "Three-Mile Territorial Sea," 731–32.

12. Selak, "High Seas Fisheries Jurisdiction," 674–75; Loring, "United States-Peruvian 'Fisheries' Dispute," 399.

13. Selak, "High Seas Fisheries Jurisdiction," 673; Loring, "United States-Peruvian 'Fisheries' Dispute," 399–400.

14. "Fishing in Troubled Waters," *New York Times*, January 7, 1970, p. 42; William R. Lux, "The Peruvian Fishing Industry: A Case Study in Capitalism at Work," *Revista de Historia de América* 71 (January-June 1971): 139–40.

15. Selak, "High Seas Fisheries Jurisdiction," 673–74; Loring, "United States-Peruvian 'Fisheries' Dispute," 400–401; Wolff, *In Pursuit of Tuna*, 22, 51.

16. Wolff, *In Pursuit of Tuna*, 22.

17. Loring, "United States-Peruvian 'Fisheries' Dispute," 401.

18. Dwight Eisenhower, as quoted in *To Protect Rights of U.S. Vessels on High Seas: Hearings before the United States*, Hearing on H.R. 9584 (Washington, D.C.: Government Printing Office, 1954), 49; Wolff, *In Pursuit of Tuna*, 52.

19. "Peru Accuses U.S. Ships; Charges Tuna Craft Are Violating Her Three-Mile Limit," *New York Times*, August 25, 1952, p. 2; "2 More U.S. Ships Held; Ecuador Acts after Releasing Others for Fishing Violations," *New York Times*, October 31, 1952, p. 9.

20. Theodor Meron, "The Fishermen's Protective Act: A Case in Contemporary Legal Strategy of the United States," *The American Journal of International Law* 69 (April 1975): 292.

21. Loring, "United States-Peruvian 'Fisheries' Dispute," 404–5.

22. Wolff, *In Pursuit of Tuna*, 23.

23. "'Tuna War' Averted in Ecuador Dispute," *New York Times*, May 29, 1963, p. 2; "U.S. Bids Ecuador Free Tuna Boats," *New York Times*, May 30, 1963, p. 3; "Ecuador Detaining 21 U.S. Tuna Boats," *New York Times*, May 31, 1963, p. 4; "Ecuador Rebuffs Rusk in Dispute," *New York Times*, June 1, 1963, p. 3; "Ecuador Sets Fines for U.S. Tuna Boats," *New York Times*, June 5, 1963, p. 4; "U.S. and Ecuador Set Fishing Talks; Envoy to Plan Negotiations in Dispute over Tuna Owners to Decide on Fines," *New York Times*, June 6, 1963, p. 12; "Tuna Boats Leave Ecuador after Protest over Fines," *New York Times*, June 11, 1963, p. 10; "U.S. Tuna Boat Is Released after Paying Ecuador Fee," *New York Times*, June 18, 1963, p. 31; Loring, "United States-Peruvian 'Fisheries' Dispute," 407.

24. Loring, "United States-Peruvian 'Fisheries' Dispute," 407.

25. Loring, "United States-Peruvian 'Fisheries' Dispute," 392, 408.

26. Meron, "Fishermen's Protective Act," 292–96.

27. Loring, "United States-Peruvian 'Fisheries' Dispute," 409.

28. Wolff, *In Pursuit of Tuna*, 55.

29. Wolff, *In Pursuit of Tuna*, 55.

30. Benjamin Welles, "U.S.-Peru Accord for Sale of Arms Is Reported Near," *New York Times*, June 15, 1969, p. 1; Everett Holles, "Tuna Fleet Gambles Millions against Taint," *New York Times*, January 2, 1971, Business and Finance, p. 34.

31. Benjamin Welles, "Ecuador Arms Aid Suspended," *New York Times*, January 19, 1971, p. 1.

32. Everett R. Holles, "Tuna War off Ecuador Coast Fades as Fish Migrate North," *New York Times*, September 24, 1972, p. S18.

33. Everett R. Holles, "Tuna Fleet Asks U.S. Aid off Ecuador," *New York Times*, March 9, 1975, p. 20.

34. "Armed Forces Oust Ecuador President in a Bloodless Coup," *New York Times*, February 16, 1972, p. 1.

35. David Binder, "Senate Approves a 200-Mile Limit on Fishing Rights," *New York Times*, January 29, 1976, Week in Review, p. 69; Geoffrey Waugh, "Development, Economics, and Fishing Rights in the South Pacific Tuna Fishing," in Philip A. Neher, Ragnar Árnason, and Nina Mollett, eds., *Rights Based Fishing* (Dordrecht: Kluwer Academic Publishers, 1989), 330.

36. "Canada Is Seizing Fishing Boats in Dispute with U.S. over Tuna; Reports on U.S. Ships," *New York Times*, September 2, 1979, p. 33; *The Economist*, September 8, 1979, p. 82; "U.S.-Canada Tuna Treaty," *New York Times*, July 30, 1981, http://www.nytimes.com/1981/07/30/business/us-canada-tuna-treaty.html?scp = 2&sq = tuna%20war&st = cse.

37. Graham Hovey, "U.S. Seeks Tuna Pact with Mexico; Called 'Pirate Ships' Permanent Agreement," *New York Times*, July 17, 1980, p. A8; Pamela G. Hollie, "The 'Tuna War' with Mexico; Many U.S. Ships Idled," *New York Times*, July 31, 1980, Business and Finance, pp. D1, D10; Patrick H. Heffernan, "Conflict over Marine Resources," *Proceedings of the Academy of Political Science, Mexico-United States Relations* 34 (1981): 172.

38. William Stockton, "U.S. and Mexico Seek End to Tuna War," *New York Times*, May 12, 1986, http://www.nytimes.com/1986/05/12/business/us-and-mexico-seek-end-to-tuna-war.html.

39. Heffernan, "Conflict over Marine Resources," 172; Stockton, "U.S. and Mexico Seek End to Tuna War."

40. Dale D. Murphy, "The Tuna-Dolphin Wars," *Journal of World Trade: Law, Economics, Public Policy* 40 (August 2006): 598.

41. Joel P. Trachtman, "United States—Restrictions on Imports of Tuna, No. DS21/R, 30 ILM 1594 (1991)," *American Journal of International Law* 86 (January 1992): 142–43; "U.S. Enforces Tuna Embargo," *New York Times*, February 3, 1992, http://www.nytimes.com/1992/02/03/business/us-enforces-tuna-embargo.html?scp = 1&sq = tuna+embargo+&st = nyt.

42. Waugh, "Development, Economics, and Fishing Rights," 332.

43. Waugh, "Development, Economics, and Fishing Rights," 333.

8. PORPOISE FISHING

1. William F. Perrin, "Early Days of the Tuna/Dolphin Problem," *Aquatic Mammals* 35 (April 2009): 293.

2. William F. Perrin, "The Porpoise and the Tuna," *Sea Frontiers* 14 (1968): 166–74; Perrin, "Using Porpoises to Catch Tuna," *World Fishing* 18 (June 1969): 42–45; Perrin, "Early Days of the Tuna/Dolphin Problem," 295–96.

3. William F. Perrin, "The Problem of Porpoise Mortality in the U.S. Tropical Tuna Fishery," in *Proceedings of the Sixth [sic] Annual Conference on Biological Sonar and Diving Mammals* (Menlo Park, Calif.: Stanford Research Institute, 1970), 45–48.

4. "Porpoise Fishing Described by Guy Silva," *Pacific Fisherman* 39 (February 1941): 36; Perrin, "Using Porpoises to Catch Tuna," 43–45; Oral History Program: An Interview with August John Felando," September 5, 1995, http://gondolin.ucsd.edu/sio/ceo-sdhsoh/OH_felando.html.

5. James Joseph and Joseph W. Greenough, *International Management of Tuna, Porpoise, and Billfish: Biological, Legal, and Political Aspects* (Seattle: University of Washington Press, 1979), 137.

6. Kenneth Brower, "The Destruction of Dolphins," *Atlantic Monthly* 263 (July 1989), http://www.theatlantic.com/past/docs/issues/89jul/dolph3.htm.

7. August Felando and Harold Medina, *The Tuna/Porpoise Controversy* (San Diego: Western Sky Press, 2011), 107–8, 110–12.

8. William F. Perrin, *Chronological Bibliography of the Tuna-Dolphin Problem, 1941–2001* (La Jolla, Calif.: U.S. Dept. of Commerce, National Oceanic and Atmospheric Administration, National Marine Fisheries Service, Southwest Fisheries Science Center, 2004), swfsc.noaa.gov/publications/TM/SWFSC/NOAA-TM -NMFS-SWFSC-356.pdf.

9. Richard Ellis, *The Empty Ocean: Plundering the World's Marine Life* (Washington, D.C.: Island Press/Shearwater Books, 2003), 222.

10. Michael J. Bean and Melanie J. Rowland, *The Evolution of National Wildlife Law*, 3rd ed. (Westport, Conn.: Praeger, 1997), 123.

11. "The Gentle Dolphin Is Threatened," *Los Angeles Times*, January 30, 1972, p. 16.

12. Scott McVay, "The Great Porpoise Massacre," *New York Times*, March 19, 1972, Week in Review, p. E15.

13. Mark Schoell, "The Marine Mammal Protection Act and Its Role in the Decline of San Diego's Tuna Fishing Industry," *San Diego's History* 45 (Winter 1999): 32–52, https://www.sandiegohistory.org/journal/99winter/tuna.htm.

14. James J. Armstrong, "The Porpoise-Tuna Controversy," *Ocean Law Memo* 4 (June 1, 1977): 2.

15. Felando and Medina, *Tuna/Porpoise Controversy*, 70–72.

16. Pamela G. Hollie, "The 'Tuna War' With Mexico; Many U.S. Ships Idled," *New York Times*, July 31, 1980, Business and Finance, p. D1.

17. "Statement on the Tuna-Porpoise Problem," Audubon Naturalist Society of the Central Atlantic States, Northern Virginia Conservation Council, May 11, 1977, as cited in Schoell, "Marine Mammal Protection Act."

18. Tom Garrett, "The Tuna-Porpoise Story," *Not Man Apart* 6 (Mid-July 1976), 1–8; "Save the Dolphins" (San Francisco: Save the Dolphins, 1976); Thomas Wolff, *In Pursuit of Tuna: The Expansion of a Fishing Industry and Its International Ramifications—The End of an Era* (Tempe: Center for Latin American Studies, Arizona State University, 1980), 143; Schoell, "Marine Mammal Protection Act," 32–52.

19. Schoell, "Marine Mammal Protection Act," 32–52.

20. Brower, "Destruction of Dolphins"; Kevin Danaher and Jason Mark, *Insurrection: Citizen Challenges to Corporate Power* (New York: Routledge, 2003), 114.

21. Danaher and Mark, *Insurrection*, 117.

22. Brower, "Destruction of Dolphins"; Eugene H. Buck, "96011: Dolphin Protection and Tuna Seining; Environment and Natural Resources Policy Division," http://digital.library.unt.edu/ark:/67531/metacrs389/m1.

23. Andis Robeznieks, "Is It Safe to Eat Fish?" *Vegetarian Times* (July 1985): 51.

24. *Mother Jones Magazine* 13 (June 1988): 1.

25. Jason Salisbury, *Just Say No to Tuna: A Pocket Conspiracy Mini-Comic* (N.p.: Argus IG, 1990); "Saving the Planet," *Orange Coast Magazine* 16 (February 1990): 95.

26. Brower, "Destruction of Dolphins."

27. Brower, "Destruction of Dolphins."

28. "Boycott Power," *Mother Jones Magazine* 16 (July-August 1991): 18.

29. Richard H. K. Victor, Forest Reinhardt, and Peggy Duxbury, *StarKist* (Boston: Harvard Business School Case Services, 1994), 11.

30. Bernice Kanner, "Forcing the Issue," *New York Magazine* 24 (February 11, 1991): 22.

31. Kanner, "Forcing the Issue," 22–23.

32. "The Truth in Tuna Labeling Act," *Congressional Record* (January 10, 2003): 410.

33. Committee on Reducing Porpoise Mortality from Tuna Fishing, Board on Biology, Board on Environmental Studies and Toxicology, Commission on Life Sciences, National Research Council, *Dolphins and the Tuna Industry* (Washington, D.C.: National Academy Press, 1992), 29.

34. Joel P. Trachtman, "GATT Dispute Settlement Panel," *American Journal of International Law* 86 (January 1992): 145–51; Keith Bradsher, "Trade Ministers at W.T.O. Talks Agree to Limit Fishing Subsidies," *New York Times*, December 15, 2005; Alessandro Bonanno and Douglas Constance, *Stories of Globalization: Transnational Corporations, Resistance, and the State* (University Park: Pennsylvania State University Press, 2008), 65–67.

35. Martin A. Hall, "An Ecological View of the Tuna-Dolphin Problem: Impacts and Trade-offs," *Review in Fish Biology and Fisheries* 8 (1) (1998): 1–34.

36. "The Truth in Tuna Labeling Act," 410.

37. Christopher Marquis, "2 Scientists Contend U.S. Suppressed Dolphin Studies," *New York Times*, January 9, 2003, http://www.nytimes.com/2003/01/09/us/2-scientists-contend-us-suppressed-dolphin-studies.html.

38. Christopher Marquis, "Rule Weakening Definition of 'Dolphin Safe' Is Delayed," *New York Times*, January 10, 2003, http://www.nytimes.com/2003/01/10/us/rule-weakening-definition-of-dolphin-safe-is-delayed.html.

39. "West; California: Defining 'Dolphin-Safe' Tuna," *New York Times*, August 12, 2004, http://www.nytimes.com/2004/08/12/us/national-briefing-west-california-defining-dolphin-safe-tuna.html.

40. Marie Wilke and Hannes Schloemann, "Not-So-Voluntary Labelling in

the WTO Tuna-Dolphin Dispute," *Bridges Trade BioRes Review* 5(3) (November 2011), http://ictsd.org/i/news/bioresreview/117757.

41. Bonanno and Constance, *Stories of Globalization*, 79–83; Ana Teixeira, "Swimming with Dolphins: A Study on Legitimacy Processes in the Southern California Tuna Industry" (PhD diss., University of North Carolina at Chapel Hill, 2009), 45–46; Humane Society of the United States, "The Dolphin Safe Label," http://www.hsus.org/about_us/humane_society_international_hsi/international_policy/treaties/the_dolphin_safe_label; Buck, "96011: Dolphin Protection and Tuna Seining," http://digital.library.unt.edu/ark:/67531/metacrs389/m1.

42. *Report of the Scientific Research Program under the International Dolphin Conservation Program Act* (La Jolla, Calif.: Southwest Fisheries Science Center, NOAA Fisheries, National Oceanic and Atmospheric Administration, 2002), 30–31.

9. PARTS PER MILLION

1. Patricia A. D'Itri and Frank M. D'Itri, *Mercury Contamination: A Human Tragedy* (New York: John Wiley & Sons, 1977), 16–28; Japanese Ministry of Environment, http://www.env.go.jp/en/chemi/hs/minamata2002/ch2.html.

2. Kathryn R. Mahaffey, "Methylmercury: A New Look at the Risks," *Public Health Reports* (September-October 1999): 397.

3. D'Itri and D'Itri, *Mercury Contamination*, 62–63.

4. Mahaffey, "Methylmercury," 398.

5. Hal Smith, "Bruce McDuffie: Discovered Mercury in Tuna," *Mother Earth News* (May/June 1971); Richard D. Lyons, "Mercury in Tuna Leads to Recall: F.D.A. Head Says They Don't Imperil Health; Million Cans of Tainted Tuna Recalled," *New York Times*, December 16, 1970, p. 1; D'Itri and D'Itri, *Mercury Contamination*, 63.

6. John J. Putman, "Quicksilver and Slow Death," *National Geographic* 142 (October 1972): 525.

7. D'Itri and D'Itri, *Mercury Contamination*, 64.

8. Grace M. Egeland and John P. Middaugh, "Balancing Fish Consumption Benefits with Mercury Exposure," *Science* 278 (December 12, 1997): 1904–5.

9. Mahaffey, "Methylmercury," 398; Edward Groth III, "Ranking the Contributions of Commercial Fish and Shellfish Varieties to Mercury Exposure in the United States: Implications for Risk Communication," *Environmental Research* 110 (April 2010): 226–36, http://mercurypolicy.org/wp-content/uploads/2010/04/dr-groth-abstract-environmental-research-April-2010-April-20101.pdf.

10. Richard A. Merrill and Michael Schewel, "FDA Regulation of Environmental Contaminants of Food," *Virginia Law Review* 66 (December 1980): 1399.

11. Al Delugach, "Packers Moving Closer to the Tuna; California Canneries Feeling the Bite," *Los Angeles Times*, March 12, 1972, p. H2.

12. *Mercury Study Report to Congress* (Washington, D.C.: Office of Air Quality Planning and Standards and Office of Research and Development, U.S. Environmental Protection Agency, 1997).

13. Mahaffey, "Methylmercury," 402–13.

14. Committee on the Toxicological Effects of Methylmercury, Board on Environmental Studies and Toxicology, Commission on Life Sciences, National Research Council, *Toxicological Effects of Methylmercury* (Washington, D.C.: National Academy Press, 2000).

15. "F.D.A. Warns Women Not to Eat Some Fish," *New York Times,* January 14, 2001.

16. Sam Roe and Michael Hawthorne, "How Safe Is Tuna?" *Chicago Tribune,* December 13, 2005.

17. Marian Burros, "EATING WELL: Mercury in Fish; What's Too Much?" *New York Times,* May 9, 2001.

18. Jeremiah Baumann, *Brain Food: What Women Should Know about Mercury Contamination of Fish* (Washington, D.C.: USPIRG: Environmental Working Group, 2001).

19. Peter Waldman, "Mercury and Tuna: U.S. Advice Leaves Lots of Questions," *Wall Street Journal,* August 1, 2005, p. A1.

20. Clark Carrington, as quoted in Roe and Hawthorne, "How Safe Is Tuna?"; Loretta Schwartz-Nobel, *Poisoned Nation: Pollution, Greed, and the Rise of Deadly Epidemics* (New York: St. Martin's Press, 2007), 65–73.

21. Schwartz-Nobel, *Poisoned Nation,* 67.

22. Jennifer Lee, "E.P.A. Raises Estimate of Babies Affected by Mercury Exposure," *New York Times,* February 10, 2004, http://www.nytimes.com/2004/02/10/science/epa-raises-estimate-of-babies-affected-by-mercury-exposure.html.

23. Schwartz-Nobel, *Poisoned Nation,* 69.

24. "EPA and FDA Advice for Women Who Might Become Pregnant, Women Who Are Pregnant, Nursing Mothers, and Young Children" (March 2004), http://www.fda.gov/food/foodsafety/product-specificinformation/seafood/foodbornepathogenscontaminants/methylmercury/ucm115662.htm.

25. Terry Rodgers, "As Canned Tuna Sales Dive, Companies Plan Ad Blitz to Reel Buyers Back In," *San Diego Union-Tribune,* July 27, 2005, http://legacy.signonsandiego.com/news/business/20050727-9999-1b27tuna.html; Schwartz-Nobel, *Poisoned Nation,* 73.

26. As quoted in Schwartz-Nobel, *Poisoned Nation,* 68.

27. Waldman, "Mercury and Tuna," A1.

28. Roe and Hawthorne, "How Safe is Tuna?."

29. "Mercury in Tuna: New Safety Concerns," *Consumer Reports,* July 2006; "Mercury in Canned Tuna Still a Concern," *Consumer Reports* (January 2011): 20–21.

30. Emily Oken et al., "Maternal Fish Consumption, Hair Mercury, and Infant Cognition in a US Cohort," *Environmental Health Perspectives* 113 (October 2005): 1376–80; Oken et al., "Maternal Fish Intake during Pregnancy, Blood Mercury Levels, and Child Cognition at Age 3 Years in a US Cohort," *American Journal of Epidemiology* 167.10 (2008): 1171–81; quote from Edward Growth III, "Re: 'Maternal Fish Intake During Pregnancy, Blood Mercury Levels, and Child Cognition at Age 3 Years in a US Cohort,'" *American Journal of Epidemiology* 168.2 (2008): 236.

31. Eighth International Conference on Mercury as a Global Pollutant, Madison, Wisconsin, August 6–11, 2006, summarized at http://www.nytimes.com/images/blogs/dinersjournal/mercury_letter.pdf.

32. Lyndsey Layton, "FDA Draft Report Urges Consumption of Fish despite Mercury Contamination," *Washington Post*, December 12, 2008, http://www.washingtonpost.com/wp-dyn/content/article/2008/12/11/AR2008121103394.html.

33. Jacob H. Lowenstein, Joanna Burger, Christian W. Jeitner, George Amato, Sergios-Orestis Kolokotronis, and Michael Gochfeld, "DNA Barcodes Reveal Species-Specific Mercury Levels in Tuna Sushi That Pose a Health Risk to Consumers," *Biology Letters*, April 21, 2010, http://rsbl.royalsocietypublishing.org/content/early/2010/04/13/rsbl.2010.0156.full?sid = 33cf4b2b-597c-470c-8842-c839 e126c09a; Ana Garcia and Fred Mamoun, "How Much Mercury Is in Your Sushi?" NBC Los Angeles, http://www.nbclosangeles.com/news/local-beat/How-Much-Mercury-is-in-Your-Sushi-Part-1-93635804.html.

34. Edward Groth III, "Ranking the Contributions of Commercial Fish and Shellfish Varieties to Mercury Exposure in the United States: Implications for Risk Communication," *Environmental Research* 110 (April 2010): 226–36, http://mercurypolicy.org/wp-content/uploads/2010/04/dr-groth-abstract-environmental-research-April-2010-April-20101.pdf.

35. "Chemistry Newsletter," no. 8 (December 1993), http://chemiris.chem.binghamton.edu:8080/newsletters/nwsltf93.htm.

36. Layton, "FDA Draft Report Urges Consumption of Fish."

37. C. A. Choy, B. Popp, J. J. Kaneko, and J. C. Drazen, "The Influence of Depth on Mercury Levels in Pelagic Fishes and Their Prey," *Proceedings of the National Academy of Sciences* 106 (August 18, 2009): 13865–69.

EPILOGUE

1. Al Delugach, "Packers Moving Closer to the Tuna; California Canneries Feeling the Bite," *Los Angeles Times*, March 12, 1972, p. H2.

2. Delugach, "Packers Moving Closer to the Tuna," H2.

3. Pamela G. Hollie, "The 'Tuna War' with Mexico; Many U.S. Ships Idled," *New York Times*, July 31, 1980, Business and Finance, p. D10.

4. Committee on Reducing Porpoise Mortality from Tuna Fishing, Board on Biology, Board on Environmental Studies and Toxicology, Commission on Life Sciences, National Research Council, *Dolphins and the Tuna Industry* (Washington, D.C.: National Academy Press, 1992), 30–31; Ana Teixeira, "Swimming with Dolphins: A Study on Legitimacy Processes in the Southern California Tuna Industry" (PhD diss., University of North Carolina at Chapel Hill, 2009), 43.

5. Delugach, "Packers Moving Closer to the Tuna," H1.

6. "Last Full Scale Tuna Cannery in California Closes," *Crow's Nest* (August 2001), http://www.casamarintl.com/CrowsNest/2001/august01.html; Alessandro Bonanno and Douglas Constance, *Stories of Globalization: Transnational Corporations, Resistance, and the State* (University Park: Pennsylvania State University Press, 2008), 62.

7. Bonanno and Constance, *Stories of Globalization*.

8. "Testimony of Christopher D. Lischewski, President/CEO Bumble Bee Foods before the U.S. International Trade Commission, March 2, 2010, United States Trans-Pacific Partnership Trade Agreement," p. 2, http://www.usitc.gov/press_room/documents/testimony/131_034_005.pdf.

9. "Pelosi's Tuna Surprise," *Wall Street Journal*, January 17, 2007, p. 11.

10. U.S. Department of Labor, *Economic Report: The Minimum Wage in American Samoa, 2007*, http://www.dol.gov/whd/AS/EconomicReport-2007.pdf.

11. The abandoned factory has recently been taken over by the Samoa Tuna Processors, a subsidiary of Tri Marine, the world's largest tuna supply company, which started in Singapore, and a portion of the facility opened for business March 2, 2011.

12. "Pelosi's Tuna Surprise," 11; Dionisia Tabureguci, "Pacific Update: Samoa's Wage Fiasco," http://www.islandsbusiness.com/islands_business/index_dynamic/containerNameToReplace = MiddleMiddle/focusModuleID = 19234/overideSkinName = issueArticle-full.tpl.

13. Dan Flynn, "Korean-Owned StarKist Tuna Says 'No' to FDA," *Food Safety News*, March 9, 2011, http://www.foodsafetynews.com/2011/03/korean-owned-starkist-tuna-says-no-to-fda.

14. Andrew Leonard, "Charlie the Tuna Swims to Korea; Whom to Blame for Starkist's Emigration? How about the Price of Oil, Cheap Labor, Dolphins, and Free Trade?" Salon.com, June 20, 2008, http://www1.salon.com/tech/htww/2008/06/20/starkist_tuna/print.html.

15. Norimitsu Onishi, "Farming Bluefin Tuna, Through Thick Stocks and Thin," *New York Times*, September 26, 2006, http://www.nytimes.com/2006/09/26/world/asia/26tuna.html; "513-Pound Tuna Auctioned for $177,000," *Bos-

ton Globe, January 6, 2010, http://www.boston.com/news/world/asia/articles/2010/01/06/513_pound_tuna_auctioned_for_177000.

16. Elisabeth Rosenthal, "Fishing Depletes Mediterranean Tuna, Conservationists Say," *New York Times,* July 16, 2006, http://www.nytimes.com/2006/07/16/world/europe/16tuna.html.

17. "Mediterranean Bluefin Tuna Stocks Collapsing Now as Fishing Season Opens," "Pretending to Be Guided by Science—Timeline of a Fishery Failure: Eastern Atlantic and Mediterranean Bluefin Tuna," and "WWF Mediterranean Tuna Collapse Trends," April 14, 2009, http://wwf.panda.org/?162001/Mediterranean-bluefin-tuna-stocks-collapsing-now-as-fishing-season-opens.

18. C. J. Hughes, "Greenpeace Takes on Nobu," May 30, 2009, http://dinersjournal.blogs.nytimes.com/2009/05/30/greenpeace-takes-on-nobu.

19. C. J. Hughes, "They Dressed for Dinner, but Had Protest in Mind," *New York Times,* June 1, 2009, http://www.nytimes.com/2009/06/01/nyregion/01nobu.html.

20. David Jolly, "Europe Leans toward Bluefin Trade Ban," *New York Times,* February 3, 2010, http://www.nytimes.com/2010/02/04/world/europe/04tuna.html.

21. "Study Shows Steep Drop in Pacific Bluefin Tuna," *Japan Today,* May 10, 2010, http://www.japantoday.com/category/national/view/study-shows-steep-drop-in-pacific-bluefin-tuna.

22. Onishi, "Farming Bluefin Tuna."

23. For more information, see *Marine Science Assessment of Capture-Based Tuna (Thunnus orientalis) Aquaculture in the Ensenada Region of Northern Baja, Mexico* (Stanford, Conn.: University of Connecticut, 2008), http://digitalcommons.uconn.edu/ecostam_pubs/1/.

24. Audrey Mcavoy, "Hawaii Regulators Approve First US Tuna Farm," *Seattle Times,* October 24, 2009, http://seattletimes.nwsource.com/html/businesstechnology/2010130167_apusfarmingtuna.html.

Bibliography

BOOKS AND ARTICLES

Anderson, A. W., W. H. Stolting, et al. *Survey of the Domestic Tuna Industry.* U.S. Fish and Wildlife Services, Special Scientific Report: Fisheries, no. 104. Washington, D.C.: Department of the Interior, 1952.

Armstrong, James J. "The Porpoise-Tuna Controversy." *Ocean Law Memo* 4 (June 1, 1977): 1–3.

Arnold, Jeanne E., Roger H. Holten, and Scott Pletka. "Contexts for Cultural Change in Insular California." *American Antiquity* 62 (April 1997): 300–318.

Bamford, Edwin Fitton. *Social Aspects of the Fishing Industry at Los Angeles Harbor.* Studies in Sociology, Sociological Monograph, no. 18, vol. 5 (January, 1921). Los Angeles: The Southern California Sociological Society, University of Southern California, [1921].

Benson, Norman G., ed. *A Century of Fisheries in North America, 1970.* Washington, D.C.: [American Fisheries Society,] 1970.

Bergin, Anthony, and Marcus Haward. *Japan's Tuna Fishing Industry: A Setting Sun or New Dawn?* Commack, N.Y.: Nova Science Publishers, 1996.

Bestor, Theodore C. "How Sushi Went Global." *Foreign Policy* 121 (November-December 2000): 54–63.

———. "Supply-Side Sushi: Commodity, Market, and the Global City." *American Anthropologist*, n.s., 103 (March 2001): 76–95.

———. *Tsukiji: The Fish Market at the Center of the World.* Berkeley: University of California Press, 2004.

Bignami, Louis. *Stories behind Record Fish.* Minnetonka, Minn.: North American Fishing Club, 1991.

Bisson, T. A. "American Trade and Japanese Aggression." *Annals of the American Academy of Political and Social Science* 211 (September 1940): 123–29.

Bitting, A. W. *Appertizing; or, the Art of Canning.* San Francisco: Trade Pressroom, 1937.

Block, Barbara A., and E. Donald Stevens, eds. *Tuna: Physiology, Ecology, and Evolution.* San Diego: Academic Press, 2001.

Bonanno, Alessandro, and Douglas Constance. *Caught in the Net: The Global Tuna Industry, Environmentalism, and the State.* Lawrence: University Press of Kansas, 1996.

———. *Stories of Globalization: Transnational Corporations, Resistance, and the State.* University Park: Pennsylvania State University Press, 2008.

Bronz, George. "The Tariff Commission as a Regulatory Agency." *Columbia Law Review* 61 (March 1961): 463–89.

Brower, Kenneth. "The Destruction of Dolphins." *Atlantic Monthly* 263 (July 1989): 35–58. http://www.theatlantic.com/past/docs/issues/89jul/dolph3.htm.

Buck, Eugene H. "96011: Dolphin Protection and Tuna Seining; Environment and Natural Resources Policy Division." http://digital.library.unt.edu/ark:/67531/metacrs389/m1.

Cesarini, Thomas J., and Kimber M. Quinney. *San Diego's Fishing Industry.* San Francisco: Arcadia Pub., 2008.

Cháirez A., José Adán. *Historia de la pesca del atún en México.* 3 vols. Ensenada, B.C., Mexico: Editorial Chairez, 1996.

Chamberlin, Eugene Keith. "The Japanese Scare at Magdalena Bay." *Pacific Historical Review* 24 (November 1955): 345–59.

Chartkoff, Joseph L., and Kerry Kona Chartoff. *The Archaeology of California.* Stanford, Calif.: Stanford University Press, 1984.

Chuman, Frank F. *The Bamboo People: The Law and Japanese-Americans.* Del Mar, Calif.: Publisher's Inc., 1976.

Clemens, Harold B., and William L. Craig. "An Analysis of California's Albacore Fishery." *Fish Bulletin* 128. Terminal Island, Calif.: Marine Resources Operations, 1965.

Clover, Charles. *The End of the Line: How Overfishing Is Changing the World and What We Eat.* New York: The New Press, 2006.

Coan, Atilio. "Eastern Pacific Skipjack Tuna." In *California's Living Marine Resources and Their Utilization*. La Jolla: NMFS / Southwest Fisheries Science Center, 2000.

Collins, James. *The Story of Canned Foods*. New York: E. P. Dutton and Company, 1924.

Committee on Reducing Porpoise Mortality from Tuna Fishing, Board on Biology, Board on Environmental Studies and Toxicology, Commission on Life Sciences, National Research Council. *Dolphins and the Tuna Industry*. Washington, D.C.: National Academy Press, 1992.

Committee to Review Atlantic Bluefin Tuna, Ocean Studies Board, Commission on Geosciences, Environment, and Resources, and the National Research Council. *An Assessment of Atlantic Bluefin Tuna*. Washington, D.C.: National Academy Press, 1994.

Corson, Trevor. *The Story of Sushi: An Unlikely Saga of Raw Fish and Rice*. New York: Harper Perennial, 2008.

———. *The Zen of Fish: The Story of Sushi from Samurai to Supermarket*. New York: HarperCollins, 2007.

Corwin, Genevieve. "A Bibliography of the Tunas." *Fish Bulletin* 22. Contribution no. 87 from the California State Fisheries Laboratory. Sacramento: California State Printing Office, 1929.

Danaher, Kevin, and Jason Mark. *Insurrection: Citizen Challenges to Corporate Power*. New York: Routledge, 2003.

Daniels, Roger. *Prejudice of Prejudice: The Anti-Japanese Movement in California and the Struggle for Japanese Exclusion*. Berkeley: University of California Press, 1977.

Detrick, Mia. *Sushi*. San Francisco: Chronicle Books, 1981.

D'Itri, Patricia A., and Frank M. D'Itri. *Mercury Contamination: A Human Tragedy*. New York: John Wiley & Sons, 1977.

Doulman, David J., ed. *The Development of the Tuna Industry in the Pacific Islands Region*. Honolulu: East-West Center, 1987.

Ellis, Arthur M. "Maurice Harris Newmark." *California Historical Society Quarterly* 9 (March 1930): 94–95.

Ellis, Richard. *Dolphins and Porpoises*. New York: Knopf, distributed by Random House, 1982.

———. *Tuna: A Love Story*. New York: Alfred A. Knopf, 2008.

Engler, George. *Hibachi Cookery in the American Manner: Japanese-American Cookbook*. Rutland, Vt., and Tokyo: Charles E. Tuttle Co., 1952.

Estes, Donald H. "Kondo Masaharu and the Best of All Fishermen." *Journal of San Diego History* 23 (Summer 1977): 1–19.

———. "'Offensive Stupidity' and the Struggle of Abe Tokunosuke." *Journal of San Diego History* 28 (Fall 1982): 248–68.

———. "Silver Petals Falling: Japanese Pioneers in San Diego's Fishery." *Mains'l Haul* 35:2 and 3 (1999): 28–46.

Farrington, S. Kip, Jr. *The Trail of the Sharp Cup: The Story of the Fifth Oldest Trophy in International Sports.* New York: Dodd, Mead, 1974.

Farrior, Michael L. *The History of the Tuna Club, 1898–1998.* Avalon, Santa Catalina Island, Calif.: Tuna Club Foundation, 2004.

Felando, August J. "California's Tuna Clipper Fleet: 1918–1963; Part 1." *Mains'l Haul* 32:4 (1996): 6–17.

———. "California's Tuna Clipper Fleet: 1918–1963; Part 2." *Mains'l Haul* 33:1 (1997): 16–27.

———. "California's Tuna Clipper Fleet: 1918–1963; Part 3." *Mains'l Haul* 33:3 (1997): 28–39.

Felando, August, and Harold Medina. *The Tuna/Porpoise Controversy.* San Diego: Western Sky Press, 2011.

Gamble, Lynn H. *The Chumash World at European Contact: Power, Trade, and Feasting among Complex Hunter-Gatherers.* Berkeley: University of California Press, 2008.

Garrett, Tom. "The Tuna-Porpoise Story." *Not Man Apart* 6 (Mid-July 1976): 1–8.

Gerstenberger, Shawn, Adam Martinson, and Joanna L. Kramer. "An Evaluation of Mercury Concentrations in Three Brands of Canned Tuna." *Toxicology and Chemistry* 29 (2010): 237–42.

Gill, Theodore. *On the Proper Generic Name of the Tunny and Albicore.* Washington, D.C.: United States National Museum, 1889.

Godsil, H. C. "The High Seas Tuna Fishery of California." *Fish Bulletin* 51. Sacramento: Bureau of Marine Fisheries, Division of Fish and Game of California, 1938.

Goode, G. Brown. *American Fishes: A Popular Treatise upon the Game and Food and Food Fishes of North America.* Boston: Estes and Lauriant, 1887.

———. *American Fishes: A Popular Treatise upon the Game and Food and Food Fishes.* 2nd ed. Revised and enlarged by Theodore Gill. Boston: L. C. Page & Company, 1903.

———. *The Fisheries and Fishery Industries of the United States.* Section I. U.S. Commission of Fish and Fisheries. Washington, D.C.: Government Printing Office, 1884.

Goodspeed, Charles E. *Angling in America: Its Early History and Literature.* Boston: Houghton Mifflin, 1939.

Greenberg, Paul. *Four Fish: The Future of the Last Wild Food.* New York: Penguin Press, 2010.

Greenwood, Roberta S., R. O. Browne, and John E. Fitch. *A Coastal Chumash Village: Excavation of Shisholop, Ventura County, California.* [Los Angeles: Southern California Academy of Sciences,] 1969.

Grescoe, Taras. *Bottomfeeder: How to Eat Ethically in a World of Vanishing Seafood.* Toronto: HarperCollins, 2008.

Grey, Zane. *Tales of Fishes.* New York: Harper & Brothers, 1919.

———. *Tales of Swordfish and Tuna.* New York: Grosset & Dunlap, 1927.

Griswold, Frank Gray. *Some Fish and Some Fishing.* New York: John Lane Company, 1921.

Guinn, J.M. *A History of California and an Extended History of Its Southern Coast Counties, Also Containing Biographies of Well-Known Citizens of the Past and Present.* Los Angeles: Historic Record Co., 1907.

Gulick, Sidney Lewis. *Anti-Japanese War-Scare Stories.* New York: Fleming H. Revell Company, 1917.

Hasegawa, Susan, et al. *Japanese Americans in San Diego.* Charleston, S.C.: Arcadia Pub., 2008.

Heffernan, Patrick H. "Conflict over Marine Resources." *Proceedings of the Academy of Political Science, Mexico-United States Relations* 34 (1981): 168–80.

Heimann, Richard, and John Carlisle Jr. "The California Marine Fish Catch for 1968 and Historical Review, 1916–68." *Fish Bulletin* 149. Sacramento: Department of Fish and Game, State of California, 1970.

Herrick, Sam. "The U.S. Pacific Tuna Industry." In *Our Living Oceans: The Economic Status of U.S. Fisheries.* [Washington, D.C.]: U.S. Department of Commerce, National Oceanic and Atmospheric Administration, National Marine Fisheries Service, 1996.

Hibbeln, Joseph R., et al. "Maternal Seafood Consumption in Pregnancy and Neurodevelopmental Outcomes in Childhood (ALSPAC Study): An Observational Cohort Study." *Lancet* 369.9561 (2007): 578–85.

Holder, Charles Frederick. *Big Game at Sea.* New York: Outing Publishing Co., 1908.

———. *The Channel Islands of California: A Book for the Angler, Sportsman, and Tourist.* Chicago: A.C. McClurg & Co., 1910.

Holder, Charles Frederick, and David Starr Jordan. *Fish Stories Alleged and Experienced.* New York: Henry Holt and Company, 1909.

Hosokawa, Bill. *JACL: In Quest of Justice.* New York: William Morrow and Co., 1982.

Howison, John. *European Colonies, in Various Parts of the World.* 2 vols. London: Richard Bentley, New Burlington Street, Publisher in Ordinary to His Majesty, 1834.

Issenberg, Sasha. *The Sushi Economy: Globalization and the Making of a Modern Delicacy.* New York: Gotham Books, 2007.

Joseph, James, and Joseph W. Greenough. *International Management of Tuna, Porpoise, and Billfish: Biological, Legal, and Political Aspects.* Seattle: University of Washington Press, 1979.

Joseph, James, Witold Klawe, and Pat Murphy. *Tuna and Billfish—Fish without a Country.* La Jolla, Calif.: Inter-American Tropical Tuna Commission, 1988.

Kamp, David. *The United States of Arugula: How We Became a Gourmet Nation.* New York: Broadway Books, 2006.

Kanai, Atsuko. "How Sushi Came to California and How Edamamé Came to Be Served There with Sushi." In William Shurtleff and Akiko Aoyagi, eds., *History of Edamamé, Green Vegetable Soybeans, and Vegetable-Type Soybeans,* 631–33. Lafayette, Calif.: Soyinfo Center, 2009.

Kaplan, Moise N. *Big Game Anglers' Paradise: A Complete, Non-Technical Narrative-Treatise on Salt Water Gamefishes and Angling in Florida and Elsewhere.* New York: Liveright Publishing Corporation, 1937.

Kawasumi, Ken. *The Encyclopedia of Sushi Rolls.* Translated by Laura Driussi. Tokyo: Graph-Sha, Japan Publications Trading Co., 2001.

Köber, Achim. "Why Everybody Loves Flipper: The Political-Economy of the U.S. Dolphin-Safe Laws." *European Journal of Political Economy* 14 (1998): 475–509.

Lawless, Edward W. *Technology and Social Shock.* New Brunswick, N.J.: Rutgers University Press, 1977.

Loring, David C. "The United States-Peruvian 'Fisheries' Dispute." *Stanford Law Review* 23 (February 1971): 391–453.

Lovatelli, A., and P. F. Holthus, eds. *Capture-Based Aquaculture: Global Overview.* FAO Fisheries Technical Paper, no. 508. Rome: FAO. 2008.

Ludwig, Ella A. *History of the Harbor District of Los Angeles, Dating from Its Earliest History.* Los Angeles: Historic Record Company, Inc., [1927].

Lux, William R. "The Peruvian Fishing Industry: A Case Study in Capitalism at Work." *Revista de Historia de América* 71 (January-June 1971): 137–46.

Macrate, Arthur N. *The History of the Tuna Club.* Avalon, Calif.: N.p., [1948].

Mahaffey, Kathryn R. "Methylmercury: A New Look at the Risks." *Public Health Reports* (September-October 1999): 396–99, 402–13.

Majkowski, Jacek. *Global Fishery Resources of Tuna and Tuna-like Species.* Rome: Food and Agriculture Organization of the United Nations, 2007.

Marquez, Ernest, and Veronique De Turenne. *Port of Los Angeles: An Illustrated History from 1850 to 1945.* Santa Monica, Calif.: Angel City Press, 2007.

Martin, Irene, and Roger Tetlow. *Flight of the Bumble Bee: The Columbia River Packers Association and a Century in the Pursuit of Fish.* Long Beach, Wash.: Chinook Observer, 2011.Mason, William A. and John A. McKinstry. *The Japanese of Los Angeles, 1869–1920.* History Division of the Los Angeles County Museum of Natural History, Contribution no. 1. Los Angeles: Los Angeles County Museum of Natural History, 1969.

Mathes, W. Michael. "Early California Propaganda: The Works of Fray Antonio de la Ascencion." *California Historical Quarterly* 50 (June 1971): 195–205.

May, Earl Chapin. *The Canning Clan: A Pageant of Pioneering Americans.* New York: The Macmillan Company, 1937.

McEvoy, Arthur F. *The Fisherman's Problem: Ecology and Law in the California Fisheries, 1850–1980.* New York: Cambridge University Press, 1990.

———. "Law, Public Policy, and Industrialization in the California Fisheries, 1900–1925." *Business History Review* 57 (Winter 1983): 494–521.

McGovern, Dan. "Strategic Alliances: Fishermen Are Exploring Partnerships with Recreational and Environmental Groups to Solve Fisheries Management Problems." *National Fishermen* 81 (July 2000): 32–33, 56.

Meade, Tom, and Paul C. Nicholson. *The Atlantic Tuna Club: Then and Now.* [South Kingstown, R.I.]: The Club, 1992.

Meltzoff, Sarah, and Edward S. LiPuma. *A Japanese Joint Venture: Worker Experience and National Development in the Solomon Islands.* ICLARM Technical Reports 12. Manila, Philippines: International Center for Living Aquatic Resources Management, 1983.

Meron, Theodor. "The Fishermen's Protective Act: A Case in Contemporary Legal Strategy of the United States." *American Journal of International Law* 69 (April 1975): 290–309.

Merrill, Richard A., and Michael Schewel. "FDA Regulation of Environmental Contaminants of Food." *Virginia Law Review* 66 (December 1980): 1399.

Miyake, Makoto, Naozumi Miyabe, and Hideki Nakano. *Historical Trends of Tuna Catches in the World.* Rome: Food and Agriculture Organization of the United Nations, 2004.

Modell, John. *The Economics and Politics of Racial Accommodation: The Japanese of Los Angeles, 1900–1942.* Urbana: University of Illinois Press, 1977.

Moriyama, Alan Takeo. *Imingaisha: Japanese Emigration Companies and Hawaii, 1894–1908.* Honolulu: University of Hawaii Press, 1985.

Mullendore, William Clinton. *History of the United States Food Administration, 1917–1919.* Stanford, Calif.: Stanford University Press, 1941.

Murphy, Dale D. *The Structure of Regulatory Competition: Corporations and Public Policies in a Global Economy.* New York: Oxford University Press, 2004.

———. "The Tuna-Dolphin Wars." *Journal of World Trade: Law, Economics, Public Policy* 40 (4) (2006): 597–617.

Nambiar, K. P. P., and N. Krishnasamy, eds. *Tuna 95 Manila: Papers of the 4th World Tuna Trade Conference, 25–27 October 1995, Manila, Philippines.* Kuala Lumpur, Malaysia: Infofish, 1996.

Nambiar, K. P. P., and Sudari Pawiro, eds. *Tuna 97 Bangkok: Papers of the 5th World Tuna Trade Conference, 25–27 October 1997, Bangkok, Thailand.* Kuala Lumpur, Malaysia: Infofish, 1998.

National Marine Fisheries Service. "Our Living Oceans: The Economic Status of U.S. Fisheries, 1996." [Washington, D.C.]: U.S. Department of Commerce,

National Oceanic and Atmospheric Administration, National Marine Fisheries Service, 1996.

———. "Our Living Oceans: The First Annual Report on the Status of U.S. Living Marine Resources, 1991." [Washington, D.C.]: U.S. Department of Commerce, National Oceanic and Atmospheric Administration, National Marine Fisheries Service, 1991.

National Research Council. *Dolphins and the Tuna Industry*. Washington, D.C.: National Academy Press, 1992.

Ng, Franklin. *The Asian American Encyclopedia*. 6 vols. New York: Marshall Cavendish, 1995.

Niiya, Brian, ed. *Encyclopedia of Japanese American History*. New York: Checkmark Books, 2001.

O'Connor, Sue, Ono Rintaro, and Chris Clarkson. "Pelagic Fishing at 42,000 Years before the Present and the Maritime Skills of Modern Humans." *Science* 334 (November 25, 2011): 1117-21.

Odo, Franklin, and Kazukp Sinoto. *A Pictorial History of the Japanese in Hawaii, 1885–1924*. Honolulu: Hawaii Immigrant Preservation Center, 1985.

Oken, Emily, et al. "Maternal Fish Consumption, Hair Mercury, and Infant Cognition in a US Cohort." *Environmental Health Perspectives* 113 (October 2005): 1376–80.

Oliver, Lawrence. *Never Backward: The Autobiography of Lawrence Oliver, a Portuguese-American*. San Diego: Neyensch Printers, 1972.

Orbach, Michael K. *Hunters, Seamen, and Entrepreneurs: The Tuna Seinermen of San Diego*. Berkeley: University of California Press, 1977.

Pacific Fisherman's Canned Fish Hand-i-Book: The Facts on Canned Seafoods. 3rd ed. [Astoria, Ore.: Pacific Fisherman, 1950].

Perrin, William F. *Chronological Bibliography of the Tuna-Dolphin Problem, 1941–2001*. La Jolla, Calif.: U.S. Dept. of Commerce, National Oceanic and Atmospheric Administration, National Marine Fisheries Service, Southwest Fisheries Science Center, 2004. swfsc.noaa.gov/publications/TM/SWFSC/NOAA-TM-NMFS-SWFSC-356.pdf.

Petit, Thomas A. "The Impact of Imports and Tariffs on the American Tuna Industry." *American Journal of Economics and Sociology* 19 (April 1960): 275–88.

Pirrone, Nicola, and Kathryn R. Mahaffey, eds. *Dynamics of Mercury Pollution on Regional and Global Scales: Atmospheric Processes and Human Exposures around the World*. New York: Springer, 2005.

Popkin, Susan A., and Roger B. Allen. *Gone Fishing: A History of Fishing in River, Bay and Sea*. Philadelphia: Philadelphia Maritime Museum, 1987.

Pourade, Richard. *The History of San Diego*. 7 vols. San Diego: Union-Tribune Pub. Co., 1960–99.

Problems of the Fishing Industry: Hearings Before the Subcommittee on Fisheries and

Wildlife Conservation of the Committee on Merchant Marine and Fisheries, House of Representatives, Eighty-First Congress, First Session, February 15–16, 1949. Washington, D.C.: Government Printing Office, 1949.

Proceedings of the United States National Museum. Vols. 3 and 4 Washington, D.C.: Smithsonian Institution, 1881.

Radcliffe, William. *Fishing from Earliest Times.* London: J. Murray, 1921.

Reiger, George, ed. *The Best of Zane Grey, Outdoorsman.* Mechanicsville, Pa.: Stackpole Books, 1972.

———. *Profiles in Saltwater Angling: A History of the Sport; Its People and Places, Tackle and Techniques.* Englewood Cliffs, N.J.: Prentice-Hall, 1973.

Rivkin, Mike. *Big-Game Fishing Headquarters: A History of the IGFA.* Dania Beach, Fla.: IGFA Press, 2005.

Robinson, William Wilcox, and Doyce Blackman Nunis. *Southern California Local History: A Gathering of the Writings of W. W. Robinson.* Los Angeles: Historical Society of Southern California, 1993.

Rockland, Steven. "The San Diego Tuna Industry and Its Employment Impact on the Local Economy." *Marine Fisheries Review* (1978): 1313.

Roeder, Mark A. *Archaeological Study of Ca-Ven-110, Ventura, California: Fish Remains.* Pacific Palisades: Greenwood and Associates, 1987.

Safina, Carl. *Song for the Blue Ocean: Encounters along the World's Coasts and beneath the Seas.* New York: Henry Holt and Co., 1997.

Saram, Henri de, and N. Krishnasamy, eds. *Tuna 93 Bangkok: Papers of the 3th World Tuna Trade Conference, 26–28 October 1993, Manila, Philippines.* Kuala Lumpur, Malaysia: Infofish, 1993.

Schaefer, Kurt M. "Comparative Study of Some Morphological Features of Yellowfin and Bigeye." *Bulletin,* vol. 21, no. 7. La Jolla, Calif.: Inter-American Tropical Tuna Commission, 1999.

Schoell, Mark. "The Marine Mammal Protection Act and Its Role in the Decline of San Diego's Tuna Fishing Industry." *San Diego's History* 45 (Winter 1999): 32–52.

Schwartz-Nobel, Loretta. *Poisoned Nation: Pollution, Greed, and the Rise of Deadly Epidemics.* New York: St. Martin's Press, 2007.

Scofield, W. L. "Purse Seines and Other Roundhaul Nets in California." *Bulletin,* no. 81. Sacramento: California Department of Fish and Game, 1951.

Selak, Charles B., Jr. "Recent Developments in High Seas Fisheries Jurisdiction under the Presidential Proclamation of 1945." *American Journal of International Law* 44 (October 1950): 670–81.

Sheehy, Colleen J. "American Angling: The Rise of Urbanism and the Romance of the Rod and Reel." In Kathryn Grover, ed. *Hard at Play: Leisure in America, 1840–1940,* 77–92. Amherst: University of Massachusetts Press; Rochester, N.Y.: Strong Museum, 1992.

Shimada, Bell, and Milner B. Schaefer. *A Study in Changes in Fishing Effort, Abundance, and Yield for Yellowfin and Skipjack Tuna in the Eastern Tropical Pacific Ocean*. La Jolla, Calif.: Inter-American Tropical Tuna Commission, 1956.

Smetherman, Bobbie B., and Robert M. Smetherman. "Peruvian Fisheries: Conservation and Development." *Economic Development and Cultural Change* 21 (January 1973): 338–51.

Smith, Bill. *Tuna*. Short Hills, N.J.: Burford Books, Inc., 2000.

Spivak, John L. *Honorable Spy*. New York: Modern Age Books, 1939.

Springer, John, and Seymour Francis. "Los Angeles-Long Beach: Development by the Fishing Industry." *Pan-American Fisherman* 3 (December 1948): 19–59.

———. "Monterey." *Pan-American Fisherman* 3 (March 1949): 11–17.

———. "San Diego." *Pan-American Fisherman* 3 (February 1949): 26–41.

Starr, Kevin. *Americans and the California Dream, 1850–1915*. New York: Oxford University Press, 1973.

State of California, Department of Fish and Game: Marine Fisheries Branch. "Commercial Fish Catch of California for the Year." Sacramento: California State Printing Office.

———. "Commercial Fish Catch of California for the Years 1936–1939." *Fish Bulletin* 57.

———. "Commercial Fish Catch of California for the Year 1940." *Fish Bulletin* 58.

———. "Commercial Fish Catch of California for the Years 1941–1942." *Fish Bulletin* 59.

———. "Commercial Fish Catch of California for the Years 1945–1946." *Fish Bulletin* 67.

———. "Commercial Fish Catch of California for the Years 1948–1949." *Fish Bulletin* 80.

———. "Commercial Fish Catch of California for the Year 1950." *Fish Bulletin* 86.

State of California, Department of Fish and Game: Marine Fisheries Branch. "Purse Seines and Other Roundhaul Nets in California, 1951." *Fish Bulletin* 81. Sacramento: California State Printing Office, 1952.

Subasinghe, S., and Sudari Pawiro, eds. *Global Tuna Industry Situation and Outlook: Resources, Production & Marketing Trends, and Technological Issues; Proceedings of the Tuna 2002, Kuala Lumpur 7th Infofish World Tuna Trade Conference, 30 May–1 June, 2002*. Kuala Lumpur, Malaysia: Infofish, 2002.

Tanabe, Eiji. "The History of Japanese Commercial Fishing." *Pacific Citizen*, March 27, 1948, pp. 5–6.

To Protect Rights of United States Vessels on High Seas: Hearings Before the Subcommittee on Fisheries and Wildlife Conservation of the Committee on Merchant

Marine and Fisheries, House of Representatives, Eighty-Fifth Congress, First Session, on H.R. 5526. Washington, D.C.: Government Printing Office, 1957.

To Protect Rights of United States Vessels on High Seas: Hearing Before the Committee on Merchant Marine and Fisheries, House of Representatives, Eighty-Third Congress, Second Session, on H.R. 9584, a Bill to Protect the Rights of the United States on the High Seas and in Territorial Waters of Foreign Countries, July 2, 1954. Washington, D.C.: Government Printing Office, 1954.

Tosches, Nick. "If You Knew Sushi." *Vanity Fair* (June 2007). http://www.vanityfair.com/culture/features/2007/06/sushi200706.

Trachtman, Joel P. "United States—Restrictions in Imports of Tuna." *American Journal of International Law* 86 (January 1992): 142–51.

Trenor, Casson. *Sustainable Sushi: A Guide to Saving the Oceans One Bite at a Time.* Berkeley: North Atlantic Books, 2008.

The Tuna Fishing and Packing Industry of California. Los Angeles: William R. Staats Co., 1949.

Tuna Imports: Hearings Before the Committee on Finance, United States Senate, Eighty-Second Congress. Washington, D.C.: Government Printing Office, 1952.

Tuna Imports: Hearings Before a Subcommittee of the Committee on Ways and Means, House of Representatives, Eighty-Second Congress. Washington, D.C.: Government Printing Office, 1951.

Twiss, John R., and Randall R. Reeves. *Conservation and Management of Marine Mammals.* Washington, D.C.: Smithsonian Institution Press, 1999.

Ulanski, Stan. *The Gulf Stream: Tiny Plankton, Giant Bluefin, and the Amazing Story of the Powerful River in the Atlantic.* Chapel Hill: University of North Carolina Press, 2008.

[United States International Trade Commission]. *Tuna: Current Issues Affecting the U.S. Industry; Report to the Committee on Finance, United States Senate, on Investigation No. 332–313 under Section 332(g) of the Tariff Act of 1930 as Amended.* Washington, D.C.: U.S. International Trade Commission, [1992].

U.S. Trade in Tuna for Canning. Terminal Island, Calif.: National Marine Fisheries Service, Southwest Region, n.d.

Vachell, Horace Annesley. "Tuna Fishing in the Pacific." *Pall Mall Magazine* 6 (November 1898): 353–60.

Vickery, Oliver. *Harbor Heritage: Tales of the Harbor Area of Los Angeles, California.* Mountain View, Calif.: Morgan Press/Farag, 1978.

Walsh, Virginia M. *Global Institutions and Social Knowledge: Generating Research at the Scripps Institution and the Inter-American Tropical Tuna Commission, 1900s-1990s.* Cambridge, Mass.: MIT Press, 2004.

Warner, Joie, and Drew Warner. *Joie Warner's Take a Tin of Tuna: 65 Inspired Recipes for Every Meal of the Day.* San Francisco: Chronicle Books, 2004.

Waugh, Geoffrey. "Development, Economics, and Fishing Rights in the South

Pacific Tuna Fishing." In Philip A. Neher, Ragnar Árnason, and Nina Mollett, eds. *Rights Based Fishing*, 323–48. Dordrecht: Kluwer Academic Publishers, 1989.

Whynott, Douglas. *Giant Bluefin*. New York: North Point Press, Farrar, Straus and Giroux, 1995.

Wilcox, Clair. "Trade Policy for the Fifties." *American Economic Review: Papers and Proceedings of the Sixty-Fifth Annual Meeting of the American Economic Association* 43 (May 1953): 61–70.

Wilder, Robert Jay. "The Three-Mile Territorial Sea: Its Origins and Implications for Contemporary Offshore Federalism." *Virginia Journal of International Law* 32 (1991–1992): 681–746.

Williams, Steve. "Understanding Japanese Seafood Markets, Part 1." *Australian Fisheries* 51 (February 1992): 32–36; "Part 2: Structure and Function." *Australian Fisheries* 51 (March 1992): 16–21; "Part 3: Recent Changes in Seafood Consumption and Purchasing Behavior." *Australian Fisheries* 51 (April 1992): 32–36.

Wilson, Peter. *Aku! The History of Tuna Fishing in Hawaii and the Western Pacific*. N.p.: Xlibris, 2011.

Wolff, Thomas. *In Pursuit of Tuna: The Expansion of a Fishing Industry and Its International Ramifications—The End of an Era*. Tempe: Center for Latin American Studies, Arizona State University, 1980.

Zierer, Clifford M. "The Los Angeles Harbor Fishing Center." *Economic Geography* 10 (October 1934): 402–18.

THESES AND DISSERTATIONS

Abrams, Jane Underhill. "A Case Study of Some of the Political Ramifications of the American Tuna Problem." Master's thesis, San Diego State College, 1957.

Constance, Douglas H. "Global-Post Fordism: The Case of the Tuna-Dolphin Controversy." PhD diss., University of Missouri at Columbia, 1993.

Corey, Roger Lyman, Jr. "Technology and Competition in the Tuna Industry." PhD diss., University of Rhode Island, 1993.

Finley, Mary Carmel. "The Tragedy of Enclosure: Fish, Fisheries Science, and U.S. Foreign Policy, 1920–1960." PhD diss., University of California, San Diego, 2007.

Kai, Gunki. "Economic Status of the Japanese in California." Master's thesis, Stanford University, 1922.

Kawasaki, Kanichi. "The Japanese Community of East San Pedro, Terminal Island, California." Master's thesis, University of Southern California, 1931.

McEvoy, Arthur F. "Economy Law and Ecology in the California Fisheries to 1925." PhD diss., University of California at San Diego, 1979.

Modell, John. "The Japanese of Los Angeles: A Study in Growth and Accommodation, 1900–1946." PhD diss., Columbia University, 1969.

Peterson, Ann M. "Recollections of Andrea Gomez: Terminal Island Fish Cannery Employee and Union Organizer, 1924–1965." Master's thesis, California State University, Long Beach, 2005.

Petit, Thomas A. "The Economics of the Southern California Tuna Industry." Master's thesis, University of Southern California, 1959.

Richardson, William C. "The Fishermen of San Diego." Master's thesis, San Diego State University, 1981.

Roesti, Robert Max. "Economic Analysis of Factors Underlying Pricing in the Southern California Tuna Canning Industry." PhD diss., University of Southern California, 1960.

Schoell, Mark. "Flipper vs. the Fishermen: The Decline of San Diego's Tuna Fishing Industry." Master's thesis, San Diego State University, 1998.

Swift, John Cornish. "The Tuna Fishery of Southern California." Master's thesis, University of California, Berkeley, 1956.

Teixeira, Ana. "Swimming with Dolphins: A Study on Legitimacy Processes in the Southern California Tuna Industry." PhD diss., University of North Carolina at Chapel Hill, 2009.

Toyama, Chotoku. "The Japanese Community in Los Angeles." Master's thesis, Columbia University, 1926.

Uono, Koyoshi. "The Factors Affecting Geographical Aggregation and Dispersion of the Japanese Residences in the City of Los Angeles." Master's thesis, University of Southern California, 1927.

Yamashita, Kanshi Stanley. "Terminal Island: Ethnography of an Ethnic Community; Its Dissolution and Reorganization to a Non-spatial Community." PhD diss., University of California, Irvine, 1985.

COOKBOOKS AND RECIPE BOOKS

Black, Andy. *A Can of Tuna: The Complete Guide to Cooking with Tuna.* Santa Rosa, Calif.: Prism Press, 1995.

Howell, Richard M. *American Samoa Fish Handling, Processing, and Marketing Training Project, April 6, 1982–December 20, 1982: Final Report; Recipes from the 22nd South Pacific Conference Tuna Cooking Contest, Pago Pago, Samoa, 1982.* Honolulu: Pacific Fisheries Development Foundation, 1982.

Johnson, Kristi. *Oodle Doodles Tuna Noodle and Other Salad Recipes.* Mankato, Minn.: Capstone Press, 2008.

Metcalf, Sheila. *The Tuna Cookbook*. Garden City, N.Y.: Doubelday & Company, 1972.

Robey, Dorothy M., and Rose G. Kerr. *Little Tuna Recipes*. Washington, D.C.: United States Department of the Interior, Fish and Wildlife Service, 1954.

Seaman, Tracy. *The Tuna Fish Gourmet*. New York: Villard Books, 1994.

Staples, Katherine S. *Recipes: Tuna & Chips Casserole, Cole Slaw, Rice Krispies Marshmallow Treats: Level 3*. [Fargo: North Dakota State University, n.d.]

Sweetser, Wendy. *50 Recipes for Tuna*. N.p.: Woodhead-Faulkner, 1989.

Teriyaki and Sushi: Selected 72 Recipes. Elmsford, N.Y.: Japan Publications Trading Co., 1963.

United States Department of the Interior. "How to Cook Tuna." *Test Kitchen Series No. 12*. 1957. Reprint, Washington, D.C.: United States Department of the Interior, 1964.

PROMOTIONAL PAMPHLETS

Canadian Fishing Co. *Gold Seal Tuna Recipes*. [Vancouver]: Canadian Fishing Co., [ca. 1970s].

Chicken of the Sea. *Hoppy's Bar-20 Ranch Recipes Featuring . . . Chicken of the Sea, Hoppy's Favorite Brand!* Los Angeles: V.C.S.F. Co., Inc., 1951.

———. *Tempting Tuna Cookbook*. New York: Rutledge Books and Benjamin Book Company, 1976.

French Sardine Company. *Food and Fun: A Book of Food Recipes, Party Games, Tricks, and Fascinating Puzzles . . . from Star-Kist Tuna*. N.p.: French Sardine Company, 1953.

———. *Star-Kist Tuna*. Terminal Island, Calif.: French Sardine Company, n.d.

Good Packaging Report, eds. *The U.S. Tuna Industry*. Terminal Island, Calif.: Star-Kist Foods, Inc., 1963.

Greenseas Division. *Collection of Popular Tuna & Salmon Recipes*. Vol. 2. Eden, N.S.W., Australia: Greenseas Division, [ca. 1990s].

———. *The Workers of Greenseas, Eden, N.S.W. Present a Collection of Popular Greenseas Tuna Recipes for All Occasions*. Eden, N.S.W., Australia: Greenseas Division, n.d. [1980s].

Halfhill, C. P. *Birth of a Mighty Industry*. Long Beach, Calif.: Halfhill Company, South Pacific Canning, 1951.

Hawaiian Tuna Packers. *Coral Tuna Cookbook*. Honolulu: Hawaiian Tuna Packers, Ltd., 1956.

Interatun. *Canned Tuna, a Food to Enjoy: The 50 Best Recipes*. [Pontevedra, Spain]: Interatun 2007.

Mitsubishi International Corp. *Three Diamonds Fancy Tuna*. New York: Mitsubishi International Corporation, n.d.

Pacific Trading Co. *30 Tested Sea Food Recipes: Tuna, Clam, Crab.* [N.p.: Pacific Trading Co., 1930.]

Premier Packing Co. *Recipes for Preparing Steeles Premium California Tuna: Packed in Perfectly Blended Oils.* San Diego: Premier Packing Co., n.d.

Sealord Products. *Fin 'N' Shell Cookery: With Favorite Recipes of Members and Friends of the Bay Shore Tuna Club, Inc., Bay Shore, Long Island, New York.* Bay Shore, N.Y.: Bay Shore Tuna Club, 1971.

———. *Simply Delicious, Simply Nutritious: Recipes from Sealord Tuna.* Nelson, N.Z.: Sealord Products, n.d.

Southern California Fish Co. *14 Tasty Recipes for Serving Blue Sea Extra Fancy Brand Tuna.* Terminal Island, Calif.: Southern California Fish Co., [ca. 1930s].

———. *Blue Sea Tuna.* Los Angeles: Southern California Fish Co., n.d.

StarKist Seafood Co. *Open a New World of Dining.* N.p.: StarKist Seafood Company, 1992.

———. *StarKist Sensational Tuna.* N.p.: Starkist Seafood Co., 1990.

———. *The Star-Kist Story.* N.p.: H. J. Heinz Co.,1962.

———. *StarKist Tuna for Today: Tempting New Ideas.* Lincolnwood, Ill.: Publications International Ltd., 1994, 1997.

———. *Tuna.* [Lincolnwood, Ill.: Publications International], 1990.

Synergistic Marketing, Inc. *Quick & Easy Recipes: Brought to You by Durkee French Fried Onions and Starkist Tuna.* New York: Synergistic Marketing, Inc., 1991.

Tuna Research Foundation. *Exploring the Tuna Industry.* Terminal Island, Calif.: Tuna Research Foundation, 1963.

———. "The Story of Tuna." Terminal Island, Calif.: Tuna Research Foundation, n.d.

———. *Tempting Tuna Recipes.* New York: Synergistic Marketing, Inc., 1992.

———. *Tuna, as You Like It: A New Anthology with a Featured Repertory of Distinguished Recipes.* Terminal Island, Calif.: Tuna Research Foundation, [1960s].

———. *Tuna, as You Like It: Recipes—History—Facts.* San Pedro, Calif.: Tuna Research Foundation, 1974.

———. *Tuna, as You Like It: Recipes, History, Facts.* Terminal Island, Calif.: Tuna Research Foundation, n.d.

———. *Tuna, a Saga of the Sea: A Collection of Easy-to-Prepare Recipes.* Terminal Island, Calif.: Tuna Research Foundation, n.d. [1950s].

Van Camp Sea Food Co. *17 Proven Recipes for Chicken of the Sea Brand Fancy Tuna.* Terminal Island, Calif.: Van Camp Sea Food Co., [ca. 1924].

———. *19 Proven Recipes, White Star Brand California Fancy Tuna Fish: Chicken of the Sea.* Terminal Island, Calif.: Van Camp Sea Food Co., n.d [1940s].

———. *86 New Proven Tuna Recipes and the Romance of Tuna.* N.p.: Van Camp Sea Food, 1926.

Westgate-California Tuna Packing Co. *Treats with Tuna: Basic Recipes, Easy Variations, Special Dishes*. San Diego: Westgate-California Tuna Packing Co., 1953.

Westgate Sea Products Co. *Breast-O'-Chicken Brand, The Finer Tuna Fish*. San Diego: Westgate Sea Products Co., n.d.

Westgate-Sun Harbor Co. *Original Tuna Recipes: Featuring Breast-O'-Chicken Tuna*. [San Diego]: Westgate-Sun Harbor Co., 1950.

Westgate-Tuna Packing Company. *Selected Tuna Recipes*. San Diego: Westgate-Tuna Packing Company, 1953.

White, Frank Decatur. *Breast-O'-Chicken Brand Recipes*. San Diego: Westgate Sea Products, 1949.

Index

Text	10/14 Palatino
Display	Bauer Bodoni and Palatino
Compositor	BookMatters, Berkeley
Printer and binder	Maple-Vail Book Manufacturing Group